Cloud-Native Applications in Java

Build microservice-based cloud-native applications that dynamically scale

Ajay Mahajan
Munish Kumar Gupta
Shyam Sundar

BIRMINGHAM - MUMBAI

Cloud-Native Applications in Java

Commissioning Editor: Aaron Lazar
Acquisition Editor: Nitin Dasan
Content Development Editor: Zeeyan Pinheiro
Technical Editor: Romy Dias
Copy Editor: Safis Editing
Project Coordinator: Vaidehi Sawant
Proofreader: Safis Editing
Indexer: Rekha Nair
Graphics: Jason Monteiro
Production Coordinator: Shantanu Zagade

First published: February 2018

Production reference: 1220218

Published by Packt Publishing Ltd.
Livery Place
35 Livery Street
Birmingham
B3 2PB, UK.

ISBN 978-1-78712-434-9

www.packtpub.com

To my son, Anurag, and my wife, Rashmi, for having patience with me on the many Sundays and a few vacations when this book was mostly written.

– Ajay Mahajan

Dedicated to the memory of my father, Shri R P Gupta.

– Munish Kumar Gupta

To my daughter, Aditi, and my wife, Nithya, for their patience and understanding.

– Shyam Sundar

`mapt.io`

Mapt is an online digital library that gives you full access to over 5,000 books and videos, as well as industry leading tools to help you plan your personal development and advance your career. For more information, please visit our website.

Why subscribe?

- Spend less time learning and more time coding with practical eBooks and Videos from over 4,000 industry professionals

- Improve your learning with Skill Plans built especially for you

- Get a free eBook or video every month

- Mapt is fully searchable

- Copy and paste, print, and bookmark content

PacktPub.com

Did you know that Packt offers eBook versions of every book published, with PDF and ePub files available? You can upgrade to the eBook version at `www.PacktPub.com` and as a print book customer, you are entitled to a discount on the eBook copy. Get in touch with us at `service@packtpub.com` for more details.

At `www.PacktPub.com`, you can also read a collection of free technical articles, sign up for a range of free newsletters, and receive exclusive discounts and offers on Packt books and eBooks.

Foreword

In a deployment diagram, internet outside the firewall was depicted using the shape of a cloud. Not until I read *Big Switch*, Nicholas G. Carr, did I realize the full potential of cloud and what was to come. Fast forwarding 10 years, now we do not think twice before drawing the cloud shape around the complete system to depict how cloud is everywhere. Cloud Native comes naturally for start-ups, but for a lot of enterprises, this is still an uncharted territory. Just doing lift-and-shift is not the right use of cloud, though it may be the first thing most large corporations are doing to mitigate the currency of their data centers or to avoid extension of leases. The power of cloud is seen when we are able to build cloud-native architecture-based applications that are business critical and can drive transformational value. Hence, I have always encouraged my team to gain knowledge on designing and building smarter applications on cloud.

Munish, Ajay, and Shyam are part of the core team that has always researched and worked on emerging technologies, using them to solve business problems. They are among the leading experts and consultants on the enterprise digital transformation with a focus on distributed systems using microservices and emerging technologies such as reactive frameworks, open source, and container technology (Dockers and Kubernetes) to name a few. Hence, I encouraged them to work on this book so as to enable the next generation of developers to jump start their journey to cloud-native applications.

This book takes a step-by-step approach to understanding, designing, and writing applications for cloud. The authors take you on a learning journey that starts with the concepts, followed by building a small REST service, and then going through the incremental journey of enhancing the service to be cloud native. They cover various aspects of cloud-specific nuances, such as how to discover a service in a distributed architecture and the role played by service discovery tools. You will also learn how to migrate your application to public cloud providers—AWS and Azure. The book covers serverless computing models such as AWS Lamda and Cloud Functions.

I encourage you to get the best out of this book to spearhead your application development journey on cloud.

Hari Kishan Burle

Vice President and Global Head Architecture Services

Wipro Limited

Contributors

About the authors

Ajay Mahajan is a Distinguished Member of Technical Staff (DMTS) at Wipro Technologies, and currently is in role of Chief Technologist of Retail vertical. In his current role, he helps customers adopt cloud-native and digital architecture for next-generation retail applications. He worked with retail and banking clients in Europe and USA on large-scale mission-critical systems. He has seen the evolution of enterprise Java from the Netscape Application Server to servlets/JSP, JEE, Spring, and now the cloud and microservices during the course of 19 years of working on Java platform.

A lot of ideas, best practices, and patterns for this book originated from our work in Emerging Technologies, which was spearheaded by Aravind Ajad Yarra. My special thanks goes to Shyam (coauthor), who is the most talented technical person I have come across. A big thanks to Munish for brainstorming the structure and content of the book. My thanks to Hari Burle, whose encouraging words and guidance helped me keep my focus on the book.

Munish Kumar Gupta is a lead system architect with Visa. Based in Bangalore, India, his day-to-day work involves solution architectures for applications with stringent non-functional requirements, application performance engineering, managing application infrastructure, and exploring the readiness of cutting-edge, open source technologies for enterprise adoption. He is the author of *Akka Essentials*. He is very passionate about software programming and craftsmanship. He blogs about technology trends, application performance engineering, and Akka.

I have to start by thanking my wife, Kompal. She urged me to keep writing, and here I am with my second book. Thanks to everyone on the Packt team who helped me so much. A special mention to Zeeyan, Nitin, and Romy.

Shyam Sundar is a senior architect with Wipro Technologies based in Bangalore. He is part of the Emerging Technologies Architecture group within Wipro. He is responsible for helping teams adopt new and emerging technologies in their projects. He focuses primarily on the client side and cloud technologies. He is a lifelong learner who cares deeply about software craftsmanship. He is constantly experimenting with new tools and technologies to improve the development experience.

I have to first thank my coauthors, Ajay and Munish, for taking me along on this incredible journey with them. For someone who is more used to expressing themselves with code rather than words, both Ajay and Munish gave a lot of thoughtful pointers on how to structure the content and simplify the concepts. I must also thank my boss, Aravind Ajad Yarra, for his continued support and encouragement.

About the reviewer

Andreas Olsson is a Java and Spring trainer, specializing in cloud-native solutions. He has been a Java developer since 2001 and started using Spring in 2004. When designing the architecture of an application, he usually finds the solution in the Spring ecosystem. He started his own company in 2011 when cloud-native platforms started to emerge, and he has been a cloud-native enthusiast ever since. Andreas lives in Sweden and is currently working as a trainer internationally. He is a certified Java and Spring professional and really enjoys learning new things on a daily basis.

Packt is searching for authors like you

If you're interested in becoming an author for Packt, please visit authors.packtpub.com and apply today. We have worked with thousands of developers and tech professionals, just like you, to help them share their insight with the global tech community. You can make a general application, apply for a specific hot topic that we are recruiting an author for, or submit your own idea.

Table of Contents

Preface

Businesses today are evolving so rapidly that they are resorting the elasticity of the cloud to provide a platform to build and deploy their highly scalable applications. This means that developers now are faced with the challenge of building build applications that are native to the cloud. For this, they need to be aware of the environment, tools, and resources they're coding against.

The book begins by explaining the driving factors for cloud adoption and shows you how cloud deployment is different from regular application deployment on a standard data centre. You will learn about design patterns specific to applications running in the cloud and find out how you can build a microservice in Java Spring using REST APIs.

You will then take a deep dive into the life cycle of building, testing, and deploying applications with maximum automation to reduce the deployment cycle time. Gradually, you will move on to configuring the AWS and Azure platforms and working with their APIs to deploy your application. Finally, you'll take a look at API design concerns and their best practices. You'll also learn how to migrate an existing monolithic application into distributed cloud-native applications.

By the end, you will understand how to build and monitor a scalable, resilient, and robust cloud-native application that is always available and fault tolerant.

Who this book is for

Java developers who want to build resilient, robust, and scalable applications that are targeted for cloud-based deployment will find this book helpful. Some knowledge of Java, Spring, web programming, and public cloud providers (AWS and Azure) should be sufficient to get you through the book.

What this book covers

Chapter 1, *Introduction to Cloud-Native*, addresses the what and why of cloud-native applications: what are the drivers of moving to cloud application? Why is cloud development and deployment different from regular applications? What is a 12-factor app?

`Chapter` 2, *Writing Your First Cloud-Native Application*, introduces the core concepts of using the microservices approach for application design. It then shows a sample bare-bones `product` service that will be enhanced as the discussion progresses in the book. You will learn how to use Spring Boot for microservice application development and appreciate the microservice principles that are used to build cloud-native applications.

`Chapter` 3, *Designing Your Cloud-Native Application*, covers some of the high-level architecture considerations in designing cloud-native applications. It includes event-driven architecture, decoupling using choreography, and using **domain-driven design** (**DDD**) concepts such as Bounded Contexts. You will learn about the architecture patterns and considerations for developing on the cloud and frontending the applications with consumer-friendly APIs instead of a system-centric service definition.

`Chapter` 4, *Extending Your Cloud-Native Application*, takes a deep dive into creating an application using various stacks, principles, and supporting components. It covers the patterns while implementing the service. This chapter highlights the differential aspects such as error handling and patterns such as **Command Query Response Segregation** (**CQRS**) and caching that have a significant impact on cloud development.

`Chapter` 5, *Testing Cloud-Native Applications*, delves into how to test your microservices and how to write tests in **behavior-driven development**.

`Chapter` 6, *Cloud-Native Application Deployment*, delves into the deployment model for the microservice, including how to package your application in a Docker container and setting up the CI/CD pipeline.

`Chapter` 7, *Cloud-Native Application Runtime*, covers the runtime aspects of the service. We will cover how configuration can be externalized in a configuration server and frontend by Zuul (Edge). We will look at Pivotal Cloud Foundry and deploying our service on PCF Dev. We will also cover container orchestrations.

`Chapter` 8, *Platform Deployment – AWS*, describes the AWS environment and discusses AWS-specific tools to do cloud development using the concepts (registry, configuration, log aggregation, and async messaging) discussed in earlier chapters.

`Chapter` 9, *Platform Deployment – Azure*, describes the Azure environment and discusses Azure-specific tools to do cloud development (including Service Fabric and Cloud Functions).

Chapter 10, *As a Service Integration*, discusses the various types of XaaS, including IaaS, PaaS, iPaaS, and DBaaS, and how to expose infrastructure elements as services. In the cloud-native mode, your application might be integrating with social media APIs or PaaS APIs or you can be hosting services that will be used by other applications. This chapter covers how to connect/use other external services or provide such services.

Chapter 11, *API Design Best Practices*, discusses how to design consumer-centric APIs that are granular and functionality oriented. It also discusses the various best practices in API design, such as whether to do orchestration at the API level or in service, how to create freemium versions of API, how to address the channel-specific concerns at the API layer so that the service remains channel agnostic, and the security aspects in API design.

Chapter 12, *Digital Transformation*, covers the impact of cloud development on the existing landscape of an enterprise and how it can achieve the transformation to move toward a digital enterprise.

To get the most out of this book

1. The book starts with an introduction and then builds on a simple service, step by step, through the chapters. Hence, the readers will benefit by following the flow of the book, unless they are looking for a particular topic.
2. Downloading the code and running it is always tempting. However, you will benefit more as you type the code out, especially in the initial chapters. The book is written in such a way that the important concepts and code are present in the chapter, thus preventing you from going back to see the source code.
3. Having said that, do try out the code samples and run them. It makes the principles concrete and easier to grasp.
4. I hope that you have invested in a good desktop/laptop, given that you will be running containers and VMs on your machine, which take resources, it is good to have a strong piece of equipment to get going.
5. Refer to the documentation links mentioned through the chapters to expand the knowledge on the frameworks and technologies discussed in the book.
6. The cloud is a technology that changes very rapidly. Hence, this book stresses on concepts and demonstrates them through code. For example, CQRS is important as a concept, so we have shown implementation on MongoDB and Elasticsearch. However, you can try out the pattern on any other set of databases.

Download the example code files

You can download the example code files for this book from your account at
`www.packtpub.com`. If you purchased this book elsewhere, you can visit
`www.packtpub.com/support` and register to have the files emailed directly to you.

You can download the code files by following these steps:

1. Log in or register at `www.packtpub.com`.
2. Select the **SUPPORT** tab.
3. Click on **Code Downloads & Errata**.
4. Enter the name of the book in the **Search** box and follow the onscreen instructions.

Once the file is downloaded, please make sure that you unzip or extract the folder using the latest version of:

- WinRAR/7-Zip for Windows
- Zipeg/iZip/UnRarX for Mac
- 7-Zip/PeaZip for Linux

The code bundle for the book is also hosted on GitHub at `https://github.com/PacktPublishing/Cloud-Native-Applications-in-Java`. We also have other code bundles from our rich catalog of books and videos available at `https://github.com/PacktPublishing/`. Check them out!

Download the color images

We also provide a PDF file that has color images of the screenshots/diagrams used in this book. You can download it here: `https://www.packtpub.com/sites/default/files/downloads/CloudNativeApplicationsinJava_ColorImages.pdf`.

Conventions used

There are a number of text conventions used throughout this book.

`CodeInText`: Indicates code words in text, database table names, folder names, filenames, file extensions, pathnames, dummy URLs, user input, and Twitter handles. Here is an example: "The `CrudRepository` interface comes with a set of default methods to implement the most common operations."

A block of code is set as follows:

```
-- Adding a few initial products
insert into product(id, name, cat_Id) values (1, 'Apples', 1)
insert into product(id, name, cat_Id) values (2, 'Oranges', 1)
insert into product(id, name, cat_Id) values (3, 'Bananas', 1)
insert into product(id, name, cat_Id) values (4, 'Carrot', 2)
```

When we wish to draw your attention to a particular part of a code block, the relevant lines or items are set in bold:

```
public class Product implements Serializable {
```

Any command-line input or output is written as follows:

```
mongoimport --db masterdb --collection product --drop --file
D:datamongoscriptsproducts.json
```

Bold: Indicates a new term, an important word, or words that you see onscreen. For example, words in menus or dialog boxes appear in the text like this. Here is an example: "Next, we click on the **Deployment credentials** link on the left-hand side."

Warnings or important notes appear like this.

Tips and tricks appear like this.

Get in touch

Feedback from our readers is always welcome.

General feedback: Email feedback@packtpub.com and mention the book title in the subject of your message. If you have questions about any aspect of this book, please email us at questions@packtpub.com.

Errata: Although we have taken every care to ensure the accuracy of our content, mistakes do happen. If you have found a mistake in this book, we would be grateful if you would report this to us. Please visit www.packtpub.com/submit-errata, selecting your book, clicking on the Errata Submission Form link, and entering the details.

Piracy: If you come across any illegal copies of our works in any form on the internet, we would be grateful if you would provide us with the location address or website name. Please contact us at copyright@packtpub.com with a link to the material.

If you are interested in becoming an author: If there is a topic that you have expertise in and you are interested in either writing or contributing to a book, please visit authors.packtpub.com.

Reviews

Please leave a review. Once you have read and used this book, why not leave a review on the site that you purchased it from? Potential readers can then see and use your unbiased opinion to make purchase decisions. Also, we at Packt can understand what you think about our products, and our authors can see your feedback on their book. Thank you!

For more information about Packt, please visit packtpub.com.

1
Introduction to Cloud-Native

The advent of cloud computing and the ubiquity of mobile devices have led to the rise of consumer-facing companies (such as Amazon, Netflix, Uber, Google, and Airbnb) that have redefined the entire customer experience. These companies have built their applications (both web and mobile interfaces) on the cloud, using features or services that allow them to scale up or down based on demand, be available at all times, and be ready to handle failures at all levels.

Traditional enterprises are looking at these consumer-facing companies and want to adopt some of their best practices. They do this to help scale up their rapidly evolving enterprise applications, allowing them to take advantage of the elasticity and scalability of the cloud.

Before we dive deep into cloud-native, let's see what this chapter holds. We will cover the following topics in this chapter:

- Why go cloud-native?
- What is cloud-native?
- Intro to the 12-factor app
- Why move from monolithic applications to distributed microservice-based applications?
- The advantages of building a distributed microservice-based application

Why go cloud-native?

Let's have a look at the following points to understand why we need to go cloud-native:

- The first wave of cloud adoption was about cost savings and business agility (especially around infrastructure provisioning and cheap storage). With increasing cloud adoption, enterprises started discovering **Infrastructure as a Service (IaaS)** and **Platform as a Service (PaaS)** services and their utilization in building applications that leverage the elasticity and scalability of the cloud, all the while embracing the inherent failures of the cloud platform.

- A lot of enterprises are adopting greenfield design and development of microservices in the area of digital initiatives. When dealing with the **Internet of Things (IoT)**, mobile devices, SaaS integration, and online business models, enterprises are working with niche players in the market. These new age business models are being designed and developed as a system of innovation on the enterprise end. The models are iterated rapidly to identify and bubble up the customer's needs, their preferences, what works, and what does not work.

- Enterprises are also developing digital services based on their product lines. The products are enhanced with IoT to enable them to emit data about the products' performance. The data is collated and analyzed for patterns such as predictive maintenance, usage models, and external factors. The data from customers is collated and aggregated to build newer models for product enhancements and new features. A lot of these new digital services use the cloud-native model.

- These modern digital solutions use APIs from various providers, such as Google Maps for location, Facebook/Google for authentication, and Facebook/Twitter for social collaborations. Mashing all these APIs with the features and functionality of enterprise business allows them to build a unique proposition for the customer. All of this integration is happening at the API level. The mobile application is not meant for tens of hundreds of users, but tens of millions of users. This means that, as the load increases, the underlying application functionality should be able to scale up to provide a seamless experience to the customer.

- One way to scale up the resources for the enterprise is to do the heavy lifting in terms of service/environment provisioning as the load goes up or in case of failures. Another way is to offload the heavy lifting of the underlying services to the cloud platform provider. This is the sweet spot where building cloud-native applications that make use of the cloud provider's platform services allows the enterprise to offload the key aspects of scalability and focus on value generation parts.

What is cloud-native?

When applications are designed and architected to take advantage of the underlying IaaS and PaaS services supported by the cloud computing platform, they are called **cloud-native applications**.

This means building reliable system applications, such as five nines (99.999%), that run on a three nines (99.9%) infrastructure and application components. We need to design our application components to deal with failures. To handle such failures, we need a structured approach for scalability and availability. To support the entire scale of applications, all the pieces need to be automated.

Cloud adoption typically happens in a series of steps, where the enterprise starts exploring the services before they start building cloud-native applications. The adoption starts with the movement of Dev/Test environments to the cloud, where rapid provisioning is the **key ask** from the business and developer community. Once the enterprise is past the environment provisioning stage, the next step/models in which the enterprise applications are migrated to the cloud-native model will be discussed in the following sections.

Lift and shift

Traditionally, enterprises started on their cloud computing journey with IaaS services. They did a lift and shift of the business application workloads from on-premises data centers and moved to the equivalent rented capacity on the cloud computing platform. This is the first wave of adoption of cloud computing platforms, where enterprises are shifted from a capital expenditure model to an operating expenditure model.

IaaS, as the names suggests, is focused on infrastructure—compute nodes, network, and storage. In this model, enterprises can take advantage of the elasticity of the cloud, where compute nodes can be added or removed based on the incoming demand or load. The **virtual machine** (**VM**) abstracts out the underlying hardware and provides the ability to scale the number of VMs up or down with just a few clicks.

Enterprises typically make use of IaaS in the first wave because of the following:

- **Variability of resources**: The ability to add/remove resources at will, which in turn allows more business agility
- **Utility model**: IaaS provides basic resources that are rented out on an hourly basis, allowing more predictability and an opex model

Going native

Once the enterprises start becoming comfortable with the IaaS, the next wave of adoption comes in terms of adoption of PaaS as part of the application workloads. In this stage, the enterprises start discovering services with the following benefits:

- **Platform services replacement**: This involves the identification of potential platform features of the enterprise, lifting and shifting the workload, and replacing it with equivalent platform services from the cloud provider. For example:
    - Replacing application messaging systems with queuing systems provided by the cloud provider (such as AWS SQS)
    - Replacing data stores or **relational database management systems** (**RDMBS**) with equivalent managed data services (such as AWS RDS)
    - Replacing security or directory services with a managed directory or security services (such as AWS Directory and AWS IAM)
    - These services allow the enterprise to do away with all the operational efforts, such as data store backup, availability, scalability, and redundancy, and replace them with a managed service that provides all these features

- **Application services replacement**: Enterprises discover new services that can replace their own platform or utility services. For example:
  - Replacing build and release services or products with equivalent DevOps services from the cloud provider (such as AWS CodePipeline, AWS CodeCommit, or AWS CodeDeploy)
  - Replacing application services or products with equivalent application platform services (such as AWS API Gateway, AWS SWF, and AWS SES)
  - Replacing analytics workload services with equivalent application analytics services (such as AWS Data Pipeline and AWS EMR)

Once the applications start adopting the platform services, the applications start abstracting out features or functionalities provided by **commercial off-the-shelf** (**COTS**) products (such as messaging, notification, security, workflow, and API Gateway) and replacing them with equivalent feature platform services. For example, instead of hosting and running the messaging IaaS, movement to an equivalent platform service means moving to a model where you pay only for the number of messages sent, without incurring any additional operational costs. This model brings significant savings, as you move from renting and operating the product to a model where the product is rented only for the time it is utilized.

Going serverless

Once the enterprise has adopted the PaaS to build the application, the next step is to abstract out the application logic as a series of smaller functions and deploy them. These functions are invoked as a reaction to an event from the user or agent, which results in these functions computing the incoming events and giving a result back. This is the highest level of abstraction, where the application has been divided into a series of functions and these functions are deployed independently of each other. The functions communicate with each other using asynchronous communication models. Cloud computing platforms provide features such as AWS Lambda and Azure Functions for going serverless.

Cloud-native and microservices

To enable the adoption of the IaaS and PaaS services, a change in how the applications are designed and architected needs to be made.

The model of designing enterprise applications on a base platform (read: application server) meant that the heavy lifting of the application's scalability and availability was the responsibility of the platform. Enterprise developers would focus on using the standardized JEE patterns and developing components (Presentation, Business, Data, and Integration) to build fully functional and transactional applications. The extent to which the application could be scaled was limited by the abilities (node clustering and distributed caching) of the underlying platform:

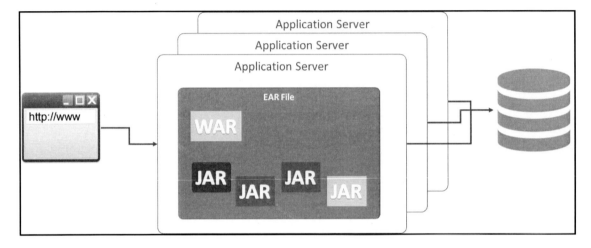

Monolithic application

A business application built as a monolithic application is typically characterized by the following factors:

- The entire application logic is packaged into a single EAR file
- The application reuse is derived by sharing JARs
- Application changes are planned months in advance, typically in a big push once a quarter
- There is one database that encompasses the entire schema for the application
- There are thousands of test cases that signify the amount of regression
- The application design, development, and deployment requires coordination among multiple teams and significant management

With the advent of social interactions and mobile users, the scale of application users and data started increasing exponentially. Enterprises soon found that the platform was becoming a bottleneck in terms of the following issues:

- **Business agility**: The operational cost of managing the application platform and making constant changes to the features/functionalities was getting hampered because of the monolithic nature of the application. Even for a small feature change, the entire cycle of regression tests and deployment across server clusters was eating into the overall speed of innovation.
  The mobile revolution meant that the problem was not just at the channel layers, but also percolated down to the integration and systems of record layers. Unless enterprises fixed the problem across these layers, the ability to innovate and be competitive in the market would be under threat.
- **Cost**: To handle the increased demand, the IT Operations team were adding new server instances to handle the load. However, with each new instance, the complexity was increasing along with license costs (that depended on the number of cores). Unlike the Facebooks of the world, enterprise cost per user was increasing with every user acquisition.

At this time, enterprises started looking at open source products and how modern applications are getting built in consumer-facing companies serving millions of users, handling petabytes of data, and deploying to the cloud.

Consumer-facing companies encounter these hurdles early in their life cycle. Lots of innovation led to the design and development of new open source products, as well as design patterns for cloud computing.

In this context, the whole premise of **service-oriented architecture** (**SOA**) was looked at and enterprises investigated how the application architecture could adopt principles of designing autonomous services that are isolated, discrete, and could be integrated and composed with other services. This has led to the rise of the microservices model, which adapts and integrates very well with the cloud services model, where everything is available as a service and as an HTTP endpoint.

Microservices is a specialization of and implementation approach for service-oriented architectures (SOA) used to build flexible, independently deployable software systems

– Wikipedia

Microservices are designed and developed, keeping in mind that a business application can be built by composing these services. The microservices are designed around the following principles:

- **Single-responsibility principle**: Each microservice implements only one business responsibility from the bounded domain context. From a software point of view, the system needs to be decomposed into multiple components where each component becomes a microservice. Microservices have to be lightweight, in order to facilitate smaller memory footprints and faster startup times.

- **Share nothing**: Microservices are autonomous, self-contained, stateless, and manage the service state (memory/storage) through container-based encapsulation models. The private data is managed by a service and there is no contention on the data from any other service. Stateless microservices scale better and start faster than stateful ones, as there is no state to be backed up on shutdown or activated on startup.

- **Reactive**: This is applicable for microservices with concurrent loads or longer response times. Asynchronous communication and the callback model allow optimal utilization of the resources, resulting in better availability and increased throughput of the microservices.

- **Externalized configuration**: This externalizes the configurations in the config server, so that it can be maintained in hierarchical structure, per environment.

- **Consistent**: Services should be written in a consistent style, as per the coding standards and naming convention guidelines.

- **Resilient**: Services should handle exceptions arising from technical reasons (connectivity and runtime), and business reasons (invalid inputs) and not crash. Patterns, such as circuit breakers and bulk headers, help isolate and contain failures.

- **Good citizens**: Microservices should report their usage statistics, the number of times they are accessed, their average response time, and so on through the JMX API or the HTTP API.

- **Versioned**: Microservices may need to support multiple versions for different clients, until all clients migrate to higher versions. There should be a clear version strategy in terms of supporting new features and bug fixing.

- **Independent deployment**: Each of the microservices should be independently deployable, without compromising the integrity of the application:

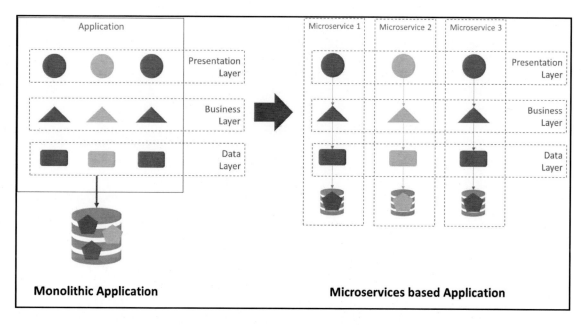

Moving from a monolithic to a microservices-based application

The microservices' design, development, and deployment considerations are covered in detail in the subsequent chapters. We will see how to build services for an e-commerce product. I am sure everyone is quite familiar with e-commerce and will understand the product requirements easily.

The 12-factor app

In order to build a distributed, microservices-based application that can be deployed across cloud providers, engineers at Heroku came up with 12 factors that need to be implemented by any modern cloud-native application:

- **Single codebase**: The application must have one codebase, tracked in revision control for every application (read: microservice) that can be deployed multiple times (development, test, staging, and production environments). Two microservices do not share the same codebase. This model allows the flexibility to change and deploy services without impacting other parts of the application.

- **Dependencies**: The application must explicitly declare its code dependencies and add them to the application or microservice. The dependencies are packaged as part of the microservice JAR/WAR file. This helps isolate dependencies across microservices and reduce any side effects through multiple versions of the same JAR.
- **Config**: The application configuration data is moved out of the application or microservice and externalized through a configuration management tool. The application or microservice will pick up the configuration based on the environment in which it is running, allowing the same deployment unit to be propagated across the environments.
- **Backing services**: All external resources, access should be an addressable URL. For example, SMTP URL, database URL, service HTTP URL, queue URL, and TCP URL.. This allows URLs to be externalized to the config and managed for every environment.
- **Build, release, and run**: The entire process of building, releasing, and running is treated as three separate steps. This means that, as part of the build, the application is built as an immutable entity. This immutable entity will pick the relevant configuration to run the process based on the environment (development, testing, staging, or production).
- **Processes**: The microservice is built on and follows the shared-nothing model. This means the services are stateless and the state is externalized to either a cache or a data store. This allows seamless scalability and allows load balance or proxy to send requests to any of the instances of the service.
- **Port binding**: The microservice is built within a container. The service will export and bind all its interfaces through ports (including HTTP).
- **Concurrency**: The microservice process is scaled out, meaning that, to handle increased traffic, more microservice processes are added to the environment. Within the microservice process, one can make use of the reactive model to optimize the resource utilization.
- **Disposability**: The idea is to build a microservice as immutable with a single responsibility to, in turn, maximize robustness with faster boot-up times. Immutability also lends to the service disposability.

- **Dev/prod parity**: The environments across the application life cycle—DEV, TEST, STAGING, and PROD—are kept as similar as possible to avoid any surprises later.
- **Logs**: Within the immutable microservice instance, the logs generated as part of the service processing are candidates for state. These logs should be treated as event streams and pushed out to a log aggregator infrastructure.
- **Admin processes**: The microservice instances are long-running processes that continue unless they are killed or replaced with newer versions. All other admin and management tasks are treated as one-off processes:

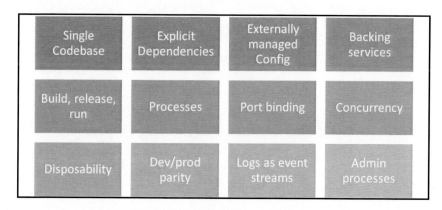

12-factor app

Applications that follow the 12 factors make no assumptions about the external environment, allowing them to be deployed on any cloud provider platform. This allows the same set of tools/processes/scripts to be run across environments and deploy distributed microservices applications in a consistent manner.

Microservices-enabling service ecosystem

In order to successfully run microservices, there are certain enabling components/services that are needed. These enabling services can be tagged as PaaS that are needed to support the building, releasing, deployment, and running of the microservices.

In the case of the cloud-native model, these services are available as PaaS services from the cloud provider itself:

- **Service discovery**: When the application is decomposed into a microservices model, a typical application may be composed of hundreds of microservices. With each microservice running multiple instances, we soon have thousands of microservice instances running. In order to discover the service endpoint, it is pertinent to have a service registry that can be queried to discover all of the instances of the microservice. In addition, the service registry tracks the heartbeat of every service instance to make sure that all services are up and running. Further, the service registry helps in load balancing the requests across the service instances. We can have two models for load balancing:
    - Client-side load balancing:
        - A service consumer asks the registry for a service instance
        - The service registry returns with the list of services where the service is running
    - Server-side load balancing:
        - The service endpoint is hidden by Nginx, API Gateway, or another reverse proxy from the consumer

Typical products in this space are Consul and Zookeeper:

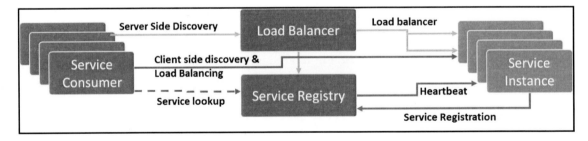

The service registry

- **Config server**: The microservice needs to be initialized with multiple parameters (for example, database URL, queue URL, functional parameters, and dependency flags). Managing properties in file or environment variables beyond a certain number can become unwieldy. To manage these properties across environments, all such configurations are managed externally in a configuration server. At boot time, microservices will load the properties by invoking the API on the config server.

Microservices also make use of listeners to listen for any changes to the properties on the config server. Any runtime change of properties can be picked up immediately by the microservices. The properties are typically categorized at multiple levels:

- **Service-specific properties**: Hold all properties tied to the microservice
- **Shared properties**: Hold properties that might be shared between services
- **Common properties**: Hold properties that are common across services

The config server can back up these properties in a source-control system. Typical products in this space are Consul, Netflix Archaius, and Spring Cloud Config server:

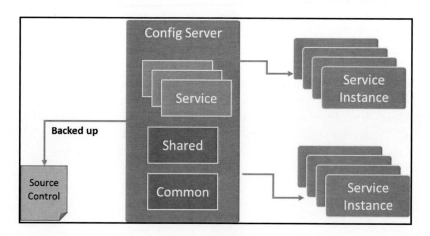

The config server

- **Service management/monitoring**: An average business application typically tends to get decomposed into about 400 microservices. Even if we ran two to three instances of these microservices, we would be talking about managing over 1,000 instances of our microservices. Without an automated model, managing/monitoring these services becomes an operational challenge. The following are the key metrics that need to be managed and monitored:
    - **Service health**: Each service needs to publish its health status. These need to be managed/tracked to identify slow or dead services.
    - **Service metrics**: Each service also publishes throughput metrics data, such as the number of HTTP requests/responses, the request/response size, and the response latency.
    - **Process info**: Each service will publish JVM metrics data (like heap utilization, the number of threads, and the process state) typically available as part of the Java VisualVM.
    - **Log events as stream**: Each service can also publish log events as a set of streaming events.

All of this information is pulled from the services and tied together to manage and monitor the application services landscape. Two types of analysis—event correlation and correction decisions—need to be done. Alerts and actuation services are built as part of the service monitoring systems. For example, if a certain number of service instances need to be maintained and the number reduces (service not available due to health check) then an actuation service can take the event as an indicator to add another instance of the same service.

Further, in order to track the service call flow through the microservices model, there is third-party software available that can help create a request identified and track how the service call flows through the microservices. This software typically deploys agents onto the containers, which weave them into the services and track the service metrics:

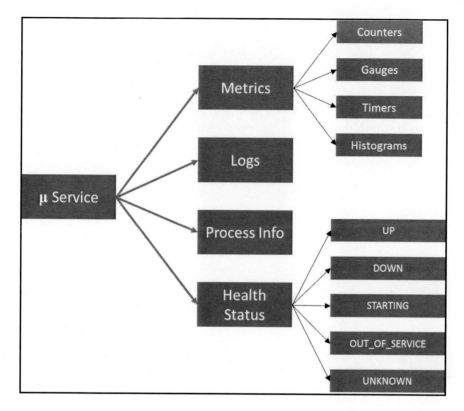

Service metrics

- **Container management/orchestration**: Another key infrastructure piece of the microservice environment is container management and orchestration. The services are typically bundled in a container and deployed in a PaaS environment. The environment can be based on an OpenShift model, a Cloud Foundry model, or a pure VM-based model, depending whether they are deployed on a private or a public cloud. To deploy and manage the dependencies between the containers, there is a need for container management and orchestration software. Typically, it should be able to understand the interdependencies between the containers and deploy the containers as an application. For example, if the application has four pieces—one for UI, two for business services, and one for data store—then all of these containers should be tagged together and deployed as a single unit with interdependencies and the right order of instantiation injected.

- **Log aggregation**: 1 of the 12 factors is treating logs as event streams. The containers are meant to be stateless. The log statements are typically stateful events that need to be persisted beyond the life of the containers. As a result, all logs from the containers are treated as event streams that can be pushed/pulled onto a centralized log repository. All the logs are aggregated and various models can be run on these logs for various alerts. One can track security and failure events through these logs, which can feed into the service management/monitoring system for further actions:

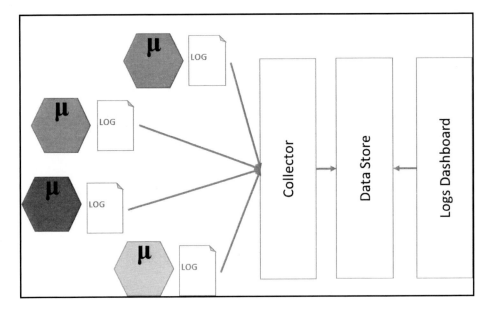

Log aggregation

- **API Gateway/management**: The services are meant to be simple and follow the single responsibility model. The question arises: who will handle other concerns, such as service authentication, service metering, service throttling, service load balancing, and service freemium/premium models? This is where the API Gateway or management software comes into the picture. The API Gateway handles all such concerns on behalf of the microservice. The API Gateway provides multiple options for managing the service endpoints and can also provide transformation, routing, and mediation capabilities. The API Gateway is more lightweight, compared to the typical enterprise service bus.

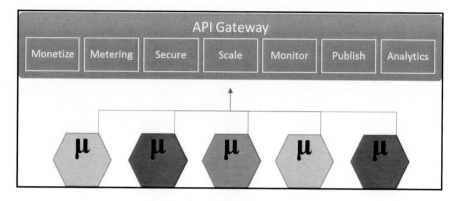

API Management Gateway

- **DevOps**: Another key aspect is the continuous integration/deployment pipeline, coupled with the automated operations that need to set up the microservice-based applications. As the developer writes code, it goes through a series of steps that need to be automated and mapped with gating criteria to allow the release of regression-tested code:

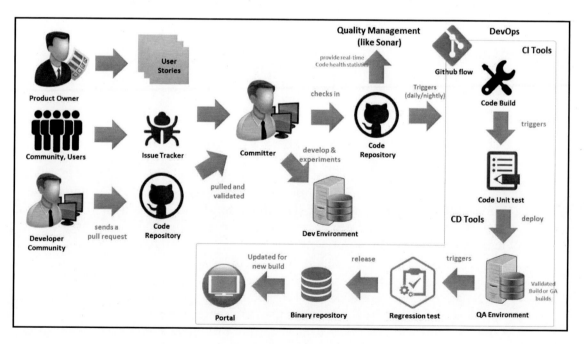

Development life cycle

Microservice adoption

Microservice adoption within an enterprise is driven by a common theme of digital transformation, whether they are looking to re-architect the existing monolithic applications in the system of innovations to increase business agility and reduce technical debt, or to develop greenfield applications that allow them to rapidly innovate and experiment with different business models.

Monolithic transformation

Enterprises have been running channel applications built on JEE principles running on clusters of application servers. These applications have accumulated a lot of technical debt over the years and have become a major issue—large, unwieldy, and resistant to constant change.

With the increase in competition in the business environment and the proliferation of the channels, businesses are looking for faster innovation and to provide seamless customer experience. On the other hand, they do not want to throw away the existing investment in the existing applications.

In this scenario, enterprises are undertaking multiple programs to re-factor and re-architect the existing applications into modern, distributed, microservice-based models that provide the currency of rapid iteration and are future-proof.

Enterprises are attacking this problem in a two-prong manner:

1. Setting the base platform that provides the core ecosystem as a set of services to deploy and run the microservices. These services include Configuration Management, Service Discovery, Elastic Compute, Container Management, Security, Management and Monitoring, DevOps pipeline, and more. Enterprises typically weigh in between using the public cloud and setting up a private cloud. The choice of cloud platform depends on the industry in question and the maturity of the enterprise strategy.
2. The second approach is to chip at the monolithic application, one functional piece at a time, and migrate the core business logic to the microservice model. The GUI part is separately migrated to an SPA model using frameworks such as AngularJS and ReactJS. For example, a lot of e-commerce enterprises have moved their catalogue and search services to elastic cloud providers. Only when the customer clicks the checkout do they bring the customer to the in-house data center.

Once the enterprise has set up the ecosystem with respect to platform services, the ability to add more microservice-based functionality becomes easy, providing the required impetus in terms of business agility and innovation.

We will cover digital transformation in more detail in Chapter 12, *Digital Transformation*.

Summary

In this chapter, we covered what cloud-native programming is and why to go for it. We saw what the various adoption models for enterprises, when it comes to cloud-native applications, are. We covered the 12 factors for distributed applications, along with the usage of microservice-based design for cloud-native enablement. We covered the enablement ecosystem for building microservices-based applications.

As we progress through the book, we will cover how to design, build, and run your cloud-native application. We will also cover cloud-native application development using two cloud provider platforms—AWS and Azure. We will make use of their platform services to build a cloud-native application.

We will also cover operational aspects of the cloud-native application—DevOps, deployment, monitoring, and management. Lastly, we will cover how to transform existing monolithic applications into modern distributed cloud-native applications. In the next chapter, we will dive right into creating our first cloud-native application.

2
Writing Your First Cloud-Native Application

This chapter looks at the essential elements of building your first cloud-native application. We will do the minimal number of steps required to get a microservice running in our development environment.

If you are an experienced Java developer using IDEs such as Eclipse, you will find yourself on familiar turf. Though most of it will be similar to building traditional applications, there are a few nuances, which we will discuss in this chapter and summarize at the end.

The setup steps to get development going will vary based on the type of developer:

- For hobbyist, self-employed, or working-from-home developers with open access to the internet, cloud development is relatively simple.
- for enterprise developers who work on projects for customers or business teams in a closed environment and has to access the internet through a proxy, you have your enterprise development guidelines to follow. You will be constrained in what you can download, run, and configure. Having said that, the benefit of being this type of developer is that you are not alone. You have the support of your team and colleagues who can help with informal help, or formal documentation in wikis.

By the end of this chapter, you will have a cloud-native microservice running in your machine. To get there, we will cover the following topics:

- The developer's toolbox and ecosystem
- Internet connectivity
- The development life cycle

- Framework selection
- Writing a cloud-native microservice
- Enabling a few cloud native behaviors
- Reviewing key aspects of cloud development

Setting up your developer toolbox

For any profession, the tools are very important, and that applies to coding as well. Before writing a line of code, we need to get the right equipment to start.

Getting an IDE

An **integrated development environment** (**IDE**) is more than a code editor; it includes the tools for autocompletion, syntax, formatting, and other miscellaneous features, such as search and replace. IDEs have advanced features such as refactoring, building, testing, and running the programs with the help of runtime containers.

The popular IDEs are Eclipse, IntelliJ IDEA, and NetBeans. Of the three, Eclipse is the most popular and open source IDE available for Java. It has a big community and is frequently updated. It has a workspace and an extensible plugin system. The development potential of applications in a whole range of languages is endless. Some other development IDEs based on Eclipse include the following:

- If you are going to do only Spring development, then the derivative of Eclipse called **Spring Tool Suite** (**STS**) is a good option.
- There are also cloud IDEs such as Eclipse Che, touted as the next-generation Eclipse. It does not need any installation. You develop in a browser that connects to a Che server, which builds a workspace remotely (containing libraries, runtime, and dependencies) in a Docker container. As a result, you can develop from any machine and anyone can contribute to your project, with just a URL. If you think that is cool and have a need for a location- and machine-independent development, give it a spin.

For the purposes of this book, let's stick to the basic and hugely popular Eclipse. The current edition, at the time of writing this book, is Neon. A large community and configurable plugin support makes it the IDE of choice for cloud-based Java development.

Download the latest version from: `https://www.eclipse.org/`. Assuming you have JDK 8 or later installed, Eclipse should start up fine.

Configure a workspace that will store your project files and settings:

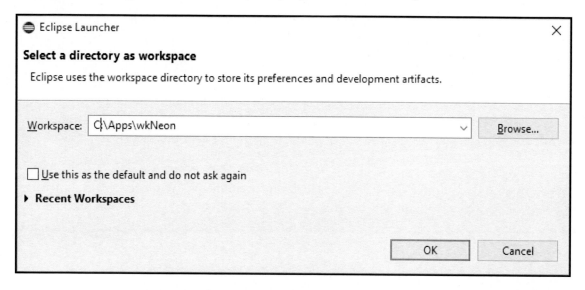

When you hit **OK**, the Eclipse IDE should open up. Eclipse Neon will automatically get you two important plugins we need for development:

- **Git client**: This will allow us to connect to a Git source control repository. This book assumes you use Git due to its popularity and features, but there are many older options in use in enterprises, such as Subversion and Perforce. In case you use the alternatives, download the respective plugin to your IDE by following the developer setup instructions given by your project team or in your team wiki. If these instructions do not exist, ask to build one for new team members to use.

- **Maven support**: Maven and Gradle are both great project management and configuration tools. They help with tasks such as getting dependencies, compiling, building, and so on. We chose Maven because of its maturity with the enterprises.

If you are coming across these two for the first time, please get familiar with both by reading up on their respective websites.

Setting up internet connectivity

If you are working in an enterprise and have to access internet through a proxy, this can be a pain based on what your enterprise policies limits you to do.

For our development purposes, we need internet connectivity for the following:

- Downloading dependency libraries such as Log4j and Spring that are configured as part of the Maven repository. This is a one-time activity, as the libraries become part of the local Maven repository once downloaded. If your organization has a repository, you need to configure that.
- Eclipse plugins from the marketplace as we evolve our sample application.
- Your program calls a service or APIs that are in the public cloud.

For writing our first service, only the first point is important. Please get your proxy details and configure them in the Maven settings from the main menu, **Windows** I **Preferences**, as follows:

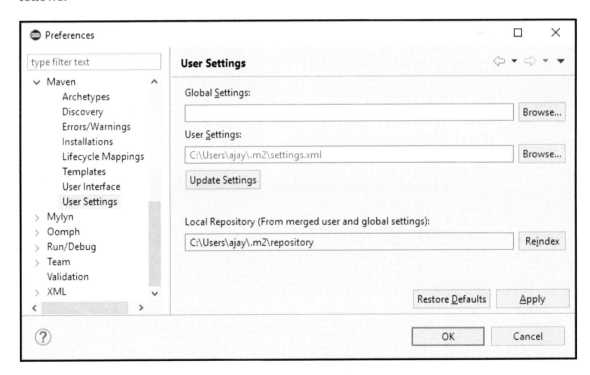

Make changes to the `settings.xml` file in **User Settings** and add a proxy section:

```xml
<proxies>
  <proxy>
      <id>myproxy</id>
      <active>true</active>
      <protocol>http</protocol>
      <host>proxy.yourorg.com</host>
      <port>8080</port>
      <username>mahajan</username>
      <password>****</password>
      <nonProxyHosts>localhost,127.0.0.1</nonProxyHosts>
  </proxy>
  <proxy>
      <id>myproxy1</id>
      <active>true</active>
      <protocol>https</protocol>
      <host> proxy.yourorg.com</host>
      <port>8080</port>
      <username>mahajan</username>
      <password>****</password>
      <nonProxyHosts>localhost,127.0.0.1</nonProxyHosts>
  </proxy>
```

Save the file and restart Eclipse. We will know whether it worked when we create a project.

Understanding the development life cycle

Professional software writing goes through various stages. In the following sections, we will talk about all the various stages we will follow while developing the application.

Requirements/user stories

It is important to know the problem statement being solved before starting any coding or design. Agile development methodology recommends breaking the overall project into modules and services, and then implementing a few features at a time as user stories. The idea is to get a **minimally viable product** (**MVP**) and then keep adding features.

The problem we have taken to solve is an area of e-commerce. Due to online shopping, most of us are familiar with e-commerce as consumers. It is time to look under the hood.

The starting point is a `product` service that does the following:

- Returns details of a product given a product ID
- Gets a list of product IDs for a given product category

Architecture

We have separate chapters dedicated to this later in the book. In brief, once the requirements are known, architecture is about taking key decisions and creating a blueprint of how the requirements will be realized, and the design is about contracts and mechanisms to implement them. For cloud-native development, we have taken a call to implement microservices architecture.

The microservices architecture paradigm recommends smaller deployment units that contain a unit of functionality. Hence, our `product` service will run its own process and have its own runtime. This makes it easier to bundle the entire runtime, and take it from development to test environments and then to production with a consistent behavior. Each `product` service will register itself in a service registry to be discoverable to other services. We will examine the technology choices later.

Design

Design takes a deeper dive into the interface and implementation decisions of the service. The `product` service will have a simple interface that takes a product ID and returns a Java object. If the product is not found in the repository, you can decide to return an exception or an empty product. The access is logged and metrics on how many times the service was accessed and how long it took are recorded. These are the design decisions.

We will discuss architecture and design principles specific to cloud development in detail in later chapters.

Testing and development

In any modern enterprise software development, testing is not an afterthought or an activity post development. It is done with or prior to the development through concepts such as **test-driven development (TDD)** and **behavior-driven development (BDD)**. The test cases are written first, which fail initially. Then, enough code is written to pass the test case. This concept is extremely important for regression testing in future iterations of the product and blends nicely with the **continuous integration (CI)** and **continuous delivery (CD)** concepts discussed later.

Building and deployment

Building and deployment are the steps to create the deployment unit from the source code and put it in the target runtime environment. The developer executes most of the steps in the IDE. However, with CI principles, an integration server does the compilation, automated test case execution, building the deployment unit, and deploying it in a target runtime.

In a cloud environment, the deployable unit is deployed on a virtual environment such as a **virtual machine (VM)** or in a container. As part of the deployment, it is important to include the necessary runtimes and dependencies as part of the build process itself. This is different from the traditional process of putting a `.war` or `.ear` in an application server running in each environment. Including all dependencies in the deployable unit makes it complete and consistent as it moves across the various environments. This reduces the chances of errors where the dependencies on server does not match with those on the local machine of the developer.

Selecting a framework

Having looked at the basics, let's write our `product` service. After IDE setup, the next step is to select a framework to write the service. The microservice architecture puts forward a few interesting design considerations that will help us select the frameworks:

- **Lightweight runtime**: The service should be small in size and fast to deploy
- **High resiliency**: It should have support for patterns such as circuit breaker and timeout

- **Measurable and monitorable**: It should capture metrics and expose hooks for monitoring agents to tap into
- **Efficient**: It should avoid blocking resources and enable high scalability and elasticity in the presence of increased load

A good comparison can be found at: `https://cdelmas.github.io/2015/11/01/A-comparison-of-Microservices-Framework s.html`. Three frameworks are gaining popularity in the Java space that meet the preceding requirements: Dropwizard, Vert.x, and Spring Boot.

Dropwizard

Dropwizard was one of the first frameworks to popularize the fat JAR concept by putting container runtime with all dependencies and libraries inside the deployment unit, instead of putting the deployment unit inside the container. It mashes up libraries such as Jetty for HTTP, Jackson for JSON, Jersey for REST, and Metrics to create a perfect blend for building RESTful web services. It was one of the early frameworks to be used in microservice development.

Its choices, such as JDBI, Freemarker, and Moustache, might sound restrictive for some organizations that want flexibility in their choice of implementation.

Vert.x

Vert.x is an excellent framework to build reactive applications that do not block resources (threads) and hence are very scalable and elastic, and hence resilient. It is a relatively new kid on the block (with major upgrades in version 3.0).

However, its Reactive programming model is not very popular in the industry yet and hence it is just gaining adoption, especially for use cases that require very high resiliency and scalability.

Spring Boot

Spring Boot is rapidly becoming the most popular of the Java frameworks for building cloud-native microservices. Here are a few good reasons:

- It has a foundation on Spring and Spring MVC, which is already popular in enterprises
- Like Dropwizard, it assembles the most reasonable defaults and takes an opinionated approach to assembling the required dependencies for the services, reducing the XML required for configuration
- It integrates Spring Cloud out of the box, which provides useful libraries such as Hystrix and Ribbon, for distributed service development that is required for cloud deployment
- It has a lower learning curve; you can get started in minutes (as we shall see next)
- It has the concept of 40+ starter Maven **Project Object Models (POMs)** that give good flexibility for choosing and developing applications

Spring Boot is suitable for a wide spectrum of the workloads that are suitable for cloud-native deployments and hence is a good first choice for most use cases.

Let's get into writing a service in Spring Boot now.

Writing a product service

For the sake of simplicity, our `product` service has two functions:

- `List<int> getProducts(int categoryId)`
- `Product getProduct(int prodId)`

The intent of the two methods is quite clear. The first returns a list of product IDs given a category ID, and the second returns product details (as an object) given a product ID.

Creating a Maven project

Open your IDE (Eclipse Neon or other) and then create a new Maven project as follows:

1. Right-click on **Package Explorer** and select **New** and **Project...**, as shown in the following screenshot:

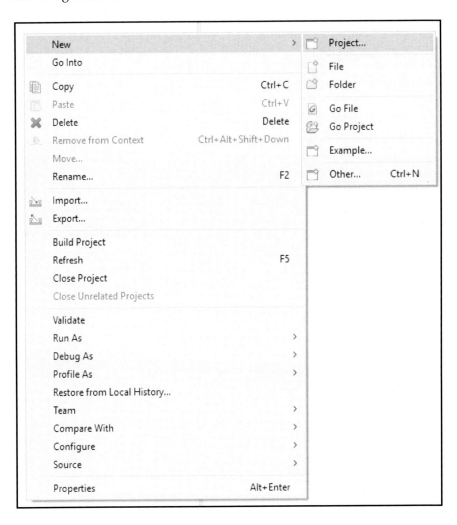

2. Select **Maven Project**:

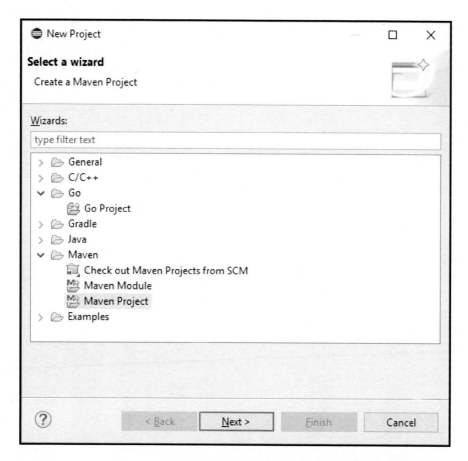

3. In the next window of the wizard, choose **Create a simple project**.

4. The next dialog will ask for many parameters. Of these, the **Group Id** (what your project name is) and the **Artifact Id** (application or service name) are important. Select reasonable names, as shown in the following screenshot:

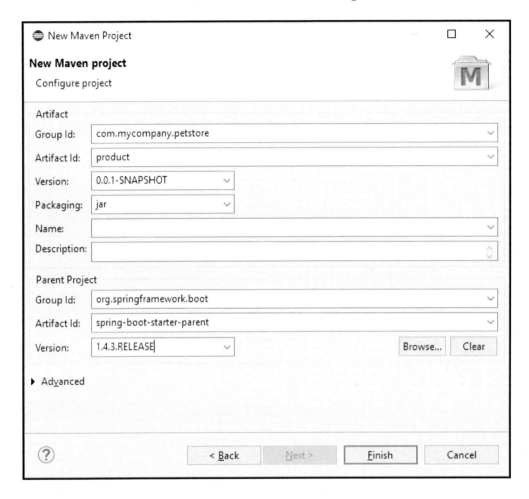

5. Select **Finish**. You should see the following structure:

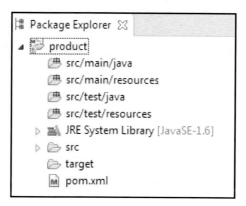

If the **JRE System Library [JavaSE-1.6]** does not exist, or you have a later version, go to the project properties and edit it to select the version that your Eclipse is configured with. You do this by changing the Properties by right-clicking **JRE System Library [JavaSE-1.6]**. Here's a screenshot after adjusting the **JRE System Library** to **1.8**.

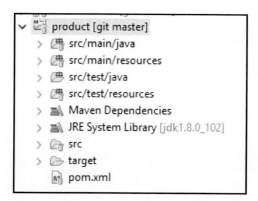

6. Now, you have a clean slate. Open the Maven file `pom.xml` and add a dependency to the `spring-boot-starter-web`. This will tell Spring Boot to configure this project to get libraries for web development:

```
<project xmlns....
  <modelVersion>4.0.0</modelVersion>
  <parent>
    <groupId>org.springframework.boot</groupId>
    <artifactId>spring-boot-starter-parent</artifactId>
```

```
        <version>1.4.3.RELEASE</version>
    </parent>
    <groupId>com.mycompany.petstore</groupId>
    <artifactId>product</artifactId>
    <version>0.0.1-SNAPSHOT</version>
<dependencies>
    <dependency>
        <groupId>org.springframework.boot</groupId>
        <artifactId>spring-boot-starter-web</artifactId>
    </dependency>
</dependencies>
</project>
```

When you save this POM file, your IDE will build the workspace and download the dependent libraries, assuming your internet connection works (directly or through a proxy as configured before), and you are all set to develop the service.

Writing a Spring Boot application class

This class contains the main method where the execution starts. This main method will bootstrap the Spring Boot application, look at the configurations, and start the respective bundled containers such as Tomcat if executing web services:

```
package com.mycompany.product;

import org.springframework.boot.SpringApplication;
import org.springframework.boot.autoconfigure.EnableAutoConfiguration;

@SpringBootApplication
public class ProductSpringApp {
  publicstaticvoid main(String[] args) throws Exception {
    SpringApplication.run(ProductSpringApp.class, args);
    }
  }
```

Note the annotation called @SpringBootApplication.

The @SpringBootApplication annotation is equivalent to using @Configuration, @EnableAutoConfiguration, and @ComponentScan, which do the following:

- @Configuration: This is a core Spring annotation. It tells Spring that this class is a source of the Bean definitions.
- @EnableAutoConfiguration: This annotation tells Spring Boot to guess how you will want to configure Spring, based on the JAR dependencies that you have added. We have added the starter web and hence the application will be considered to be a Spring MVC web application.
- @ComponentScan: This annotation tells Spring to scan for any components, for example, the RestController that we are going to write. Note the scan happens in current and child packages. Hence, the class having this component scan should be at the top of the package hierarchy.

Writing service and domain objects

The annotations in Spring Boot make it easy to extract parameters and path variables and execute the service. For now, let's mock the response instead of getting the data from the database.

Create a simple Java entity called the Product class. For now, it is a simple **Plain Old Java Object (POJO)** class with three fields:

```
publicclass Product {
   privateint id = 1 ;
   private String name = "Oranges " ;
   privateint catId = 2 ;
```

Add the getter and setter methods and a constructor that accepts the product ID:

```
public Product(int id) {
   this.id = id;
   }
```

Also, add an empty constructor that will be used by the service client, as we will see later:

```
public Product() {
 }
```

Then, write the `ProductService` class as follows:

```
M product/pom.xml        J ProductSpringApp.java        J ProductService.java ⨉    J
 1   package com.mycompany.product;
 2
 3⊖ import java.util.Arrays;
 4   import java.util.List;
 5
 6   import org.springframework.web.bind.annotation.PathVariable;
 7   import org.springframework.web.bind.annotation.RequestMapping;
 8   import org.springframework.web.bind.annotation.RequestParam;
 9   import org.springframework.web.bind.annotation.RestController;
10
11   @RestController
12   public class ProductService {
13
14⊖     @RequestMapping("/product/{id}")
15       Product getProduct(@PathVariable("id") int id) {
16           return new Product(id);
17       }
18
19⊖     @RequestMapping("/productIds")
20       List<Integer> getProductIds(@RequestParam("id") int id) {
21           return Arrays.asList(id + 1, id + 2, id + 3);
22       }
23   }
```

Running the service

There are many ways to run the service.

Right-click on the project and select **Run As | Maven build** and configure the **Run Configurations** to execute the `spring-boot:run` target as follows:

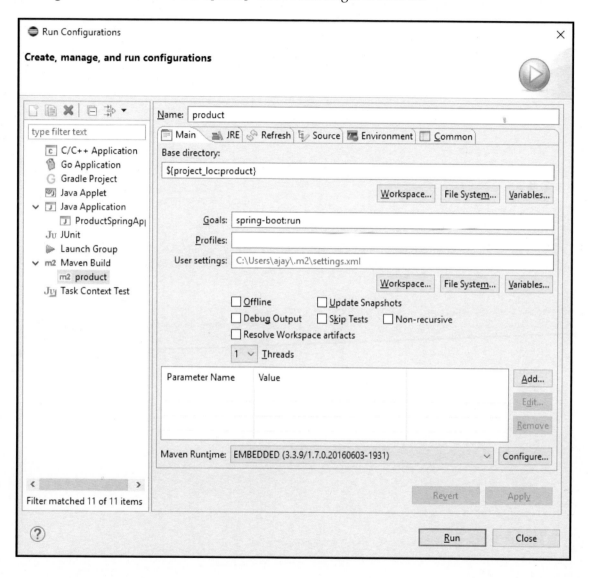

On clicking **Run**, if the internet connection and configuration are fine, you will see the following console output:

```
[INFO] Building product 0.0.1-SNAPSHOT
...
[INFO] Changes detected - recompiling the module!
[INFO] Compiling 3 source files to C:Appswkneonproducttargetclasses
...
 :: Spring Boot ::          (v1.4.3.RELEASE)

2016-10-28 13:41:16.714  INFO 2532 --- [         main]
com.mycompany.product.ProductSpringApp   : Starting ProductSpringApp on
L-156025577 with PID 2532 (C:Appswkneonproducttargetclasses started by
MAHAJAN in C:Appswkneonproduct)
...
2016-10-28 13:41:19.892  INFO 2532 --- [         main]
s.b.c.e.t.TomcatEmbeddedServletContainer : Tomcat initialized with port(s):
8080 (http)
...
2016-10-28 13:41:21.201  INFO 2532 --- [         main]
s.w.s.m.m.a.RequestMappingHandlerMapping : Mapped "{[/product/{id}]}" onto
com.mycompany.product.Product
com.mycompany.product.ProductService.getProduct(int)
2016-10-28 13:41:21.202  INFO 2532 --- [         main]
s.w.s.m.m.a.RequestMappingHandlerMapping : Mapped "{[/productIds]}" onto
java.util.List<java.lang.Integer>
com.mycompany.product.ProductService.getProductIds(int)
...
...
2016-10-28 13:41:21.915  INFO 2532 --- [         main]
s.b.c.e.t.TomcatEmbeddedServletContainer : Tomcat started on port(s): 8080
(http)
2016-10-28 13:41:21.922  INFO 2532 --- [         main]
com.mycompany.product.ProductSpringApp   : Started ProductSpringApp in
6.203 seconds (JVM running for 14.199)
```

Note the stages of the Maven execution:

1. First, the Maven task compiles all the Java files. We have three simple Java classes as of now.
2. The next step runs it as an application, where a Tomcat instance starts.
3. Note the mapping of the URLs `/product/` and `/productIds` to the `Bean` methods.
4. Tomcat listens on port `8080` for service requests.

You can also run the service by just right-clicking the class that has the main method (`ProductSpringApp`) in **Package Explorer** and then selecting **Run As | Java Application**.

Testing the service on the browser

Open a browser and hit the following URL: `http://localhost:8080/product/1`.

You should get back the following response:

```
{"id":1,"name":"Oranges ","catId":2}
```

Now, try the other service (URL—`http://localhost:8080/productIds`). What response do you get? An error, as follows:

```
There was an unexpected error (type=Bad Request, status=400).
Required int parameter 'id' is not present
```

Can you guess why? It is because the service definition that you wrote had a method expecting a request parameter:

```
@RequestMapping("/productIds")
List<Integer> getProductIds(@RequestParam("id") int id) {
```

So, the URL is expecting an `id` and as you did not supply it, it gives an error.

Give the parameter and try `http://localhost:8080/productIds?id=5` again.

You will now get back a correct response:

```
[6,7,8]
```

Creating a deployable

We are not going to run our service on Eclipse. We would like to deploy it on a server. There are two options for doing this:

- Create a WAR and deploy it in Tomcat or any other web container. This is the traditional method.
- Create a JAR with the runtime (Tomcat) included so that you just need Java to execute the service.

In cloud application development, the second option, also called fat JAR or uber JAR, is becoming popular for the following reasons:

- The deployable is self-contained with all the dependencies it needs. This reduces the chances of environment mismatch as the deployable unit is deployed to Dev, Test, UAT, and Production. If it works in development, there is a good chance it will work across all the other environments.
- The host, server, or container where the service is deployed need not have a preinstalled application server or servlet engine. Just a basic JRE is good enough.

Let's look at the steps to create a JAR file and run it.

Include the following dependencies of the POM file:

```
<build><plugins><plugin>
        <groupId>org.springframework.boot</groupId>
        <artifactId>spring-boot-maven-plugin</artifactId>
</plugin></plugins></build>
```

Now, run it by right-clicking the project in the explorer and choosing **Run As | Maven Install**.

You will see `product-0.0.1-SNAPSHOT.jar` in the target directory of the project folder structure.

Navigate to the `product` folder so that you see the target directory in the command line and then run the JAR through a Java command, as shown in the following screenshot:

You will see Tomcat listening to the port at the end of the startup. Test it through the browser again. Milestone achieved.

Enabling cloud-native behaviors

We have just developed a basic service with two APIs that respond to requests. Let's add a few capabilities that will enable to it to be a good cloud citizen. We will discuss the following:

- Externalizing configuration
- Instrumentation—health and metrics
- Service registration and discovery

Externalizing configuration

Configuration can be any property that is likely to differ between environments or production deployments. Typical examples are queue and topic names, ports, URLs, connection and pool properties, and so on.

A deployable should not have configuration in it. A configuration should be injected from outside. This makes the deployable unit immutable as it goes through the various stages of the life cycle, such as Dev, QA, and UAT.

Let's assume we have to run our `product` service in different environments, where the URL differentiates the environment. Therefore, the small change we make in the request mapping is as follows:

```
@RequestMapping("/${env}product/{id}")
Product getProduct(@PathVariable("id") int id) {
```

We can inject this variable in various ways. Once injected, the value is not expected to change for the life of the deployment. The simplest is to pass it in the command-line argument. Bring up the **Run Configurations** dialog and in the **Arguments**, add the command-line parameter `-env=dev/` as follows:

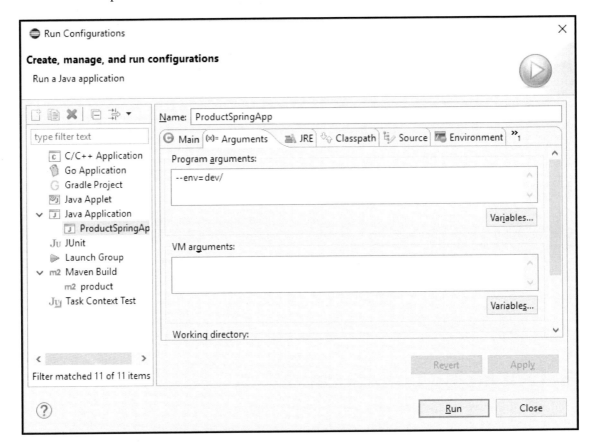

Now, **Run** the configuration. During startup, you will find the value substituted in the log statement as follows:

```
... Mapped "{[/dev/product/{id}]}" onto com.mycompany.product.Product
com.mycompany.product.ProductService.getProduct(int)
```

The configuration can also be provided through configuration files, database, operating system environment properties, and so on.

Spring applications popularly use `application.properties` to store a few properties such as port numbers. Recently, YAML, which is a superset of JSON, is becoming more popular due to the hierarchical definition of the properties.

Create an `application.yml` file in the `/product/src/main/resources` folder of the application and put in the following:

```
server:
  port: 8081
```

This tells the `product` service to run at port `8081` instead of the default `8080`. This concept is further extended to profiles. So, it is possible to load different profiles by loading the configuration specific to the profile.

Spring Cloud Config as a project handles this well. It uses a `bootstrap.yml` file to get the application started up with a name and details of the source to further load the configuration. Hence, `bootstrap.yml` contains the application name and config server details, and then loads the respective profile configuration.

Create a `bootstrap.yml` file in the `resources` folder of the application and put in the following:

```
spring:
  application:
    name: product
```

We will come back to these files when we discuss service registration later.

Metering your services

Instrumentation is important for cloud applications. Your service should expose health check and metrics so that it can be monitored better. Spring Boot allows for easier instrumentation through the `actuator` module.

Include the following in your POM:

```xml
<dependency>
    <groupId>org.springframework.boot</groupId>
    <artifactId>spring-boot-starter-actuator</artifactId>
</dependency>
```

Run the service. During startup, you will see a number of mappings being created.

You can access these URLs (such as `http://localhost:8080/env`) directly and see the information displayed:

```json
{
  "profiles": [],
  "server.ports": {
    "local.server.port": 8082
  },
  "commandLineArgs": {
    "env": "dev/"
  },
  "servletContextInitParams": {},
  "systemProperties": {
    "java.runtime.name": "Java(TM) SE Runtime Environment",
    "sun.boot.library.path": "C:\Program Files\Java\jdk1.8.0_73\jrebin",
    "java.vm.version": "25.73-b02",
    "java.vm.vendor": "Oracle Corporation",
    "java.vendor.url": "http://java.oracle.com/",
    "path.separator": ";",
    "java.vm.name": "Java HotSpot(TM) 64-Bit Server VM",
    "file.encoding.pkg": "sun.io",
    "user.country": "IN",
    "user.script": "",
    "sun.java.launcher": "SUN_STANDARD",
    "sun.os.patch.level": "Service Pack 1",
    "PID": "9332",
    "java.vm.specification.name": "Java Virtual Machine Specification",
    "user.dir": "C:\Apps\wkneon\product",
```

The metrics are especially interesting (`http://localhost:8080/metrics`):

```
{
  "mem": 353416,
  "mem.free": 216921,
  "processors": 4,
  "instance.uptime": 624968,
  "uptime": 642521,
  . . .
  "gauge.servo.response.dev.product.id": 5,
  . . .
    threads.peak": 38,
  "threads.daemon": 35,
  "threads.totalStarted": 45,
  "threads": 37,
  . . .
```

The information includes the counters and gauges which store the number of times the service was accessed and the response times.

Service registration and discovery

Why is service registration and discovery important? So far, we have been calling the service through its URL, which includes the IP address—for example, `http://localhost:8080/prod`—thus we expect the service to run at that address. Even though we might substitute the test and the production URLs, the step of calling the service at a particular IP address and port is still static.

However, in a cloud environment, things are quite dynamic. If the service goes down at a given IP, it can come up in a different IP address as it comes up on some container. Although we can mitigate that with virtual IPs and reverse proxies, it would be better to look up a service dynamically at the time of the service call and then call the service at the IP address. The lookup addresses can be cached in the client, so that the dynamic lookup need not be performed for each service call.

A registry (referred to as a service registry) helps in this case. When the service boots up, it registers itself in a registry. There is also a heartbeat between registry and service to ensure that the registry keeps only live services in its registry. If the heartbeat stops, the registry deregisters that instance of the service.

For this quick starter, we are going to use Spring Cloud Netflix, which nicely integrates with Spring Boot. We need three components now:

- **Product service**: We have already written this
- **Service registry**: We are going to use Eureka, which is part of Spring Cloud
- **Service client**: Instead of calling our service directly through a browser, we will write a simple client to our service

Running a service registry

Consul and Eureka are two popular dynamic service registries. There are subtle conceptual differences between them with respect to the method of heartbeats and agent-based operations, but the fundamental concept of registry is similar. The selection of the registry will be driven by the needs and the decisions of the enterprise. For our example, let's continue with Spring Boot and the Spring Cloud ecosystem and use Eureka for this example. Spring Cloud includes Spring Cloud Netflix, which has support for the Eureka registry.

Perform the following steps to get a service registry running:

1. Create a new Maven project with `artifactId` as `eureka-server`.
2. Edit the POM file and add the following:
    - Parent as `spring-boot-starter-parent`
    - The dependency to `eureka-server` as `spring-cloud-starter-eureka-server`
    - The `dependencyManagement` to `spring-cloud-netflix`:

```
M eureka-server/pom.xml ⊠

 1⊖ <project xmlns="http://maven.apache.org/POM/4.0.0" xmlns:xsi="http://www.w3.org/2001/XMLSchema-instance"
 2    xsi:schemaLocation="http://maven.apache.org/POM/4.0.0 http://maven.apache.org/xsd/maven-4.0.0.xsd">
 3    <modelVersion>4.0.0</modelVersion>
 4
 5    <groupId>com.mycompany.infra</groupId>
 6    <artifactId>eureka-server</artifactId>
 7    <version>0.0.1-SNAPSHOT</version>
 8
 9⊖   <parent>
10        <groupId>org.springframework.boot</groupId>
11        <artifactId>spring-boot-starter-parent</artifactId>
12        <version>1.4.1.RELEASE</version>
13    </parent>
14
15⊖   <dependencyManagement>
16⊖       <dependencies>
17⊖           <dependency>
18                <groupId>org.springframework.cloud</groupId>
19                <artifactId>spring-cloud-netflix</artifactId>
20                <version>1.2.1.RELEASE</version>
21                <type>pom</type>
22                <scope>import</scope>
23            </dependency>
24        </dependencies>
25    </dependencyManagement>
26
27⊖   <dependencies>
28⊖       <dependency>
29            <groupId>org.springframework.cloud</groupId>
30            <artifactId>spring-cloud-starter-eureka-server</artifactId>
31        </dependency>
32    </dependencies>
33
34 </project>
```

3. Create an application class similar to the one we created for the `product` project. Note the annotations. The annotation `@EnableEurekaServer` starts Eureka as a service:

```
M eureka-server/pom.xml      J EurekaApplication.java ⊠

 1   package com.mycompany.infra.eureka;
 2
 3⊖ import org.springframework.boot.SpringApplication;
 4   import org.springframework.boot.autoconfigure.SpringBootApplication;
 5   import org.springframework.cloud.netflix.eureka.server.EnableEurekaServer;
 6
 7   @SpringBootApplication
 8   @EnableEurekaServer
 9   public class EurekaApplication {
10
11⊖      public static void main(String[] args) throws Exception {
12            SpringApplication.run(EurekaApplication.class, args);
13        }
14   }
```

4. Create an `application.yml` file in the `/product/src/main/resources` folder of the application and put in the following:

```
server:
  port: 8761
```

5. Create a `bootstrap.yml` file in the `resources` folder of the application and put in the following:

```
spring:
  application:
    name: eureka
```

6. Build the `eureka-server` Maven project (as we did for `product`) and then run it.

7. Apart from a few connectivity errors (more on this later), you should see a Tomcat started message as follows:

```
: Initializing Spring FrameworkServlet 'dispatcherServlet'
: FrameworkServlet 'dispatcherServlet': initialization started
: FrameworkServlet 'dispatcherServlet': initialization completed in 19 ms
: Registered instance EUREKA/localhost:eureka:8761 with status UP (replication=false)
: DiscoveryClient_EUREKA/localhost:eureka:8761 - registration status: 204
: Disable delta property : false
: Single vip registry refresh property : null
: Force full registry fetch : false
: Application is null : false
: Registered Applications size is zero : true
: Application version is -1: true
: Getting all instance registry info from the eureka server
: The response status is 200
: Registered instance EUREKA/localhost:eureka:8761 with status UP (replication=true)
: Got 1 instances from neighboring DS node
: Renew threshold is: 1
: Changing status to UP
: Started Eureka Server
```

Once the startup is completed, access the Eureka server at `localhost:8761` and check whether you get the following page:

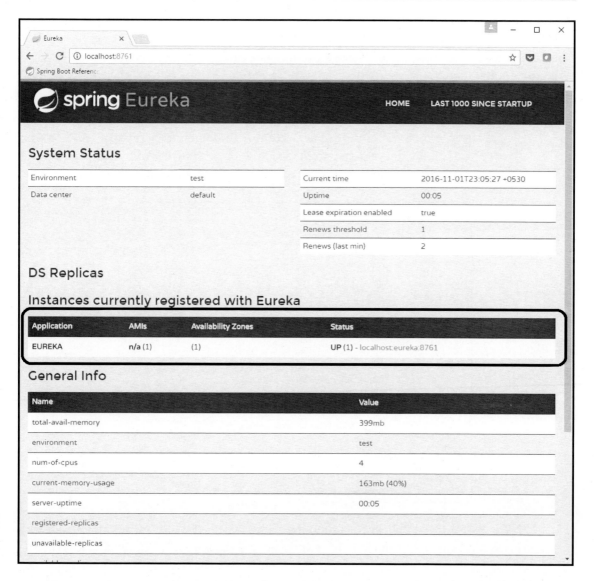

Look at the circled section in the preceding screenshot. The instance currently registered with Eureka is EUREKA itself. We can correct this later. Now, let's focus on registering our product service with this Eureka service registry.

Registering a product service

The `product` service boots up and listens on port `8081` for `product` service requests. We will now add the necessary instructions so that the service instance registers itself with the Eureka registry. Thanks to Spring Boot, we only have to do a few configurations and annotations:

1. Add the `dependencyManagement` section with dependency on `spring-cloud-netflix` and the dependency in the existing dependencies section to `spring-cloud-starter-eureka` to the `product` service POM as follows:

```xml
<dependencyManagement>
    <dependencies>
        <dependency>
            <groupId>org.springframework.cloud</groupId>
            <artifactId>spring-cloud-netflix</artifactId>
            <version>1.2.1.RELEASE</version>
            <type>pom</type>
            <scope>import</scope>
        </dependency>
    </dependencies>
</dependencyManagement>

<dependencies>
    <dependency>
        <groupId>org.springframework.boot</groupId>
        <artifactId>spring-boot-starter-web</artifactId>
    </dependency>
    <dependency>
        <groupId>org.springframework.boot</groupId>
        <artifactId>spring-boot-starter-actuator</artifactId>
    </dependency>
    <dependency>
        <groupId>org.springframework.cloud</groupId>
        <artifactId>spring-cloud-starter-eureka</artifactId>
    </dependency>
</dependencies>
```

2. The `product` service keeps renewing its lease every specific interval. Reduce it to 5 seconds, by defining an entry explicitly in the `application.yml` as follows:

```yaml
server:
  port: 8081

eureka:
  instance:
    leaseRenewalIntervalInSeconds: 5
```

3. Include the annotation @EnableDiscoveryClient in the startup application class of the product project, in other words, ProductSpringApp. The @EnableDiscoveryClient annotation activates the Netflix Eureka DiscoveryClient implementation as that is the one we have defined in the POM file. There are other implementations for other service registries, such as HashiCorp Consul or Apache Zookeeper:

```
┌─────────────────────────────────────────────────────────────────────────────────┐
│ 📄 bootstrap.yml      M product/pom.xml      J ProductServi...   J ProductSprin... ⊠ │
├─────────────────────────────────────────────────────────────────────────────────┤
│  1   package com.mycompany.product;                                               │
│  2                                                                                │
│  3⊕ import org.springframework.boot.SpringApplication;                            │
│  6                                                                                │
│  7   @SpringBootApplication                                                       │
│  8   @EnableDiscoveryClient                                                       │
│  9                                                                                │
│ 10   public class ProductSpringApp {                                             │
│ 11                                                                                │
│ 12⊖      public static void main(String[] args) throws Exception {                │
│ 13           SpringApplication.run(ProductSpringApp.class, args);                 │
│ 14       }                                                                        │
│ 15   }                                                                            │
└─────────────────────────────────────────────────────────────────────────────────┘
```

4. Now, start the product service as before:

```
com.netflix.discovery.DiscoveryClient              : Getting all instance registry info from the eureka server
com.netflix.discovery.DiscoveryClient              : The response status is 200
com.netflix.discovery.DiscoveryClient              : Starting heartbeat executor: renew interval is: 10
c.n.discovery.InstanceInfoReplicator               : InstanceInfoReplicator onDemand update allowed rate per min is 4
com.netflix.discovery.DiscoveryClient              : Discovery Client initialized at timestamp 1478022547463 with initial
c.n.e.EurekaDiscoveryClientConfiguration           : Registering application product with eureka with status UP
com.netflix.discovery.DiscoveryClient              : Saw local status change event StatusChangeEvent [timestamp=147802254
com.netflix.discovery.DiscoveryClient              : DiscoveryClient_PRODUCT/localhost:product:8081: registering service.
com.netflix.discovery.DiscoveryClient              : DiscoveryClient_PRODUCT/localhost:product:8081 - registration status
s.b.c.e.t.TomcatEmbeddedServletContainer           : Tomcat started on port(s): 8081 (http)
c.n.e.EurekaDiscoveryClientConfiguration           : Updating port to 8081
com.mycompany.product.ProductSpringApp             : Started ProductSpringApp in 10.099 seconds (JVM running for 10.567)
```

At the end of the initialization of the product service, you will see log statements that register the service with the Eureka server.

To check whether the `product` service has registered, refresh the Eureka server page that you just accessed:

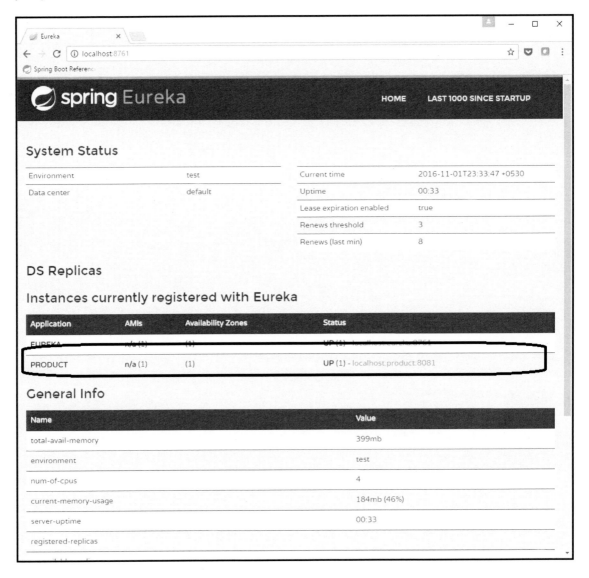

Also keep a tab on the Eureka log. You will find the lease renewal log statements of the `product` service.

Creating a product client

We have created a dynamic product registry and even registered our service. Now, let's use this lookup to access the `product` service.

We will use the Netflix Ribbon project, which provides a load balancer as well as having address lookup from the service registry. Spring Cloud makes it easier to configure and use this.

For now, let's run the client within the same project as the service itself. The client will make an HTTP call to the service after looking up the product definition in Eureka. All this will be done by the Ribbon library, and we will just be using it as an endpoint:

1. Add a dependency to the Maven POM of the `product` project as follows:

```xml
<dependencies>
    <dependency>
        <groupId>org.springframework.boot</groupId>
        <artifactId>spring-boot-starter-web</artifactId>
    </dependency>
    <dependency>
        <groupId>org.springframework.boot</groupId>
        <artifactId>spring-boot-starter-actuator</artifactId>
    </dependency>
    <dependency>
        <groupId>org.springframework.cloud</groupId>
        <artifactId>spring-cloud-starter-eureka</artifactId>
    </dependency>
    <dependency>
        <groupId>org.springframework.cloud</groupId>
        <artifactId>spring-cloud-starter-ribbon</artifactId>
    </dependency>
</dependencies>
```

2. Create a `ProductClient` class, which simply listens on `/client` and then forwards the request after doing a lookup to the actual `product` service:

```
@RestController
public class ProductClient {

    @Autowired
    private RestTemplate rTemplate ;

    @Value("${env}")
    private String env ;

    @RequestMapping("/client/{id}")
    Product getProduct(@PathVariable("id") int id) {

        Product product = rTemplate.getForObject(
                "http://PRODUCT/" + env +"/product/" + id,
                Product.class);
        return product ;
    }
}
```

 The URL construction `http://PRODUCT/` will be translated at runtime by Ribbon after doing a lookup. We are nowhere giving an IP address of the service.

3. The `restTemplate` is injected here through auto-wiring. However, it needs to be initialized in the latest Spring versions. Hence, declare it as follows in the main application class, which also acts as a configuration class:

```
@SpringBootApplication
@EnableDiscoveryClient
public class ProductSpringApp {

    public static void main(String[] args) throws Exception {
        SpringApplication.run(ProductSpringApp.class, args);
    }

    @Bean
    @LoadBalanced
    public RestTemplate restTemplate() {
        return new RestTemplate();
    }
}
```

The @LoadBalanced annotation tells Spring to use the Ribbon load balancer (as Ribbon is in the classpath due to Maven).

Seeing the lookup in action

Now, we are all set to run the product client. To recap, at this stage, we have a Eureka server project and a product project with the following structure:

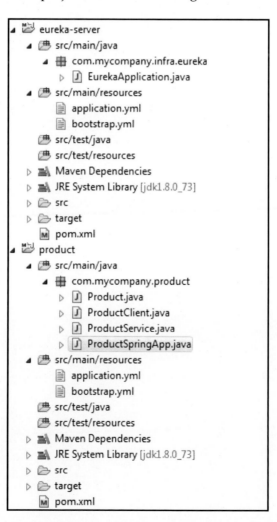

Let's take a few minutes to review what we did:

1. We created a Maven project and defined the starters and dependencies.
2. We created the YML files for bootstrapping and application properties.
3. We created the `ProductSpringApp` class containing the main method that is the starting point of the applications.
4. For the `product` project, we had the following classes:
    - `Product`: The domain or entity which we will enhance later
    - `ProductService`: The microservice responsible for implementing the services and APIs
    - `ProductClient`: The client to test out the service lookup

Now, let's see it in action:

1. Run the `EurekaApplication` class (or run a Maven build on the `eureka-server` project). Observe the last few lines in the logs:

```
Initializing Spring FrameworkServlet 'dispatcherServlet'
FrameworkServlet 'dispatcherServlet': initialization started
FrameworkServlet 'dispatcherServlet': initialization completed in 34 ms
Registered instance EUREKA/L-156025577.wipro.com:eureka:8761 with status UP (replication=false)
DiscoveryClient_EUREKA/L-156025577.wipro.com:eureka:8761 - registration status: 204
Registered instance EUREKA/L-156025577.wipro.com:eureka:8761 with status UP (replication=true)
Disable delta property : false
Single vip registry refresh property : null
Force full registry fetch : false
Application is null : false
Registered Applications size is zero : true
Application version is -1: true
Getting all instance registry info from the eureka server
The response status is 200
Registered instance EUREKA/L-156025577.wipro.com:eureka:8761 with status UP (replication=true)
Got 1 instances from neighboring DS node
Renew threshold is: 1
Changing status to UP
Started Eureka Server
```

2. Run the `ProductSpringApp` class (or run a Maven build on the `product` project). Note the last few lines in the the log:

```
InstanceInfoReplicator onDemand update allowed rate per min is 4
Discovery Client initialized at timestamp 1478077808353 with initial instances count: 1
Registering application product with eureka with status UP
Saw local status change event StatusChangeEvent [timestamp=1478077808403, current=UP, previous=STARTING]
DiscoveryClient_PRODUCT/L-156025577.wipro.com:product:8082: registering service...
DiscoveryClient_PRODUCT/L-156025577.wipro.com:product:8082 - registration status: 204
Tomcat started on port(s): 8082 (http)
Updating port to 8082
Started ProductSpringApp in 11.65 seconds (JVM running for 12.316)
```

3. Access the `product` service directly
   at: `http://localhost:8081/dev/product/4`.
   You will see the following response:

   `{"id":4,"name":"Oranges ","catId":2}`

4. Now, access the client URL, `http://localhost:8081/client/4`, which does a lookup of the `product` service from the service registry and directs it to the respective `product` service.
   You will see the following response:

   `{"id":4,"name":"Oranges ","catId":2}`

   You may see an internal server error (`No instances available for PRODUCT`). This can happen while the heartbeat completes and the addresses are re-picked by the Ribbon load balancer. Wait a few seconds for the registry to update and then try again.

A lot has happened under the hood in getting this response:

1. The HTTP request to get `/client/4` was handled by the `getProduct` method in the `ProductClient` class.

2. It did a lookup of the service from the Eureka registry. This is where we find log statements as follows:

```
c.n.l.DynamicServerListLoadBalancer: Using serverListUpdater
PollinServerListUpdater
c.netflix.config.ChainedDynamicProperty: Flipping property:
PRODUCT.ribbon.ActiveConnectionsLimit to use NEXT property:
niws.loadbalancer
c.n.l.DynamicServerListLoadBalancer: DynamicServerListLoadBalancer for
client PRODUCT intiated: DynamicServerListLoadBalancer:
```

3. After it did the lookup, it forwarded the request to the actual `ProductService` through the Ribbon load balancer library.

This was just a simple mechanism of a client invoking services through a dynamic lookup. In later chapters, we will add functionality to make it resilient and functional in terms of getting data from the database.

Summary

Let's review the key concepts of the cloud applications that we have discussed so far. We made our application **lightweight** by making it run on a servlet engine and start in less than 15 seconds. Our application is **self-contained**, as the fat JAR has all libraries to run our service. We just need a JVM to run this JAR file. It has **externalized configuration** (to some extent) by injecting environment from the command line and properties from `application.yml` and `bootstrap.yml`. We take a deeper look at the next stages of externalization in `Chapter 7`, *Cloud-Native Application Runtime*. The Spring actuator helped capturing all metrics and made their URL available for consumption, thus enabling **instrumentation**. The **location abstraction** was implemented by Eureka.

In the next chapters, we will enhance this service by adding to it a data tier and resiliency, and adding cache behavior and other enhancements that we skipped in this chapter.

3

Designing Your Cloud-Native Application

In this chapter, we pause application development and take a step back to look at the bigger picture of designing cloud applications. As seen in the first chapter, applications in the cloud have more unique challenges than the traditional enterprise applications that we have been developing so far. Also, the business requirement of agility has to be met by not compromising on performance, stability, and resiliency. Hence, a look at the first principles becomes important.

In the first chapter, we had a look at the differences between cloud environments and traditional enterprises, and how the concepts of DevOps, 12-factor app, microservices, and ecosystems are important. Here, we will look at the various principles and techniques that enable us to design robust, scalable, and agile applications.

Some of the areas we will cover include the dominance of the REST, HTTP, and JSON for building APIs, the role of the API gateways, how to decouple applications, how to identify microservices, various microservice design guidelines, the role of the data architecture, and the role of security in designing the APIs.

We will cover the following topics in this chapter:

- Popularity of REST, HTTP, and JSON
- Rise and popularity of the APIs
- Role of API gateways
- Decoupling—the need for smaller application boundaries
- Microservice identifications

- Microservice design guidelines
- Microservice patterns
- Data architecture
- Role of security

The trio – REST, HTTP, and JSON

The web has made HTTP tremendously popular and is the de facto integration mechanism for accessing content on the internet. Interestingly, this technology was not hugely popular within applications that relied on native and binary protocols, such as RMI and CORBA for inter-application access.

When social consumer companies, such as Google, Amazon, Facebook, and Twitter, started publishing APIs to connect/integrate with their products, the de facto standard for integration across the web became HTTP/REST. Social consumer companies started investing in platforms for onboard developers to develop various applications leading to the proliferation of applications that relied on HTTP as the protocol.

The applications on the browser side are a mix of HTML and JavaScript. Information returned from the server or across other applications needs to be in a simple and usable format. JavaScript supports data manipulation, and the data format that it suited most is **JavaScript Object Notation (JSON)**.

REST is a state representational style that provides a way to deal with interchange over HTTP. REST has a lot factors in its favor:

- Utilizes the HTTP protocol standard, giving it an immense leg up for anything and everything on WWW
- Mechanism to isolate the access to entities (GET/PUT/POST/DELETE) while still utilizing the same HTTP request model
- Supports JSON as the data format

REST with JSON has become the dominant model over the SOAP/XML model. According to one statistic from ProgrammableWeb:

73% of the APIs on Programmable Web use REST. SOAP is far behind but is still represented in 17% of the APIs.

Let's cover some high-level reasons why the REST/JSON model is favored over the SOAP/XML model of service development:

- SOAP model of contract first approach makes crafting web services difficult.
- SOAP is complex compared to REST, giving a steeper learning curve as compared to REST.
- REST is lightweight compared to SOAP and does not tax the bandwidth as much as SOAP.
- Support for SOAP outside of the Java world is limited, relegating SOAP primarily to the enterprise world.
- XML parsing on the client side is memory and compute intensive, which does not lend well to the mobile world.
- XML Schema/markup provides structure definitions and validation models but at the expense of additional parsing. JSON has a loose syntax allowing rapid iterations on the data model.

Today, the reality is REST/JSON has been adopted as the standard for integration across programming languages providing an easy and simple way to integrate APIs over the internet.

Rise and popularity of the APIs

An **Application Programming Interface** (**API**) provides a standard interface or contract to consume its services over the internet. The API defines the structure of the input and output and remains constant over the life of an API version.

APIs are the contract between the client layer and the enterprise. They are consumer-oriented, that is, designed by the client, and they abstract the service implementation details from the client.

Coming back to the advent of social consumer companies, creating new applications meant not starting from scratch. For example, if my application needs to use geographical maps, I can make use of the Google Map APIs and build my application on top of that. Similarly, instead of building my own authentication model, I can make use of OAuth and use Google, Facebook, or Twitter as some of the OAuth providers.

This entire model of making a repeatable but often complex functionality available as a reusable service led to a model where the developer started building the applications using these pre-existing APIs, which in turn led to increased developer productivity and evolution of the modern day applications or mobile applications economy.

Companies started to look to see if they could monetize the APIs, which meant multiple companies were writing/publishing APIs that provided similar functionalities. This led to the democratization of the APIs allowing anyone and everyone access to features/functions.

This whole democratization of the API meant, suddenly, every process or functionality could be provided as a set of APIs that could be orchestrated or choreographed to build new features or functions. What took months or years earlier, now only takes weeks or days. All this productivity means shorter development cycles, allowing rapid iteration to provide new and innovative features.

Today, all kinds of APIs are available: from social companies such as Facebook, Google, and Twitter to enterprises such as Salesforce, NetSuite, and PaaS/IaaS providers, such as AWS, Azure, **Google Cloud Engine** (**GCE**), and so on, that all provide functionality from provisioning a VM to a database instance, to AI providers such as Watson, AWS AI, and Azure ML.

Role of API gateways

An API gateway is a singular interface that handles all the incoming requests before redirecting to the internal servers. An API gateway typically provides the following functions:

- Routes the incoming traffic to the appropriate service hosted with the provider's data center/cloud. Provides a reverse proxy model to limit the exposure of various APIs and services hosted within the provider's data center/cloud.
- Filters all the incoming traffic from all kind of channels—web, mobile, and so on.
- Implements security mechanisms (such as OAuth) to authenticate and log the service usage.
- Provides ability to throttle and limit traffic to certain services.
- Transforms data between the service consumer and provider.
- Provides one or more APIs that map to an underlying service provider. For example, for different kind of consumers—mobile, web, paid service, or a free service, the same underlying service can be split into multiple custom APIs that are exposed to a different set of consumers, so that the consumer sees only the features it needs:

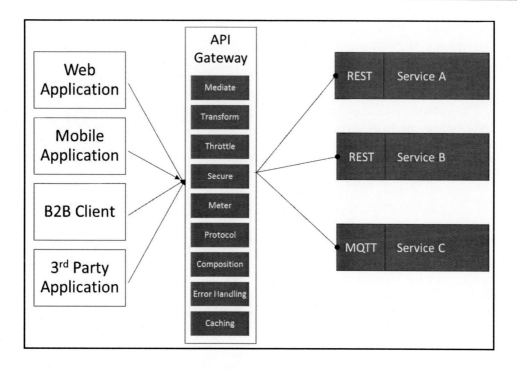

Benefits of an API gateway

Use of API gateways provides the following benefits:

- **Separation of concerns**: Insulates the microservice providers from the service consumers on the application side. This allows the separation of the application tier from the service requesting clients.
- **Consumer oriented**: API gateways provide a unified hub for a large number of APIs and microservices. This allows the consumer to focus on API utility instead of locating where a service is hosted, managing service request limits, security, and so on.
- **API oriented**: Provides an optimum API based on the type of the client and required protocols.
- **Orchestration**: Provides the ability to orchestrate multiple services calls into one API call, which in turn simplifies the logic for a client. Now, instead of calling multiple services, it can invoke one API. Fewer requests means less invocation overhead and improve the consumer experience overall. An API gateway is essential for mobile applications.

- **Monitor**: An API gateway also provides the ability to monitor API invocations, which in turn allows enterprises to evaluate the success of APIs and their usage.

Besides the overall benefits, API gateways add more pieces to the overall puzzle. Meaning more infrastructure to manage, more configurations to manage, more points of failure, and additional hops to the requests. So, unless the benefits outweigh the drawbacks, use of API gateways needs be carefully scrutinized for the business requirements and benefits.

Next, we will see the process of breaking down the application functionalities as a set of APIs or microservices.

Application decoupling

The traditional model of application development, where all the features and functionalities were bundled in a large package called a monolithic application, is becoming less popular for multiple reasons. Monolith applications take on too many responsibilities in the form of function and logic. It is this characteristic which leaves them with high coupling and low cohesion. The reuse factor in monoliths tends to be low since one part of the functionality cannot be separated from the rest of the function and logic.

As we start breaking down the monolith functionality or even designing a new application, the focus needs to be on defining the service boundaries. Defining the right set of service boundaries and their related interactions is what leads to high cohesion and low coupling models.

The question becomes, what is the basis on which the application should be decoupled into services and defined service boundaries?

Bounded context/domain-driven design

As part of the application design, the business domain needs to be broken down into smaller subdomains or business capabilities. We need to carefully examine the business entities and their attributes to define service boundaries. For example, in the case of customer ID entity, the address of the customer might be integral to the customer. Within the context of the application, address maintenance might be a separate activity and might need to be handled separately. Similarly, customer preferences or shopping habits might be required for personalization. In this case, the personalization engine is more interested in this set of attributes.

Should we be slapping together one big customer service having all kind of attributes or can it be divided based on the perspectives derived from the business? These different perspectives are what led to the definition of bounded context as part of the domain-driven design.

The bounded context is a domain-driven design paradigm that helps to add a seam and create service groups. Bounded contexts work in solution-space to indicate that the services are related and belong to a common functional domain. It is built by one team that works with one business unit as per Inverse Conway's law. A bounded context may communicate with the other services/business capabilities through:

- Exposing internal APIs or services
- Emitting events on the Event Bus

A bounded context may have its own data store common to services or adopt a data store per service paradigm.

Each bounded context has a life of its own and forms a product. Teams are organized around these bounded contexts and they take the full responsibility of the full stack implementation of the services. The teams are cross-functional and bring skills from development, testing, user experience, database, deployment, and project management. Each product might be split into smaller sets of services that communicate asynchronously with each other. Remember, the focus is not on a set of functionalities but rather on business capability.

We start building our services around business capabilities. The service owns its business data and functionality. The service is the master of such data, and other services cannot own any of this service data.

Classification into up/downstream services

Another way to break down the application systems is to categorize them by upstream and downstream data flow models. Core entities in the system comprise the upstream services. These upstream services than raise events that are subscribed by the downstream services to augment their functionality. This is aimed at decoupling the systems and help improve the overall business agility. This works well with Reactive, also known as event-driven, architecture concepts.

Let's take a simplified view of an e-commerce application, where the core entities are **CUSTOMER** and **PRODUCT**. The **ORDER** service depends on information about customers and products from the core entities. Next, we are building services that provide **RECOMMENDATION** and **PERSONALIZATION** services to the customer. The **RECOMMENDATION** and **PERSONALIZATION** services depend upon data from the core entities—**CUSTOMER, PRODUCT,** and **ORDER**. When there is a change to any of the core entities, changes are published. These changes are picked up by the **RECOMMENDATION** and **PERSONALIZATION** services, where they augment this data with additional attributes to provide relevant services. The **RECOMMENDATION** and **PERSONALIZATION** services downstream these services:

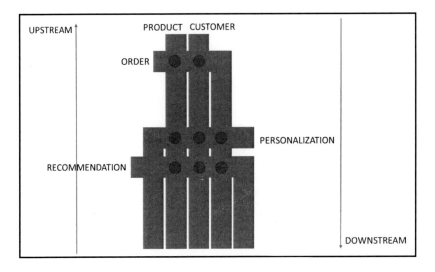

This model of classifying the business capabilities into **UPSTREAM** and **DOWNSTREAM** help define the dependency relationships between services and change the impact of any upstream services on the downstream services.

Business events

As the system evolves, the services will start aggregating into natural allies. This means finding out whether the services are depending on a similar set of data elements or providing overlapping/side-kick functionality, and can potentially be part of the same bounded context.

Services within the bounded context working within the same domain might need to rely on the master for accurate functioning. This might mean, some of the master service data attributes need to be made available to the associated bounded context services. For example, in our previous example, we talked of customer preferences. Now, these preferences might need to be mapped to the location (address) of the customer. In this case, should the customer preference call the customer address service every time to build the preferences or can it copy the relevant attributes to its own domain? Without duplication of data, the two services start getting coupled tightly, leading to a two-way communication model. To break this tight coupling, we allow the customer preferences service to cache or duplicate the relevant customer attributes using the events. This asynchronous model breaks the temporal tight coupling between the services. Whenever there is a change of customer address, the service publishes a business event for the requisite change. The change is subscribed by the customer preferences, which picks up the change to update its preferences model.

This asynchronous model allows us to make sure:

- Ownership of data is still clear. Any change to data is declared to the dependent services. The dependent services are allowed to hold or duplicate data, but not change the local copy unless the master copy is updated (golden source principle). The dependent services store only the subset of data that is required and functionally relevant (need-to-know principle).
- Asynchronous business events lead to low coupling between services. Core service changes result in an event. Events travel downstream to interested dependent services. The only dependency is the format of the business event published.
- Downstream services follow the eventual consistency principle; all business events are stored in a sequential manner to construct/state a later time (event sourcing/CQRS). Query models can be different from the system of record.
- Asynchronous models of business events also promote choreography over orchestration, leading to loosely coupled systems/services.

At times, when teams start on a new product, an upfront definition of bounded context or services decomposition might not be possible. So, teams start building the application as a monolithic application by exposing its functionality as a set of services. As the team implements more stories, they can identify pieces of functionality that are changing at a fast pace (typically experience or channel services) versus slow changing pieces (typically core services or entity services).

The team can start putting the services into two categories—experience and system services. System services can further be grouped together around entities and interrelations. Experience services are mapped to the customer journeys. Teams will typically have sprints just to clean/refactor the code to clear the technical debt that accumulates with every cycle.

So, the next question is, what identifies a service as a microservice?

Microservice identification

The name microservice does not necessarily mean that the service has to be small in size. But it has the following characteristics:

- **Single responsibility principle**: This is the core design principle of microservices. They should do one business unit of a task and do it completely. If there is low coupling, the services will be easier to modify and deploy or even replace altogether.
- **Granular**: Microservice granularity is contained within the intersection of a single functional domain, a single data domain and its immediate dependencies, a self-sufficient packaging, and a technology domain.
- **Bounded**: A service should have access to resources within its bounded context, which is managed by the same team. However, it should not access resources of other modules, such as cache and databases, directly. If a service needs to access other modules it should do so through an internal API or service layer. This helps reduce coupling and promotes agility.
- **Independent**: Each microservice is developed, tested, and deployed independently, in its own source. It can use third-party or shared libraries.

Differences between microservices and service-oriented architecture (SOA)

Here are the differences between microservices and **service-oriented architecture (SOA)**:

- A service executes the entire business unit of work. For example, if a service requires customer or product data, it is preferable to store it within the service data stores. Typically, there is no need to go to a customer service for getting a customer record through ESB.

- A service has its own private database or a database that is shared only in its bounded context and can store the information required to service the business unit of work.
- A service is a smart endpoint and typically exposes a REST interface with a contract definition in Swagger or similar repository. Some of the services that are consumed by other divisions or clients are exposed through an API platform.

Service granularity

Here are the types of services:

- **Atomic or system services**: These are the services that do a unit level of work and are enough to service the request by either referring to a database or a downstream source.
- **Composite or process services**: These services depend on the coordination between two or more atomic services. Typically, composite microservices are discouraged unless the business case already involves using existing atomic services. An example is a credit card payment from a savings account that calls two services, one to debit the savings account, and an other to credit the card account. Composite microservices also introduce inherent complexity such as state management and transactions that are difficult in a distributed scenario.
- **Experience services**: These services are tied to the customer journey and are deployed at the edge of the infrastructure. These services handle requests from the mobile and web applications. These services are exposed through a reverse proxy using tools such as API gateways.

Microservice design guidelines

The whole notion of microservices is about the separation of concerns. This requires a logical and architectural separation between the services with different responsibilities. Here are a few guidelines to design the microservices.

These guidelines are in line with the 12-factor applications guidelines given by Heroku engineers:

- **Lightweight**: Microservices have to be lightweight in order to facilitate smaller memory footprints and faster startup times. This facilitates faster MTTR, and allows for services to be deployed on smaller runtime instances, hence horizontally scaling better. Compared to heavy runtime times, such as application servers, smaller runtimes such as Tomcat, Netty, Node.js, and Undertow are more suited. Also, the services should exchange data in lightweight text formats, such as JSON, or binary formats, such as Avro, Thrift, or Protocol Buffers.

- **Reactive**: This is applicable to services with highly concurrent loads or slightly longer response times. Typical server implementations block threads to execute imperative programming styles. As microservices could depend on other microservices or I/O resources such as a database, blocking threads could increase operating system overheads. The Reactive style operates on non-blocking I/O, uses call back handlers, and reacts to events. This does not block threads and as a result, increases the scalability and load handling characteristics of the microservices much better. Database drivers have started supporting reactive paradigms, for example, MongoDB Reactive Streams Java Driver.

- **Stateless**: Stateless services scale better and start faster as there is no state to be stored on disk on shutdown or activated on start-up. They are also more resilient, as termination of a service will not result in a loss of data. Being stateless is also a step towards being lightweight. If a state is required, a service can delegate state storage to a high speed persistent (key value) store, or hold it in distributed caches.

- **Atomic**: This is the core design principle of microservices. They should be easy to change, test, and deploy. All these can be achieved if the services are reasonably small and do the smallest business unit of work that can be done independently. If there is low coupling, the services will be easier to modify and independently deploy. Composite microservices may be required on a need basis but should be limited in design.

- **Externalized configuration**: Typical application properties and configurations were traditionally managed as configuration files. Given the multiple and large deployments of microservices, this practice will start getting cumbersome, as the scale of the services increase. Hence, it is better to externalize the configurations in the configuration server, so that it can be maintained in a hierarchical structure per environment. Features such as hot changes can also be easier to reflect many services at once.

- **Consistent**: Services should be written in a consistent style as per the coding standards and naming convention guidelines. Common concerns such as serialization, REST, exception handling, logging, configuration, property access, metering, monitoring, provisioning, validations, and data access should be consistently done through reusable assets, annotations, and so on. It should be easier for another developer from the same team to understand the intent and operation of the service.

- **Resilient**: Services should handle exceptions arising from technical reasons (connectivity, runtime), and business reasons (invalid inputs) and not crash. They should use patterns such as timeouts and circuit breakers to ensure that the failures are handled carefully.

- **Good citizens**: Report their usage statistics, number of times accessed, average response times, and so on through JMX API, and/or publish it through libraries to central monitoring infrastructures, log audit, error, and business events in the standards prescribed. Expose their condition through health check interfaces, for example, as done by Spring Actuator.

- **Versioned**: Microservices may need to support multiple versions for different clients, till all clients migrate to higher versions. Hence the deployments and URL should support semantic versioning, that is, X.X.X.

In addition, microservices will need to leverage additional capabilities that are typically built at an enterprise level such as:

- **Dynamic service registry**: Microservice registers itself with a service registry when up.

- **Log aggregation**: The logs generated by a microservice can be aggregated for central analysis and troubleshooting. The log aggregation is a separate infrastructure and typically built as an async model. Products such as Splunk and ELK Stack in conjunction with event streams such as Kafka are used to build/deploy the log aggregation systems.

- **External configuration**: The microservice can get the parameters and properties from an external configuration such as Consul and Zookeeper to initialize and run.

- **Provisioning and auto-scaling**: The service is automatically started by a PaaS environment if it detects a need to start an additional instance based on incoming load, some services failing, or not responding in time.

- **API gateway**: A microservice interface can be exposed to the clients or other divisions through an API gateway that provides abstraction, security, throttling, and service aggregation.

We cover all the service design guidelines in subsequent chapters as we start building and deploying the services.

Design and deployment patterns

As you start designing the applications, you need to be aware of the various service design and integration patterns.

Design patterns

The microservice design patterns can be categorized into multiple categories depending upon the problem being solved. The most common categories and the relevant patterns are discussed in the following sections.

Content aggregation patterns

With microservices and bounded context, there is an additional responsibility of content aggregation. A client may need information that spans multiple domains or business areas (or in solution terms, the bounded contexts). The content required may not be available with one service. These patterns help identify and model the experience services category mostly. Hence there are various patterns for aggregation that can be applied.

Aggregation by client

Aggregation at the last mile. This applies to web browsers or a reasonable *processing capable* user interface, which is showing content from various domains. This pattern is typically used in the home page that aggregates various subject areas. Also, it's the pattern popularly used by Amazon:

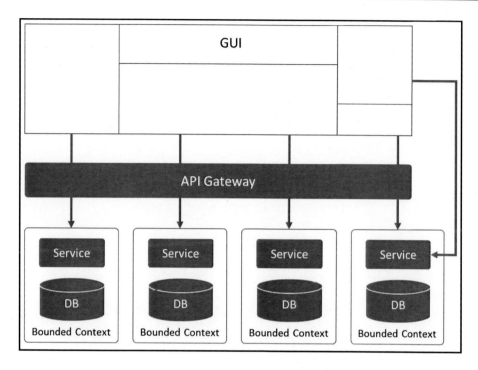

Benefits

The benefits of using the aggregation by the client pattern are as follows:

- Decoupled approach at the services layer. Easier for agility and maintainability at each individual service.
- Faster perceived performance at the UI layer, since the requests, can run in parallel to populate the various areas on the screen. More enhanced when there is a higher bandwidth available to fetch data in parallel.

Trade-offs

The trade-offs associated with the aggregation by the client pattern are as follows:

- Sophisticated user interface processing capabilities, such as Ajax and single-page application required
- The knowledge of aggregation is exposed at the UI layer, hence if the similar output was given as a dataset to a third-party, aggregation would be required

API aggregation

Aggregation at the gates. This applies to mobile or third-party use cases that do not want to know the details of the aggregation and instead would want to expect one data structure over a single request. The API gateways are designed to do this aggregation and then expose a unified service to the client. The API gateways can also select to eliminate any data sections in the aggregate service if it is not required to be shown during content aggregation:

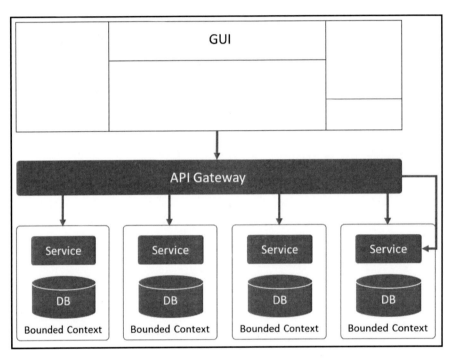

Benefits

The benefits of using the API aggregation pattern are as follows:

- The individual service details are abstracted from the client by the API gateway. Hence it gives the flexibility to change the services internally without affecting the client tier.
- Better in bandwidth constrained scenarios where running parallel HTTP requests may not be a good idea.
- Better in UI processing constrained scenarios where processing power might not be enough for concurrent page generation.

Trade-offs

The trade-offs associated with the API aggregation pattern are as follows:

- Where there is sufficient bandwidth, the latency of this option is higher than the aggregation by the client. This is because the API gateway waits for all the content to be aggregated before sending the data out to the client.

Microservice aggregation

Aggregation at the business tier. In this approach, a microservice aggregates the responses from the various constituent microservices. This pattern is useful if there is any real-time business logic to be applied while aggregating data. For example, showing the total value of customer holdings across various businesses:

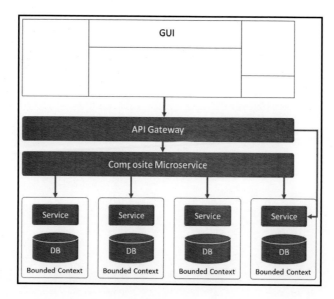

Benefits

The benefits of using the microservice aggregation pattern are as follows:

- Finer control on the aggregation. Also, there is a possibility of incorporating the business logic based on aggregated data. Thus, offering richer content aggregation capabilities.
- Lower dependency on API gateway capabilities.

Trade-offs

The trade-offs associated with the microservice aggregation pattern are as follows:

- Lower latency and more code, as there is an additional hop introduced due to an additional step.
- More chances of failure or making mistakes. Parallel aggregation from microservices will need sophisticated code such as reactive or call back mechanisms.

Database aggregation

Aggregation at the data tier. In this approach, data is pre-aggregated into an **operational data store (ODS)** typically a document database. This approach is useful for scenarios where there is additional business inference on the aggregated data that is difficult to compute in real time through a microservice, and hence can be pre-computed by an analytical engine:

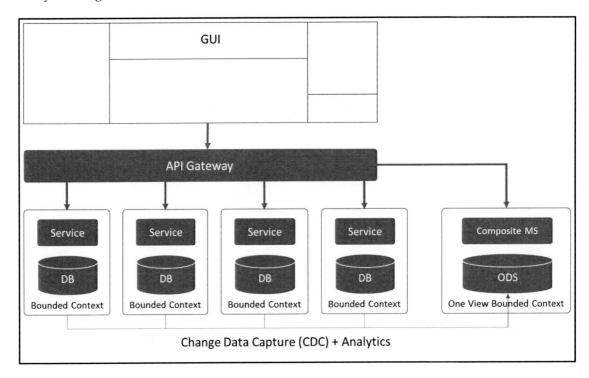

Benefits

The benefits of using the database aggregation pattern are as follows:

- Additional enrichment of data by analytical jobs is possible. For example, in a customer 360° view, based on the customer portfolio aggregated in the ODS, additional analytics can be applied for **next-best-action** (**NBA**) scenarios.
- More flexible and capable as compared to the earlier approaches, and finer control on the data model can be exercised.

Trade-offs

The trade-offs associated with the database aggregation pattern are as follows:

- Higher complexity
- Data duplication and more data storage requirements
- Additional ETL or **change data capture** (**CDC**) tools required to send the data from the system of a record to a central ODS store

Coordination patterns

Ideally, microservices should be capable of doing a business unit of work. However, in some business scenarios, microservices have to leverage other services as a dependency, or as a composition. For example, consider a credit card payment that first debits a savings account and then credits a card account. In this case, the two underlying services, such as debit and credit, could be exposed by the respective savings account and credit card domains and coordination is required between them.

Business process management (BPM)

Complex coordination that involves long-running processes are better done by BPM. An enterprise might already have a BPM product. However, BPM might be overkill for simple two- or three-step coordination.

Composite services

The guideline is to use composite services for low complexity (or simple) coordination that is high in volume. Such coordination can be referred to as microflows for the rest of the discussion.

Why composite services?

In microservices architecture, the implementation of the service definition is done by smaller deployable units instead of large monolith applications that run in application servers. This makes the services easier to write, faster to change and test, and quicker to deploy. But this also creates a challenge for microflows that span two or more microservices, perhaps across multiple bounded contexts. In a monolith application, such microflows could be coordinated as a single transaction across two modules deployed in a single deployable unit. In microservices architecture, distributed transactions are discouraged and hence, microflows have to be solved using a composition approach.

Capabilities for microservices coordination

This section lists the capabilities that the composite services require:

- **State management**: Often the state manager component is required to manage the output state of the services that it is coordinating. This state will need to be held in a persistent store that is immune to **server-side state management (SSM)** failure. Another SSM instance should be able to retrieve the state and start where it left off.
- **Transaction control**: Transaction boundaries are affected by microservices. Two separate function calls to two methods in a single transaction now become two separate service calls through a composite service. There are two approaches to handle this scenario.
  - **Distributed transactions**: These support the two-phase commit protocol. They are not scalable, increase latency and deadlocking scenarios, and need expensive products and infrastructure to support them. They may not be supported over selected protocols, such as REST or messaging. The benefit of this style is that the system is always in a consistent state.
  - **Compensating transactions**: Where the transaction control is functionally enforced by running functionally reverse transactions instead of trying to roll back to an earlier transaction. This is a more decoupled, and hence scalable, approach.
    We would recommend compensating transactions over distributed transactions due to simplification in the technical product requirements.

- **Post service call coordination**: Atomic service calls can result in success, that is, when the constituent services have finished their work successfully; or a failure, when either of the coordination services has either not responded or failed in processing due to a technical or functional error. The composite service will need to get the response of the completed services and decide on the next step of action.
- **Timeout handling**: Initiate a timer when starting a microflow. If the services do not respond in a particular time from starting the microflow, then raise an event to send to the event bus.
- **Configurability**: Multiple instances of the SSM component will run to cater for various microflows. In each of the microflows, the service coordination, timer, and actions will differ. Hence, it is important to provide a framework that can have parameterized configuration of the timers, compensation transactions, and post-processing actions.

Coordination models

We will discuss the following coordination styles of composite service micro flows.

Asynchronous parallel

A composite service initiates the service calls asynchronously to the constituent atomic services and then listens to the service response. If either services fails, it sends a compensating transaction to the other service.

This is similar to the Scatter-Gather or Composed Message Processor patterns of the EIP:

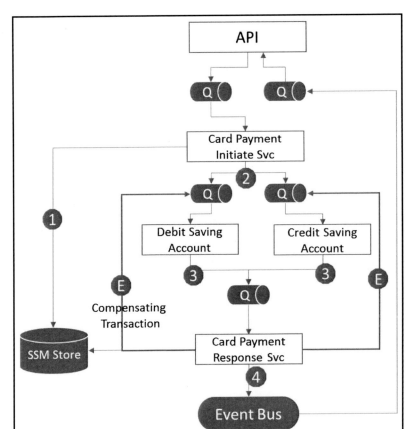

Asynchronous sequential

In pipeline processing, composite services send messages to atomic services sequentially. It waits for the previous service to return success before calling the next service. If anyone service fails, then the composite service sends the compensating transaction to previously successful services. This is similar to the Process Manager pattern in the EIP:

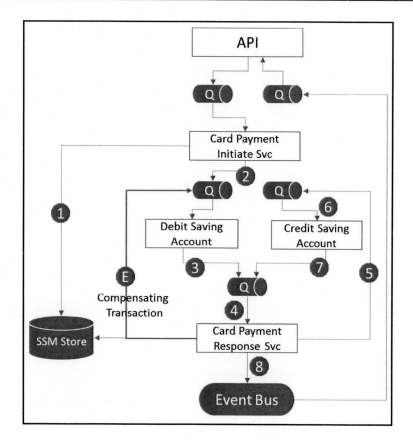

Orchestration using request/response

Similar to the preceding section, but in request/response and sync fashion instead of async messaging.

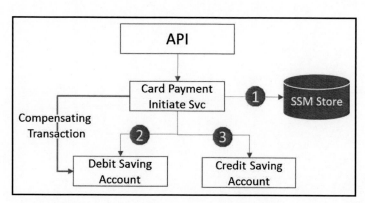

Collapsing the microservices

An option for when there seems to be a coupling between composite and its constituent microservice collapsing the services, and run as a single component. For example, transferring funds can be implemented by an account service, with an additional method `transferFunds` accepting `fromAcc`, `toAcc`, and the fund amount. It can then issue the `debit` and `credit` method calls as part of a single transaction. However, this approach needs to be decided after due consideration. The drawbacks include coupling deploying of debit and credit services of the credit card and savings domain:

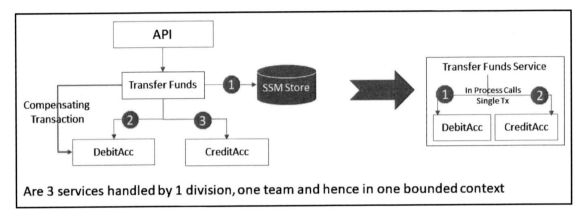

Are 3 services handled by 1 division, one team and hence in one bounded context

Deployment patterns

Microservices attempt to solve monolith problems such as dependencies, and achieve agility by having separate deployable units. We can deploy the microservices on the target runtime in various styles. The options are described in the order of increasing isolation (good) and cost (bad).

Multiple services per WAR file

Although development might be in a microservice style (separate code base for services, different teams working on different services), the deployment essentially follows the monolith style:

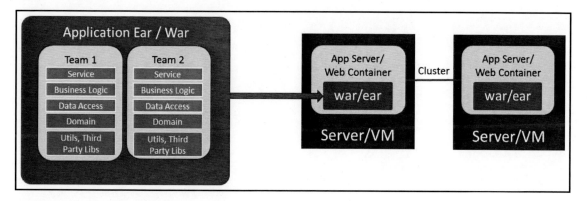

Benefits and trade-offs

The only benefit compared to a complete monolith style is that due to separate code bases and lesser dependencies, there is lower dependency on common code elements. However, it does not offer any runtime isolation between service behavior, and hence does not have the true benefits of a microservice architecture model such as independent releases, scaling individual services, or limiting the impact of one service problem on the other services.

Suitability

There are not many scenarios in which this is useful as it does not offer runtime isolation. However, it might be an intermediary step toward releasing the full separation.

Service per WAR/EAR

This model separates the build process for the services to create separate `.war`/`.ear` files per service. However, they end up being deployed to the same web container or application server:

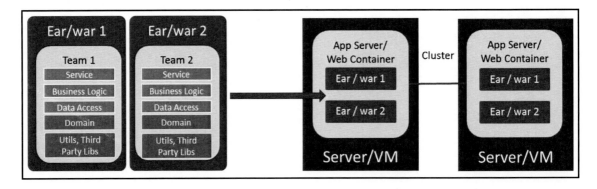

Benefits and trade-offs

This style takes the isolation a step further, by separating the build process for each service to create a deployable unit. However, since they are deployed on the same web container or application server, they share the same process. Hence, there is no runtime isolation between the services.

Suitability

Some teams might experience constraints on target deployment to use the same software or hardware that they were using in monolith style development. In this case, this deployment style is suitable, as the teams can still do independent development without getting under each other's feet, but will have to coordinate the releases with other teams during deployment to their traditional production infrastructure.

Service per process

This style uses the concept of the fat JAR discussed earlier to include the application server or web container as part of the deployment unit. Thus, the target runtime environment only needs a JVM to run the service. Dropwizard and Spring Boot frameworks encourage this type of deployment build. We have also seen an example of creating such a deployment unit in Chapter 2, *Writing Your First Cloud-Native Application*:

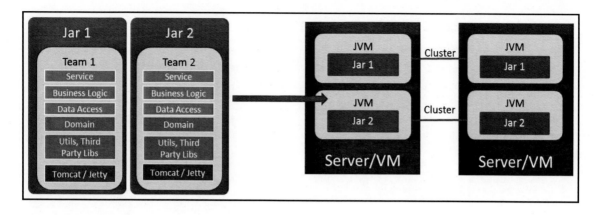

Benefits and trade-offs

The benefits and trade-offs associated with the service per process style are as follows:

- This approach helps in separating the runtime processes on which the services run. Thus, it creates an isolation between the services, so that a memory leak or fat exception in one process does not affect the other services to some extent.
- This allows for selective scaling of service, by allowing more deployments of a service compared to other services on the existing hardware.
- It also gives the freedom to teams of using a different application server/web container based on specific use cases or the needs of the team.
- However, it cannot prevent any one service from hogging system resources (such as CPU, I/O, and memory) that can affect the performance of the other services.
- It also reduces the control over the runtime of the operations team, as there is no central web container or application server present in this model.
- This style requires good governance to limit variability in the deployment estate and having substantial use cases to support the divergence.

Suitability

This style offers the best compromise for teams that are constrained to using their existing production infrastructure and do not have Docker containers or small VM configurations in place yet.

Service per Docker container

In this style, a service deploys as a fat JAR in a Docker container, which has the necessary prerequisites, such as JVM. It takes the isolation a step higher than that provided by the Linux container technology:

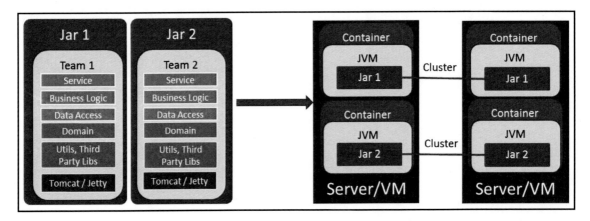

Benefits and trade-offs

The benefits and trade-offs associated with the service per Docker container style are as follows:

- The Linux container technology limits the CPU and memory consumption of the service in addition to providing networking and file access isolation. This level of isolation is sufficient for many services.
- Containers are fast to start up from an image. Hence, new containers based on an application or service image can be spawned very quickly to address the fluctuating demands of the application.
- Containers can be orchestrated through various orchestration mechanisms, such as Kubernetes, Swarm, and DC/OS so that the entire application configuration can be created automatically based on a well-defined application blueprint.
- As in the previous style, it is possible to run a variety of service technologies within a container. For example, running Node.js services in addition to Java services is possible as the container image would be at OS level and hence can be started seamlessly by the orchestration framework.

- Containers have much lower overheads compared to the virtual machines in terms of resource requirements, as they are more lightweight. Hence, they are cheaper compared to running each service in its own virtual machine.
- However, containers reuse the kernel of the host system. Hence, it is not possible to run workloads demanding different operating systems, for example, Windows or Solaris on container technology.

Suitability

This style of deployment is a good balance of isolation and cost. It is the recommended style and suitable for most service deployments.

Service per VM

In this style, the fat JAR is deployed directly on the VM, as in the *Service per process* section. However, here there is only one service deployed per VM. This ensures a complete isolation of the service from the other services.

The deployment is automated through tools such as Chef and Puppet, that can take a base image (such as having Java installed) and then run through a series of steps to install the application JAR and other utilities on the VM:

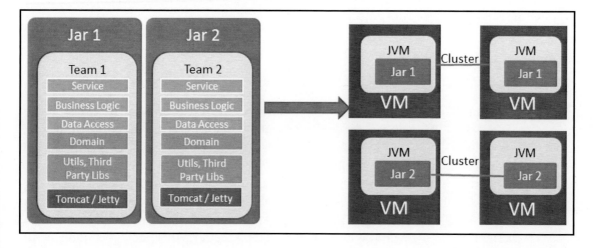

Benefits and trade-offs

The benefits and trade-offs associated with the service per VM style are as follows:

- If there are any use cases that require a complete OS level isolation, then this style is suitable
- This style also allows us to mix completely different workloads, such as Linux, Windows and Solaris, together on the VMs
- However, this style is more resource-intensive and slower to start up as compared to the previous style, as VMs include a complete guest OS start-up
- As a result, it is less cost efficient as compared to earlier options

Suitability

This style of deployment is tilting toward the increased cost. It is the recommended style, and suitable for cloud image based deployments such as creating **Amazon Machine Images (AMI)**.

Service per host

This takes the isolation from the hypervisor (for VMs) to the hardware level by deploying the services on different physical hosts. The concept of microservers or specialized appliances can be used for this purpose.

Benefits and trade-offs

The benefits and trade-offs associated with the service per host style are as follows:

- The hardware (such as processors, memory, and I/O) can be exactly tuned to the use case of the service. Intel offers a range of microservers that are tuned for specific tasks such as graphics processing, web content serving, and so on.
- A very high density of components can be achieved in this solution.
- This style of deployment is for very few use cases that would benefit from hardware-level isolation or specialized hardware needs.
- This is a maturing technology and hence not many data center cloud providers offer it yet. However, it will have matured by the time this book gets published.

Suitability

This style of deployment is extremely rare, as very few use cases require this high level of isolation or specialized hardware requirements. Appliances for web content or graphics processing are a few, specialized use cases that will benefit from this deployment style.

Release patterns

Following are the different release patterns used in services:

- **Fat JAR**: As discussed in `Chapter 2`, *Writing Your First Cloud-Native Application* the fat JAR helps to bundle the web container with the deployable. This ensures that there is no inconsistency between the versions of the deployment in the development, test, and production environment.

- **Blue-green deployment**: This pattern suggests maintaining two production environments that are identical. A new release goes to one of the unused environments, say green. The switch is done from a router to send traffic to the green deployment. If successful, the green environment becomes the new production environment and the blue environment can be made inactive. If there is an issue, rollback is easier. The next cycle happens in reverse, with deployment to the blue environment, thus alternating between the two environments. There are a few challenges such as databases upgrades. For async microservices, this technique can be used to release one microservice or a set of microservices with different input queues. The configuration loaded from connection parameters decides to drop the request message in one queue versus the other.

- **Semantic versioning**: Semantic versioning is about releasing software with version numbers, the way they change the meaning of the underlying code, and what has been modified from one version to the next. Refer to `http://semver.org/` for more details. In async microservices, a similar strategy of using an input queue per microservice applies. However, in this case, both services are active, one for the legacy and one with the new changes. Based on the request, content-based routing pattern can be used to switch the queue to send the request.

- **Canary release**: This pattern is used to introduce a change to a small set of users using a routing logic that selects a group of customers for a new service. In terms of asynchronous services, this can be handled by two sets of input queues, and the redirection logic now decides the queue to drop the request message to.

- **Immutable server / immutable delivery**: Immutable Server and Immutable Delivery are related. The intent is to automatically build the server, (VM or container) and its software and applications from the configuration management repository. Once built, it is not changed, not even when moving from one environment to other. Only the configuration parameters are injected via the environment, JNDI, or separate config servers, such as Consul or using Git. This ensures that there are no ad-hoc changes made to the production deployment that are not recorded in the version control system.
- **Feature toggle**: This allows features released in production to be toggled on or off from some configuration settings. This toggle is typically implemented at the frontend or API gates so that it can be made visible or not visible to the end users of the service/feature. This pattern is very useful for a dark launch capability, which is discussed in the following sections.
- **Dark launch**: Popularized by Facebook. Dark launch means releasing the service/capability into the production well before its scheduled release. This gives the opportunity to test out the integration points and complex services in production environments. Only frontend or API changes are done using a Canary release and feature toggle as discussed earlier.

Data architecture for microservices

One of the key design philosophies of microservices is the bounded context and the service(s) managing the data store. Within a bounded context, multiple services might have access to a common data store, or adopt a per service data store paradigm.

Since there are potentially multiple instances of a service running, how do we make sure the data read/update operations do not lead to a deadlock in resources?

Command Query Responsibility Segregation (CQRS)

CQRS introduces an interesting paradigm challenging the conventional thought of using the same data store to create/update and also query the systems. The idea is to separate the commands that change the state of the system from the queries that are idempotent. The materialized view is an example of this pattern. The separation also gives the flexibility to use a different data model for updates and queries. For example, the relational model could be used for updates, but the events generated from the updates can be used to update caches or document databases that are more read-friendly.

The user requests can be broadly classified into two parts, such as commands that change the state of the system, and queries that get the state of the system for user consumption. For the command processing, the system of engagement collects enough business data so that it can call the respective service on a system of record to execute the commands. For queries, the system of engagement can choose to either call the system of record, or get the information from a local store that is designed for read workloads. This separation of strategy can yield immense benefits, such as reducing the load on the system of record and reducing the latency:

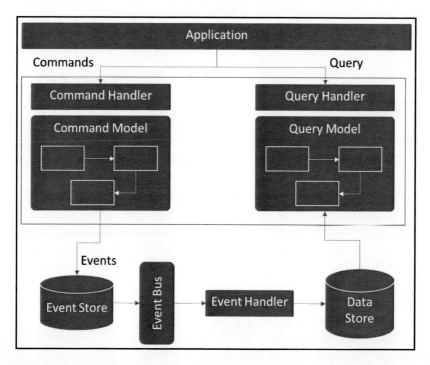

The CQRS pattern helps to leverage legacy systems of records in conjunction with the newer document databases, and caches as well. We will cover how to implement CQRS in your service in the next chapter.

Duplicating data

Within the bounded context, the services are the custodians of the data. But what if another service requires a subset of your data? Some of the questions/solutions that arise are as follows:

- Should I invoke the service to get that data?
  - Increased chattiness among the services
  - Tight coupling of two services
- Can I access the data store directly from another bounded context?
  - Breaks the bounded context model

So, how does another service (residing in another bounded context) get access to the subset of the data? (For example, requiring address attributes for a customer (from customer service) in the personalization services.)

In this case, the best way is to duplicate data from the master domain. The required changes are published as events by the master domain, which are subscribed to by any domain interested in those changes. The events are picked up from the event bus, and data from the event is used to update the changes in the duplicate data store:

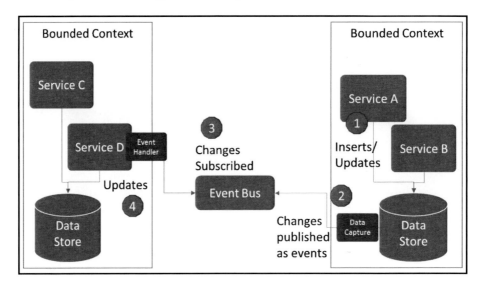

Benefits

The benefits of duplicating data are as follows:

- Helps decouple the service boundaries
- A business event containing the data is the only relationship between the services
- Helps avoid expensive distributed transaction models across boundaries
- Allows us to make changes to our service boundaries without impeding progress of other parts of the system
- We can decide how quickly or slowly we want to see the rest of the outside world and eventually become consistent
- Ability to store the data in our own databases using the technology appropriate for our service model
- Flexibility to make changes to our schema/databases
- Allows us to become much more scalable, fault tolerant, and flexible

Cons

The cons associated with duplicating data are as follows:

- Large volume of data changes might mean a more robust infrastructure at both ends and the ability to handle lost events requires event durability
- Leads to an eventual consistency model
- Complicated system and very difficult to debug

Fit for purpose

The bounded context model means the data encompassed can be modified only through the defined service interfaces or APIs. This means the actual schema or the storage technology used to store the data has no bearing on the API functionality. This opens us up to the possibility of using a fit for purpose data store. If we are building a search functionality and an in-memory data store is a better fit for the given business requirement, we can go ahead with it.

Since, access to the data is governed by the service APIs, the choice and structure of the data store is immaterial to the actual service consumers:

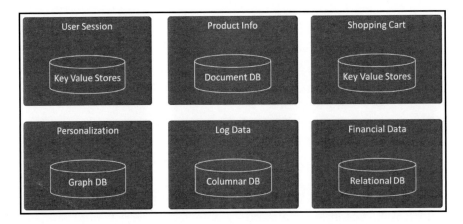

The service APIs model also provides the flexibility to move from one data store to another, without an impact on the other consuming services, as long as the service contracts are maintained. Martin Fowler has termed it, polyglot persistence.

The role of security

With the proliferation of microservices, the challenges of managing security for these services becomes a challenge. Some of the questions that need to be answered, besides the **Open Web Application Security Project** (**OWASP**) top ten web vulnerabilities, are as follows:

- Does the service require the client to authenticate before service invocation (such as OAuth)?
- Can a client call any service or only the service for which it is authorized?
- Does the service know the identity of the client from where the request originated and does it get passed down to the downstream services? Do the downstream services have a mechanism to verify the authorization of their invocation?
- Is the traffic between service to service invocation secured (HTTPS)?
- How do we verify that a request received from an authenticated user hasn't been tampered with?
- How do we detect and reject a replay of a request?

In the distributed microservice model, we need to control and limit the privileges the calling party has, and how much data is accessible (least privilege) on each call in case of a security breach. A large number of microservices and supporting databases means there is a large attack surface that need to be protected. Server hardening across the services becomes an important and key activity to secure the network. It is very important to monitor the service access and model the threats to break down the processes where we are most vulnerable and focus our effort there. We will see the role of API gateways in addressing some of the security concerns.

Summary

This brings us to the conclusion of the design principles for your cloud applications. In this chapter, you learned about the reasons for the popularity of the APIs, how to decouple your monolith application, and various categories of microservice patterns and data architecture principles for microservices design. We also saw the role of security in microservices and the role of API gateways.

In the next chapter, we will take our example from Chapter 2, *Writing Your First Cloud-Native Application*, and start adding more meat to it to make it more production grade. We will add data access, options to do caching and their considerations, applying CQRS, and error handling.

4

Extending Your Cloud-Native Application

Having understood the design principles, let's take the skeleton services developed in Chapter 2, *Writing Your First Cloud-Native Application*, and do some real work on them to make them production-ready.

We defined two get services; getProduct for a given a product ID, and getProducts for a given category. These two services have highly non-functional requirements. They always have to be available and serve the data with the lowest possible latency. The following steps will take us there:

1. **Accessing data**: Service access to data across various resources
2. **Caching**: Options to do caching and their considerations
3. **Applying CQRS**: Enable us to have different data models to service different requests
4. **Error handling**: How to recover, what return codes to send, and implementation of patterns such as a circuit breaker

We will also look at adding methods to modify the data, such as `insert`, `update`, and `delete`. In this chapter, we will cover:

- **Validations**: Ensuring that the data is clean before being processed
- **Keeping two models of CQRS in sync**: For data consistency
- **Event driven and asynchronous updates**: How it scales the architecture and decouples it at the same time

Implementing the get services

Let's take our `product` project developed in `Chapter 2`, *Writing Your First Cloud-Native Application*, forward. We will incrementally enhance it while discussing the concepts.

Let's think carefully about the database of our two services. `getProduct` returns the product information, while `getProducts` searches a list of products that fall into this category. To begin with, for simple and standard requirements, both queries can be answered by a single data model in a relational database:

1. You would store a product in a product table with a fixed number of columns.
2. You would then index the category so that the queries against it can run quickly.

Now, this design will be fine for most requirements for an average-sized company.

Simple product table

Let's use a product table in a standard relational database and access it in our service using Spring Data. Spring Data provides excellent abstractions to use the **Java Persistence API (JPA)** and makes coding **data access objects (DAO)** much easier. Spring Boot further helps in writing minimal code to begin with and extending it as we go ahead.

Spring Boot can work with embedded databases, such as H2, HSQLDB, or the external database. In-process embedded database starts with our Java service in a process and then terminates when the process dies. This is fine to begin with. Later on, the dependencies and URLs can be changed to point to actual databases.

You can take the project from `Chapter 2`, *Writing Your First Cloud-Native Application,* and add the following steps, or just download the completed code from GitHub (`https://github.com/PacktPublishing/Cloud-Native-Applications-in-Java`):

1. **Maven POM**: Including POM dependencies:

```xml
<dependency>
    <groupId>org.springframework.boot</groupId>
    <artifactId>spring-boot-starter-actuator</artifactId>
</dependency>
<dependency>
    <groupId>org.springframework.cloud</groupId>
    <artifactId>spring-cloud-starter-eureka</artifactId>
</dependency>
<dependency>
    <groupId>org.springframework.cloud</groupId>
    <artifactId>spring-cloud-starter-ribbon</artifactId>
</dependency>
<dependency>
    <groupId>org.springframework.boot</groupId>
    <artifactId>spring-boot-starter-data-jpa</artifactId>
</dependency>
<dependency>
    <groupId>org.hsqldb</groupId>
    <artifactId>hsqldb</artifactId>
    <scope>runtime</scope>
</dependency>
</dependencies>
```

This will tell Spring Boot to include the Spring Boot starter JPA and use HSQLDB in embedded mode.

2. **Entity**: As per the JPA, we will start using the concept of entity. We already have a domain object named `Product` from our previous project. Refactor it to put in an entity package. Then, add the notations of `@Entity`, `@Id`, and `@Column`, as shown in the following `Product.java` file:

```java
package com.mycompany.product.entity ;

import javax.persistence.Column;
import javax.persistence.Entity;
import javax.persistence.GeneratedValue;
import javax.persistence.GenerationType;
import javax.persistence.Id;
```

```
@Entity
public class Product {

    @Id
    @GeneratedValue(strategy=GenerationType.AUTO)
    private int id ;
    @Column(nullable = false)
    private String name ;
    @Column(nullable = false)
    private int catId ;
```

The rest of the code, such as constructors and getters/setters, remains the same.

3. **Repository**: Spring Data provides a repository, which is like a DAO class and provides methods to do **Create**, **Read**, **Update**, and **Delete** (**CRUD**) operations on the data. A lot of standard operations are already provided in the CrudRepository interface. We will be using only the query operations from now on.

   In our case, since our domain entity is Product, the repository will be ProductRepository, which extends Spring's CrudRepository, and manages the Product entity. During extension, the entity and the data type of the primary key needs to be specified using generics, as shown in the following ProductRepository.java file:

   ```
   package com.mycompany.product.dao;

   import java.util.List;
   import org.springframework.data.repository.CrudRepository;
   import com.mycompany.product.entity.Product;

   public interface ProductRepository extends CrudRepository<Product,
   Integer> {

       List<Product> findByCatId(int catId);
   }
   ```

The first question that would come to mind is whether this code is sufficient enough to work. It has just one interface definition. How can it be enough to handle our two methods, namely getProduct (given a product ID) and getProducts (for a given category)?

The magic happens in Spring Data, which helps with the boilerplate code. The CrudRepository interface comes with a set of default methods to implement the most common operations. These include save, delete, find, count, and exists operations which suffice for most of the query and update tasks. We will look at the update operations in the second half of this chapter, but let's focus on the query operations first.

The operation of finding a product given an ID is already present in the CrudRepository as a findOne method. Hence, we do not need to call it explicitly.

The task of finding products for a given category is done by the findByCatId method in our ProductRepository interface. The query builder mechanism built into the Spring Data repository infrastructure is useful for building queries over entities of the repository. The mechanism strips the prefixes, such as find, read, query, count, and get from the method and starts parsing the rest of it based on the entity. This mechanism is very powerful because the choice of keywords and the combinations means the method name is enough to do most of the query operations including operators (and/or) distinct clauses, and so on. Do refer to the Spring Data reference documentation (https://docs.spring.io/spring-data/jpa/docs/current/reference/html/) to see the details.

These conventions allow Spring Data and Spring Boot to inject implementations of the methods based on parsing the interfaces.

4. **Changing the service**: In Chapter 2, *Writing Your First Cloud-Native Application*, our product service was returning dummy hard-coded data. Let's change it to something useful that goes against the database. We achieve this by using the ProductRepository interface that we defined earlier, and injecting it through @Autowiring annotation into our ProductService class, as shown in the following ProductService.java file:

```
@RestController
public class ProductService {

    @Autowired
    ProductRepository prodRepo ;
    @RequestMapping("/product/{id}")
    Product getProduct(@PathVariable("id") int id) {
        return prodRepo.findOne(id);
    }
    @RequestMapping("/products")
    List<Product> getProductsForCategory(@RequestParam("id") int id)
```

```
{
            return prodRepo.findByCatId(id);
    }
}
```

The `findOne` method from the repository gets the object given a primary key, and the `findByCatId` method we defined helps to find products given a category.

5. **Schema definition**: For now, we will leave the schema creation to the `hibernate` capability to auto generate a script. Since we do want to see what script got created, let's enable `logging` for the classes as follows in the `application.properties` file:

```
logging.level.org.hibernate.tool.hbm2ddl=DEBUG
logging.level.org.hibernate.SQL=DEBUG
```

6. **Test data**: Since we are going to insert the products later, we need our database to be initialized with some products. Hence, add the following lines into `import.sql` and place it in resources (where the `application.properties` and bootstrap files reside):

```
-- Adding a few initial products
insert into product(id, name, cat_Id) values (1, 'Apples', 1)
insert into product(id, name, cat_Id) values (2, 'Oranges', 1)
insert into product(id, name, cat_Id) values (3, 'Bananas', 1)
insert into product(id, name, cat_Id) values (4, 'Carrot', 2)
```

7. **Leave Spring Data and Spring Boot to figure out the rest:** But in a production application, we would want to have fine-grained control over the connection URL, user ID, password, connection pool properties, and so on.

Running the service

To run our `product` service, perform the following steps:

1. Fire up the Eureka server (as we did in Chapter 2, *Writing Your First Cloud-Native Application*) using the `EurekaApplication` class. We are going to keep the Eureka service running at all times.
2. Once the `Eureka` project starts, run the `product` service.

Notice the logs generated by `hibernate`. It first uses an HSQLDB dialect automatically, and then creates and runs the `Product` table SQL as follows:

```
HHH000227: Running hbm2ddl schema export
drop table product if exists
create table product (id integer generated by default as identity (start
with 1), cat_id integer not null, name varchar(255) not null, primary key
(id))
HHH000476: Executing import script '/import.sql'
HHH000230: Schema export complete
```

Once the service starts to listen on a port, fire a query in your browser: `http://localhost:8082/product/1`. This will return the following:

```
{"id":1,"name":"Apples","catId":1}
```

When you see the logs, you will observe the SQL that ran in the background:

```
select product0_.id as id1_0_0_, product0_.cat_id as cat_id2_0_0_,
product0_.name as name3_0_0_ from product product0_ where product0_.id=?
```

Now, fire another query that returns products for a given category: `http://localhost:8082/products?id=1`. This will return the following:

```
[{"id":1,"name":"Apples","catId":1},{"id":2,"name":"Oranges","catId":1},{"i
d":3,"name":"Bananas","catId":1}]
```

The SQL that ran for this condition was as follows:

```
select product0_.id as id1_0_, product0_.cat_id as cat_id2_0_,
product0_.name as name3_0_ from product product0_ where product0_.cat_id=?
```

And trying with a different category, `http://localhost:8082/products?id=2`, will return something as follows:

```
[{"id":4,"name":"Carrot","catId":2}]
```

This completes a simple query service going against a data source.

For production purposes, this will need enhancement to take a standard database as an Oracle, PostgreSQL, or MySQL database. You will introduce an index on the category column so that the queries run faster.

Limitations of traditional databases

But what happens as the company expands its products and customers in the following scenarios?

- The scalability of a relational database (in terms of volume of products and number of concurrent requests) becomes a bottleneck.
- The product structure is different based on the category and is difficult to model in a fixed schema of a relational database.
- The search criteria starts increasing in scope. As of now, we are searching only by category; later on, we might want to search by product description, filter fields, and also by category description.

Will a single relational database suffice for all requirements?

Let's address the concerns with a few design techniques.

Caching

As the service scales in terms of the amount of data and concurrency of requests, the database will start becoming a bottleneck. In order to scale, we can adopt a caching solution that will reduce the number of hits to the database by servicing the requests from a cache if the value is available in the cache.

Spring provides mechanisms to include caching through annotations, so that Spring can return cached values instead of calling the actual processing or retrieval methods.

Conceptually, caching comes in two types, as discussed in the following sections.

Local cache

The local cache is present in the same JVM as that of the service. Its scope is limited as it can be accessed by the service instance and has to be entirely managed by the service instance.

Let's start by making our products cacheable in a local cache.

Spring 3.1 introduced its own notations for returning cached entries, evicting, or populating entries. But later on, JSR 107 JCache introduced different notations. Spring 4.1 and higher supports these as well.

Let's use the Spring notations to begin with:

1. Tell the Spring application to enable caching and look for cacheable instances. This is a one-time declaration and hence is best done in the start-up class. Add the @EnableCaching annotation into the main class:

```
@SpringBootApplication
@EnableDiscoveryClient
@EnableCaching
public class ProductSpringApp {
```

2. Enable the cache in our ProductRepository for getting products by category, by adding a cacheable notation. We will give a cache name that is explicit and will be used for this method:

```
public interface ProductRepository extends CrudRepository<Product,
Integer> {

    @Cacheable("productsByCategoryCache")
    List<Product> findByCatId(int catId);
}
```

Now, run the service again and observe the logs when you run the following set of queries in your browser:

1. http://localhost:8082/products?id=1
2. http://localhost:8082/products?id=2
3. http://localhost:8082/products?id=1
4. http://localhost:8082/products?id=2

You will see that the following SQL has been fired only twice:

```
select product0_.id as id1_0_, product0_.cat_id as cat_id2_0_,
product0_.name as name3_0_ from product product0_ where product0_.cat_id=?
```

This means that the repository executed the findByCatId method only when it did not find a category entry in the cache.

Under the hood

While it is nice that Spring handles a lot of concerns such as caching implementation under the hood, it is important to understand what is happening and be aware of the limitations.

Internally, caching is implemented by internal classes such as cache manager and cache resolver. When no caching product or framework is supplied, Spring uses `ConcurrentHashMap` by default. Spring's caching implements many other local caches such as EHCache, Guava, and Caffeine.

Check out the Spring documentation (https://docs.spring.io/spring/docs/current/ javadoc-api/org/springframework/cache/annotation/Cacheable.html) for more intricacies such as `sync=true` and conditional caching.

Limitations of a local cache

Local cache is useful in limited use cases (such as non-changing static data) as the updates done in one service using Spring annotations such as `@CachePut`, `@CacheEvict`, and so on cannot be synchronized with a cache on the other instance of services if we are running more than one instance of a service for load balancing or resiliency purposes.

Distributed cache

A distributed cache such as Hazelcast, Gemfire, and/or Coherence is network-aware and the cache instances operate either as an in-process model (peer-peer model), where the cache is part of the service runtime, or a client-server model, where the cache request goes from the service to separate dedicated cache instances.

For this example, we have selected Hazelcast, as it is a very lightweight but powerful distributed caching solution. It also integrates very well with Spring Boot. Here is how:

1. In the POM (Maven file), add a dependency to `hazelcast-spring`. The `hazelcast-spring` has a `HazelcastCacheManager` that configures a Hazelcast instance to be used:

```
<dependency>
    <groupId>org.springframework.boot</groupId>
    <artifactId>spring-boot-starter-cache</artifactId>
</dependency>
<dependency>
    <groupId>com.hazelcast</groupId>
    <artifactId>hazelcast-spring</artifactId>
</dependency>
```

2. Since Hazelcast is a distributed cache, it needs the elements to be serializable. Hence, we need to ensure that our `Product` entity is serializable:

```
public class Product implements Serializable {
```

3. A simplified Hazelcast configuration file that tells the various Hazelcast instances to discover and synchronize with each other:

```
<hazelcast xmlns:xsi="http://www.w3.org/2001/XMLSchema-instance"
    xsi:schemaLocation="http://www.hazelcast.com/schema/config
http://www.hazelcast.com/schema/config/hazelcast-config-3.6.xsd"
    xmlns="http://www.hazelcast.com/schema/config">

<group>
        <name>ProductCluster</name>
        <password>letmein</password>
</group>
<network>
        <join>
            <multicast enabled="true"/>
        </join>
    </network>
</hazelcast>
```

Now, let's test these changes. For this, we have to run two instances of the `product` service to check if it works. We can run two instances by changing the port number:

1. Run the service with port `8082` (which is configured).
2. Change the `application.properties` to `8083`.
3. Run the service again.

You will see Hazelcast messages on one service that starts as follows:

```
Loading 'hazelcast.xml' from classpath.
[LOCAL] [ProductCluster] [3.6.5] Picked Address[169.254.104.186]:5701,
using socket
[169.254.104.186]:5701 [ProductCluster] [3.6.5] Hazelcast 3.6.5 (20160823 -
e4af3d9) starting
Members [1] {
Member [169.254.104.186]:5701 this
}
```

But as soon as the second service is started, the member definitions get updated by 2:

```
Members [2] {
    Member [169.254.104.186]:5701
    Member [169.254.104.186]:5702 this
}
```

Now, on the browser, run the following queries and observe the logs in the console:

1. http://localhost:8082/products?id=1
2. http://localhost:8082/products?id=2
3. http://localhost:8082/products?id=1
4. http://localhost:8082/products?id=2
5. http://localhost:8083/products?id=1
6. http://localhost:8083/products?id=2

You will find that in the SQL, debug logs come only twice in the first service. The other four times, the cache entries are picked from Hazelcast. Unlike the previous local cache, the cache entries are synchronized between two instances.

Applying CQRS to separate data models and services

A distributed cache is one way to solve the scaling problem. However, it introduces certain challenges, such as cache staleness (keeping the cache in sync with the database) and additional memory requirements.

Also, caching is the beginning of the transition to the CQRS paradigm. Revisit the concepts of CQRS that we discussed in Chapter 3, *Designing Your Cloud-Native Application*.

The queries are answered from the cache (apart from the first hit), which is query segregation from the commands that go from the system of record (which is the database) and update the query model (cache update) later.

Let's take the next step in CQRS to do this segregation cleanly. The complexity that CQRS introduces is:

- Having two (or multiple) models to maintain instead of one
- Overheads of updating all models when the data changes
- Consistency guarantees between the different models

Hence, this model should be followed only if the use case demands separation for high concurrency, high volume, and rapid agility requirements.

Materialized views on a relational database

Materialized views are the simplest form of CQRS. If we assume that the updates to products happen less frequently as compared to the reads on the product and category, then we can have two different models supporting the getProduct (for an ID) and getProducts (for a given category).

The search query getProducts goes against this view, while the traditional getProduct based on the primary key goes to the regular table.

This should be pretty easy if supported by a database such as Oracle. If a database does not support a materialized view by default, it can be done manually if there is a need, by manually updating statistics or summary tables when the main product table is updated using triggers or better event-driven architecture, such as business events. We shall see this in the second half of this chapter, when we add addProduct functionality to our set of services.

Elasticsearch and a document database

To address limitations of flexible schema, high search ability, and higher volume handling, we can go for NoSQL technologies:

- For serving different types of products, we could choose to use a document database with its flexible schema, for example, MongoDB.
- For serving search requests, Elasticsearch, a Lucene based technology, will be beneficial due to its powerful indexing capability.

Why not use only a document database or Elasticsearch?

It is quite possible to think of these options as well:

- Elasticsearch is typically a complementary technology and not used as a master database. Hence, the product information should be maintained in a reliable, relational, or NoSQL database.
- A document database such as MongoDB can build indexes too. However, the performance or indexing capability cannot equal Elasticsearch.

This is a classic example for fit for purpose. Your choice will depend on your use case:

- Whether you have flexible schema needs
- Scalable and high volume applications
- Highly flexible search requirements

Core product service on a document database

Keeping the REST interface the same, let's change the internal implementation from using a relational database (HSQLDB, in our example) to MongoDB. Instead of running MongoDB in a process such as HSQLDB, we will run it separately as a server.

Getting MongoDB ready with test data

The steps to download and install MongoDB are as follows:

1. Install MongoDB. It is fairly easy to follow the instructions for various platforms on the MongoDB website (`https://www.mongodb.com/`).
2. Run `mongod.exe` to start an instance of MongoDB.
3. Create a test file with our sample data (similar to `import.sql`). This time, however, we will keep the data in JSON format instead of SQL statements. The `products.json` file is as follows:

   ```
   {"_id":"1","name":"Apples","catId":1}
   {"_id":"2","name":"Oranges","catId":1}
   {"_id":"3","name":"Bananas","catId":1}
   {"_id":"4","name":"Carrot","catId":2}
   ```

   Note the _id, which is the primary key notation for MongoDB. If you do not provide an _id, MongoDB will auto generate that field with the `ObjectId` definition.

4. Load the sample data into MongoDB. We will create a database called `masterdb` and load into a collection called `product`:

   ```
   mongoimport --db masterdb --collection product --drop --file
   D:datamongoscriptsproducts.json
   ```

5. Check whether the data got loaded on the command line, by using the `db.product.find()` command, after `use masterdb` as follows:

```
D:\Program Files\MongoDB\Server\3.4\bin>mongo
MongoDB shell version v3.4.1
connecting to: mongodb://127.0.0.1:27017
MongoDB server version: 3.4.1
Server has startup warnings:
2016-12-30T11:03:23.012+0530 I CONTROL  [initandlisten]
2016-12-30T11:03:23.012+0530 I CONTROL  [initandlisten]
2016-12-30T11:03:23.013+0530 I CONTROL  [initandlisten]
2016-12-30T11:03:23.014+0530 I CONTROL  [initandlisten]
> use masterdb
switched to db masterdb
> db.product.find()
{ "_id" : 1, "name" : "Apples", "catId" : 1 }
{ "_id" : 2, "name" : "Oranges", "catId" : 1 }
{ "_id" : 3, "name" : "Bananas", "catId" : 1 }
{ "_id" : 4, "name" : "Carrot", "catId" : 2 }
>
```

Creating the product service

The steps to create a `product` service are as follows:

1. It is better to start with a clean slate. Copy your project from the earlier example with Hazelcast and HSQLDB or pull from the GitHub repository (https://github.com/PacktPublishing/Cloud-Native-Applications-in-Java).

2. Adjust the Maven POM file to have the following dependencies. Remove the other ones since they are not required for our small example:

```
<dependencies>
        <dependency>
                <groupId>org.springframework.boot</groupId>
                <artifactId>spring-boot-starter-web</artifactId>
        </dependency>
        <dependency>
                <groupId>org.springframework.boot</groupId>
                <artifactId>spring-boot-starter-
    actuator</artifactId>
        </dependency>
        <dependency>
                <groupId>org.springframework.cloud</groupId>
                <artifactId>spring-cloud-starter-eureka</artifactId>
        </dependency>
        <dependency>
                <groupId>org.springframework.boot</groupId>
```

```
                        <artifactId>spring-boot-starter-data-
                        mongodb</artifactId>
                </dependency>
        </dependencies>
```

3. The `Product` entity should just have an `@Id` field. It is optional to put a `@Document` annotation at the class level. If not, the first insert performance suffers. For now, let's have the annotation in the `Product.java` file:

```
@Document
public class Product   {

    @Id
    private String id ;
    private String name ;
    private int catId ;

    public Product() {}

    .... (other constructors, getters and setters)
```

Note that the `id` here is `String` instead of `int`. The reason for that is that NoSQL databases are much better at generating the ID as a string (GUID) compared to incrementing integers in relational systems such as databases. The reason for that is databases are getting more distributed, so generating incrementing numbers reliably is a little more difficult compared to generating GUIDs.

4. The `ProductRepository` now extends the `MongoRepository` which has methods for retrieving the product from MongoDB as follows in the `ProductRepository.java` file:

```
package com.mycompany.product.dao;

import java.util.List;
import org.springframework.data.mongodb.repository.MongoRepository;
import com.mycompany.product.entity.Product;

public interface ProductRepository extends MongoRepository<Product,
String> {

    List<Product> findByCatId(int catId);
}
```

5. We just add one property to `application.properties` to tell the service to get our data from the `masterdb` database in MongoDB. Also, it is probably better to run it on a different port so that we can run the services in parallel if we want to do so later:

```
server.port=8085
eureka.instance.leaseRenewalIntervalInSeconds=5
spring.data.mongodb.database=masterdb
```

The `ProductService` class does not change as there is no change in the interface.

Now, start the Eureka server, then the service, and fire the following queries in the browser:

1. `http://localhost:8085/products?id=1`
2. `http://localhost:8085/products?id=2`
3. `http://localhost:8085/product/1`
4. `http://localhost:8085/product/2`

You will get the same JSONs back as before. This is an internal implementation change of the microservice.

Splitting the services

Let's go with a simple implementation of the suggested separation from a learning perspective. Since we are separating the master and search models, it makes sense to split the services, as the functionality of the search can be considered a downstream function to the **Product** master.

The `getProducts` function for a category is part of the search functionality, which can become a complex and independent business area in itself. Hence, it is time to rethink whether it makes sense to keep them both in the same microservice or split them into core **Product** service and **Product Search** services.

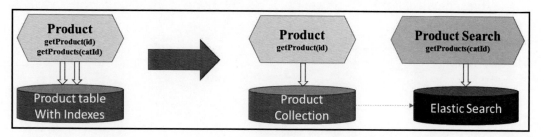

The product-search service

Let's create a new microservice that specializes in high speed, high volume searches. The search data store backing the search microservice need not be a master of the product data, but can act as a complementary search model. Elasticsearch has been extremely popular for a variety of search use cases and fits the need for extreme search requirements.

Getting Elasticsearch ready with test data

The following are the steps to get Elasticsearch ready with test data:

1. Install the Elastic version. Use version 2.4.3, since the recent 5.1 versions are not compatible with Spring Data. Spring Data uses Java drivers that communicate on port `9300` with the server, and hence having the same version on the client and server is important.

2. Create a test file with our sample data (similar to `products.json`). The format is only slightly different from the previous case, but for Elasticsearch instead of MongoDB. The `products.json` file is as follows:

   ```
   {"index":{"_id":"1"}}
   {"id":"1","name":"Apples","catId":1}

   {"index":{"_id":"2"}}
   {"id":"2","name":"Oranges","catId":1}

   {"index":{"_id":"3"}}
   {"id":"3","name":"Bananas","catId":1}

   {"index":{"_id":"4"}}
   {"id":"4","name":"Carrot","catId":2}
   ```

3. Use Postman or cURL to call a REST service on Elasticsearch to load the data. See the following screenshot for output in the Postman extension. In Elasticsearch, the equivalent of a database is an index, and we can name our index `product`. Elasticsearch also has a concept of type, but more on that later:

4. Check whether the data got loaded by running a simple * query in Postman, the browser, or cURL:

```
http://localhost:9200/product/_search?q=*&pretty
```

As a result, you should get the four products added.

Creating the product-search service

With two databases done so far, you must be familiar with the drill by now. It is not very different from what we did for HSQLDB and MongoDB. Copy the Mongo project to create a `productsearch` service and make the changes as before to the Maven POM, entity, repository classes, and the application properties:

1. In the Maven POM, `spring-boot-starter-data-elasticsearch` replaces `spring-boot-starter-data-mongodb` or `spring-boot-starter-data-jpa` in the earlier two service examples.

2. In the `Product` entity, `@Document` now represents an Elasticsearch document. It should have an `index` and `type` defined the same since we used to load the test data as shown in the `Product.java` file:

```
package com.mycompany.product.entity ;

import org.springframework.data.annotation.Id;
import org.springframework.data.elasticsearch.annotations.Document;

@Document(indexName = "product", type = "external" )
public class Product   {

    @Id
    private String id ;
    private String name ;
    private int catId ;              //Remaining class is same as
before
```

3. The `ProductRepository` now extends `ElasticsearchRepository` as shown in the `ProductRepository.java` file:

```
package com.mycompany.product.dao;

import java.util.List;
import
org.springframework.data.elasticsearch.repository.ElasticsearchRepo
sitory;
import com.mycompany.product.entity.Product;

public interface ProductRepository extends
ElasticsearchRepository<Product, String> {

    List<Product> findByCatId(int catId);
}
```

4. Make changes in the `application.properties` to indicate a server model of `elasticsearch` (versus the embedded model, like we did for HSQLDB):

```
server.port=8086
eureka.instance.leaseRenewalIntervalInSeconds=5

spring.data.elasticsearch.repositories.enabled=true
spring.data.elasticsearch.cluster-name=elasticsearch
spring.data.elasticsearch.cluster-nodes=localhost:9300
```

Now, start the Eureka server and then the `productsearch` service and fire the following queries in the browser, in the following order:

1. `http://localhost:8085/products?id=1.`
2. `http://localhost:8085/products?id=2.`

You will get the same JSONs back as before. This is an internal implementation change of the microservice from the hard coded implementation in `Chapter 2`, *Writing Your First Cloud-Native Application,* to HSQLDB, MongoDB, and now Elasticsearch.

Due to the Spring Data framework, the code to access the driver and communicate with it has been heavily abstracted from us, so all we need to do is add the following:

1. Dependencies in the Maven POM file.
2. Base class to extend from in the case of a repository.
3. Annotations to use for the entities.
4. Properties to configure in application properties.

Data update services

So far, we have looked at getting the data. Let's look at some of the data modification operations, such as creating, updating, and deleting (CRUD operations).

Given the popularity of REST for cloud-based API operations, we will do our data manipulation through REST methods.

Let's pick the HSQLDB example with Hazelcast that we worked on previously in this chapter.

REST conventions

The `GET` method was a no-brainer, but the choice of the methods for operations such as creating, inserting, and deleting require some deliberation. We will follow the conventions as per industry guidelines:

URL	HTTP operation	Service method	Description
`/product/{id}`	GET	`getProduct`	Gets a product given an ID

`/product`	`POST`	`insertProduct`	Inserts the product and returns a new ID
`/product/{id}`	`PUT`	`updateProduct`	Updates a product for a given ID with the data in the request body
`/product/{id}`	`DELETE`	`deleteProduct`	Deletes the product with a provided ID

Let's look at the implementations in the `ProductService` class. We already had the `getProduct` implementation from earlier in the chapter. Let's add the other methods.

Inserting a product

Leaving aside validations for a minute (which we will cover in a while), the insertion looks very simple to implementing the REST interface.

We map the `POST` operation to the `insertProduct` method and in the implementation, we just call `save` on the repository that was already defined:

```
@RequestMapping(value="/product", method = RequestMethod.POST)
ResponseEntity<Product> insertProduct(@RequestBody Product product) {
    Product savedProduct = prodRepo.save(product) ;
    return new ResponseEntity<Product>(savedProduct, HttpStatus.OK);
}
```

Notice a few differences from the `getProduct` method we coded earlier:

- We have added a `POST` method in `@RequestMapping` so that the URL will map to the `insertProduct` method when HTTP `POST` is used.
- We are capturing the `product` details from the `@RequestBody` annotation. This is expected to be supplied when inserting a new product. Spring does the job of mapping JSON (or XML) to the `Product` class for us.
- We are returning a `ResponseEntity` instead of just a `Product` object as we did in the `getProduct` method. This allows us to customize the HTTP responses and headers, which is important in REST architecture. For a successful insert, we are returning an HTTP `OK` (200) response, telling the client that his request to add a product was successful.

Testing

The steps to test our `insertProduct` method are as follows:

1. Start the Eureka server, then the `product` service (assuming it is listening on `8082`).
2. Note that a browser will not suffice now, as we want to indicate the HTTP methods and provide a response body. Use Postman or cURL instead.
3. Set the content-type to **application/json**, since we will be submitting the new product information as a JSON.
4. Provide the production information in JSON format, such as `{"name":"Grapes","catId":1}`. Note we are not providing a product ID:

5. Hit **Send**. You will get a response with the product JSON. This time, an ID will be populated. This is the ID generated by the repository (which in turn got it from the underlying database).

Updating a product

Here, instead of POST, we will use a PUT method indicating the ID of the product to be updated in the URL pattern. Like the POST method, the details of the product to be updated are provided in the @RequestBody annotation:

```
@RequestMapping(value="/product/{id}", method = RequestMethod.PUT)
ResponseEntity<Product> updateProduct(@PathVariable("id") int id,
@RequestBody Product product) {
    // First fetch an existing product and then modify it.
    Product existingProduct = prodRepo.findOne(id);
    // Now update it back
    existingProduct.setCatId(product.getCatId());
    existingProduct.setName(product.getName());
    Product savedProduct = prodRepo.save(existingProduct) ;
    // Return the updated product with status ok
    return new ResponseEntity<Product>(savedProduct, HttpStatus.OK);
}
```

The implementation involves:

1. Retrieving an existing product from the repository.
2. Making changes to it as per business logic.
3. Saving it back to the repository.
4. Returning the updated product (for client verification) with an OK status as before.

If you hadn't noticed, the last two steps are exactly like the insert case. It is just the retrieval and update of the product that are the new steps.

Testing

The steps to test our insertProduct method are as follows:

1. As we did for inserting a product, fire up Eureka and ProductService again.
2. Let's change the product description of the first product to Fuji Apples. So, our JSON looks like {"id":1,"name":"Fuji Apples","catId":1}.
3. Prepare Postman to submit the PUT request as follows:

4. Hit **Send**. You will get a response **200 OK** with the body containing the JSON
   `{"id":1,"name":"Fuji Apples","catId":1}`.
5. Fire a `GET` request `http://localhost:8082/product/1` to check the change.
   You will find `apples` changed to `Fuji Apples`.

Deleting a product

The mapping and implementation for deleting a product looks as follows:

```
@RequestMapping(value="/product/{id}", method = RequestMethod.DELETE)
ResponseEntity<Product> deleteProduct(@PathVariable("id") int id) {
    prodRepo.delete(id);
    return new ResponseEntity<Product>(HttpStatus.OK);
}
```

We invoke the `delete` operation on the repository and return `OK` to the client, assuming
everything is fine.

Testing

To test, fire a DELETE request through Postman on the product ID 1:

You will get a **200 OK** response. To check whether it really got deleted, try a GET request on the same product. You will get an empty response.

Cache invalidation

If you do a get operation that populates the cache, then either the cache updates, or invalidation has to take place when PUT/POST/DELETE operations occur that update the data.

If you recollect, we had a cache that held the products corresponding to a category ID. As we add and remove products using the APIs created for inserting, updating, and deleting, the cache needs to be refreshed. Our first preference is to check if we can update the cache entry. However, the business logic of pulling the categories corresponding to the cache is present in the database (through a WHERE clause). Hence, it is best to invalidate the cache containing the relations when a product update happens.

The general assumption for a caching use case is that the reads are much higher than inserts and updates.

To enable cache eviction, we have to add the methods in the `ProductRepository` class and provide an annotation. Hence, we add two new methods to the interface in addition to the existing `findByCatId` method, and mark eviction to be false:

```
public interface ProductRepository extends CrudRepository<Product, Integer>
{

    @Cacheable("productsByCategoryCache")
    List<Product> findByCatId(int catId);
    @CacheEvict(cacheNames="productsByCategoryCache", allEntries=true)
    Product save(Product product);
    @CacheEvict(cacheNames="productsByCategoryCache", allEntries=true)
    void delete(Product product);
}
```

Though the preceding code is a valid solution, it is not efficient. It clears the entire cache. Our cache could have 100s of categories and it is not right to clear the ones that are not related to the product being inserted, updated, or deleted.

We could be a little more intelligent in only clearing the entries related to the category being operated upon:

```
@CacheEvict(cacheNames="productsByCategoryCache", key = "#result?.catId")
Product save(Product product);
@CacheEvict(cacheNames="productsByCategoryCache", key = "#p0.catId")
void delete(Product product);
```

The code is a little cryptic because of the **Spring Expression Language (SpEL)**, and the documentation of `CacheEvict`:

1. `key` indicates what cache entry we want to clear.
2. `#result` indicates the return result. We extract the `catId` out of it and use it to clear the data.
3. `#p0` indicates the first parameter in the method called. This is the `product` object that we want to use the category from and then delete the object.

To test whether cache removal is working fine, start the service and Eureka, fire the following requests, and observe the results:

Request	Result
`http://localhost:8082/products?id=1`	Gets the product corresponding to category 1 and caches it. SQL will be displayed in the out log.
`http://localhost:8082/products?id=1`	Gets the products from cache. No entry in the SQL updated.
`POST` to `http://localhost:8082/product` Add `{"name":"Mango","catId":1}` as `application/json`	Adds the new Mango product to the database.
`http://localhost:8082/products?id=1`	Reflects the newly added Mango. SQL indicates the data was refreshed.

Validations and error messages

So far, we have been treading in very safe territory and assuming happy paths. But not everything will be right all the time. There are many scenarios such as:

1. `GET`, `PUT`, `DELETE` requests for products that don't exist.
2. `PUT` and `POST` missing critical information, for example, no product name or category.
3. Business validations, such as products, should belong to known categories and names should be more than 10 characters.
4. Incorrect formats of the data submitted, such as alphanumeric for category ID where only an integer was expected.

And these are not exhaustive. Therefore, it is always important to do validations and return appropriate error codes and messages when things go wrong.

Format validations

If the request has errors in the format of the request body being submitted (for example, invalid JSON), then Spring throws an error before it reaches the method.

For example, for a `POST` request to `http://localhost:8082/product`, if the submitted body is missing commas, such as `{"id":1 "name":"Fuji Apples" "catId":1}`, then the error returned is `400` as follows. This indicates it is a badly formed request:

```
{
    "timestamp": 1483701698917,
    "status": 400,
    "error": "Bad Request",
    "exception":
"org.springframework.http.converter.HttpMessageNotReadableException",
    "message": "Could not read document: Unexpected character ('"' (code
34)): was expecting comma to separate Object entriesn at ...
```

Likewise, a letter instead of a number, for example, in ID, will be caught early enough. For example, `http://localhost:8082/product/A` will result in a `Failed to convert value` error:

Data validations

A few errors can be caught at the entity level, if they are not allowed. For example, not providing a product description when we have annotated the `Product` entity as follows:

```
@Column(nullable = false)
private String name ;
```

This will cause the error message while trying to save the product supplied in the request without the name, for example, `{"id":1, "catId":1}`.

The server returns a `500` internal server error and gives a detailed message as follows:

```
could not execute statement; SQL [n/a]; constraint [null]; nested exception
is org.hibernate.exception.ConstraintViolationException:
```

This is not a very clean message to return to the client. Therefore, it is better to catch the validations upfront and return a `400` error code back to the client.

Business validations

This will typically be done in code, as it is specific to the functionality or business use case being addressed. For example, checking for a product before updating or deleting it. This is a simple code-based validation as follows:

```
@RequestMapping(value="/product/{id}", method = RequestMethod.DELETE)
ResponseEntity<Product> deleteProduct(@PathVariable("id") int id) {
    // First fetch an existing product and then delete it.
    Product existingProduct = prodRepo.findOne(id);
    if (existingProduct == null) {
        return new ResponseEntity<Product>(HttpStatus.NOT_FOUND);
    }
    // Return the inserted product with status ok
    prodRepo.delete(existingProduct);
    return new ResponseEntity<Product>(HttpStatus.OK);
}
```

Exceptions and error messages

In case of error, the simplest thing to begin with is to indicate an error message telling us what went wrong, especially in case of a bad input request or business validations since the client (or requestor) may have no idea of what went wrong. For example, in the preceding case, the `NOT_FOUND` status code is returned, But no other details are supplied.

Spring provides interesting notations such as `ExceptionHandler` and `ControllerAdvice` to handle this error. Let's see how this works.

Secondly, the service method earlier was directly manipulating the `ResponseEntity` by sending HTTP codes. We will revert it back to return business objects such as `Product` instead of `ResponseEntity`, making it more POJO-like. Revert back the `deleteProduct` code discussed earlier to the following:

```
@RequestMapping(value="/product/{id}", method = RequestMethod.DELETE)
Product deleteProduct(@PathVariable("id") int id) {
    // First fetch an existing product and then delete it.
    Product existingProduct = prodRepo.findOne(id);
    if (existingProduct == null) {
      String errMsg = "Product Not found with code " + id ;
      throw new BadRequestException(BadRequestException.ID_NOT_FOUND,
errMsg);
    }
    // Return the deleted product
    prodRepo.delete(existingProduct);
    return existingProduct ;
}
```

In the preceding code:

1. We are returning `Product` instead of `ResponseEntity`, as handling error codes and responses will be done externally.
2. An exception is thrown (a runtime exception or its extended version) that tells us what was wrong in the request.
3. The scope of the `Product` method ends here.

The `BadRequestException` class is a simple class that provides an ID and extends from the `RuntimeException` class:

```
public class BadRequestException extends RuntimeException {

    public static final int ID_NOT_FOUND = 1 ;
    private static final long serialVersionUID = 1L;
    int errCode ;
    public BadRequestException(int errCode, String msg) {
        super(msg);
        this.errCode = errCode ;
    }
}
```

When you execute the service now, instead of just getting a 404 Not Found status, we will get a proper message indicating what went wrong. See the screenshot of the request sent and the exception received:

However, sending 500 and getting an exception stack in the logs is not clean. 500 gives an indication that the error handling is not robust and stack traces are thrown around.

Therefore, we should capture and handle this error. Spring provides @ExceptionHandler that can be used in the service. This annotation on a method enables Spring to call the method to handle the error:

```
@ExceptionHandler(BadRequestException.class)
void handleBadRequests(BadRequestException bre, HttpServletResponse
response) throws IOException {
    int respCode = (bre.errCode == BadRequestException.ID_NOT_FOUND) ?
```

```
        HttpStatus.NOT_FOUND.value()  : HttpStatus.BAD_REQUEST.value() ;
    response.sendError(respCode, bre.errCode + ":" + bre.getMessage());
}
```

When we execute the service now, and call the `DELETE` method with a product ID that is not available, the error code becomes more specific and looks clean enough:

```
{
    "timestamp": 1483780958138,
    "status": 404,
    "error": "Not Found",
    "exception": "com.mycompany.product.exception.BadRequestException",
    "message": "1:Product Not found with code 156",
    "path": "/product/156"
}
```

Now, taking a step further, what if we want all our services to follow this pattern of raising a `BadRequestException` and returning the correct error codes? Spring provides a mechanism called `ControllerAdvice` which when used in a class, the exception handlers within the class can be applied universally to all services in the scope.

Create a new class as follows and put it in the exception package:

```
@ControllerAdvice
public class GlobalControllerExceptionHandler {

    @ExceptionHandler(BadRequestException.class)
    void handleBadRequests(BadRequestException bre, HttpServletResponse
response) throws IOException {
        ... Same code as earlier ...
    }
}
```

This allows the exceptions to be handled across the services in a consistent way.

Data updates for CQRS

As discussed in the previous chapter, and we saw in action in the previous section, the CQRS pattern provides an efficient and fit for purpose data model for handling commands and queries separately. To recap, we had a flexible document model in MongoDB to handle the command pattern with transaction guarantees. We had a flexible query model in Elasticsearch to handle complex search conditions.

Though this pattern allows easier queries due to fit for purpose query models, the challenge comes in updating data across the various models. In the previous chapter, we discussed multiple mechanisms of keeping the information updated across the models, such as distributed transactions, and eventually consistent models using Publish-Subscribe messaging.

In the following sections, we will look at using messaging and the asynchronous mechanism of updating data.

Asynchronous messaging

HTTP/REST provides for a request response mechanism to execute the service. The client waits (or rather, blocks) till the processing is complete and uses the result provided at the end of the service. Therefore, the processing is said to be synchronous.

In asynchronous processing, the client does not wait for the response. Asynchronous processing can be used in two scenarios, such as **fire-and-forget** and **request/response**.

In fire and forget, the client sends a command or request to the downstream service, and then does not require a response. It is used typically in pipeline processing architecture, where one service does enrichment and processing of the request and sends it to the other service, which sends to a third service, and so on.

In asynchronous request/response, the client sends a request to the service, but unlike synchronous processing, it does not wait or block for the response. When the service finishes processing, it has to notify the client so that the client can use the response.

In CQRS, we use messaging to send update events to the various services, so that the read or query models can be updated.

To begin with, we will use ActiveMQ as a reliable messaging mechanism in this chapter and then look at Kafka as a scalable distributed messaging system in the chapters ahead.

Starting ActiveMQ

The steps to set up ActiveMQ are as follows:

1. Download ActiveMQ from the Apache website (`http://activemq.apache.org/`).
2. Unzip it to a folder.
3. Navigate to the `bin` folder.
4. Run the `activemq start` command.

Open the console to see messages and manage ActiveMQ at
`http://localhost:8161/admin` and log in with `admin/admin`. You should see the UI
interface as follows:

Creating a topic

Click on the **Topics** link and create a topic named `ProductT`. You can follow the naming convention you are used to. This topic will get all the updates for a product. These updates can be used for various downstream processing purposes, such as keeping the local data models up to date. Once you create a topic, it will appear in the list of topics on the admin console which is shown as follows. The other two topics are ActiveMQ's own topics and we will leave them alone:

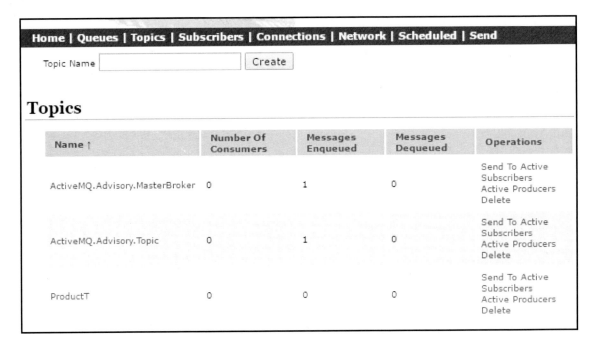

Golden source update

When there are multiple models in CQRS, we follow the golden source pattern, as discussed earlier:

1. One model (command model) is considered the golden source.
2. All validations are performed before updating to the golden source.
3. The update to the golden source happens in a transaction to avoid any inconsistent update and failure states. So, the update operation is automatic.

4. Once the update is complete, a broadcast message is put on a topic.
5. If there is an error in putting the message on topic, the transaction is rolled back and the client is sent an error.

We did a CQRS implementation using MongoDB and Elasticsearch. In our case, MongoDB is the golden source of the product data (also the command model). Elasticsearch is the query model that contains the data organized from a search perspective.

Let's first look at updating the command model or the golden source.

Service methods

We did three methods in HSQLDB implementation: inserting, updating, and deleting. Copy the same methods to the MongoDB-based project, so that the service class in this project is exactly the same as that in the HSQLDB project.

Also, copy the exception class and `ControllerAdvice` that we did in the HSQLDB project. Your package structure should look identical to the HSQLDB project, which is shown as follows:

The difference in this project is that the ID is a string, as that supports better native handling in MongoDB for ID creation. Therefore, the method signatures will be string for ID instead of integer as in our HSQLDB project.

A PUT operation that updates the MongoDB is shown as follows:

```
@RequestMapping(value="/product/{id}", method = RequestMethod.PUT)
Product updateProduct(@PathVariable("id") String id, @RequestBody Product
product) {
    // First fetch an existing product and then modify it.
    Product existingProduct = prodRepo.findOne(id);
    if (existingProduct == null) {
        String errMsg = "Product Not found with code " + id ;
        throw new BadRequestException(BadRequestException.ID_NOT_FOUND,
errMsg);
    }
    // Now update it back
    existingProduct.setCatId(product.getCatId());
    existingProduct.setName(product.getName());
    Product savedProduct = prodRepo.save(existingProduct) ;
    // Return the updated product
    return savedProduct ;
}
```

Test whether the get, insert, update, and delete operations run as they should.

Raising an event on data updates

When an insert, delete, or update operation happens, it is important for the golden source system to broadcast the change, so that a lot of downstream actions can happen. This includes:

1. Cache clearance by dependent systems.
2. Update of the local data models in the system.
3. Doing further business processing, for example, sending emails to interested customers on the addition of a new product.

Using Spring JMSTemplate to send a message

The steps to use JMSTemplate are as follows:

1. Include Spring starter for ActiveMQ in our POM file:

```
<dependency>
    <groupId>org.springframework.boot</groupId>
    <artifactId>spring-boot-starter-activemq</artifactId>
</dependency>
```

2. We have to enable JMS support for our Spring application. Therefore, include an annotation in the `ProductSpringApp.java` file as follows, and provide a message converter. The message converter will help convert objects to JSON and vice versa:

```
@SpringBootApplication
@EnableDiscoveryClient
@EnableJms
public class ProductSpringApp {
```

3. Create an entity that encapsulates the `Product` and the action, so that whoever gets the product message will also know if the action performed was delete or insert/update, by adding the entity in the `ProductUpdMsg.java` file as follows:

```
public class ProductUpdMsg {

    Product product ;
    boolean isDelete = false ;
// Constructor, getters and setters
```

If there are more actions, feel free to change the `isDelete` flag to a string action flag based on your use case.

4. Configure the JMS properties in the `application.properties` file. The `pub-sub-domain` indicates a topic should be used instead of a queue. Note that by default, the message is persistent:

```
spring.activemq.broker-url=tcp://localhost:61616
jms.ProductTopic=ProductT
spring.jms.pub-sub-domain=true
```

5. Create a message producer component that will do the job of sending messages:
   - This is based on Spring's `JmsMessagingTemplate`
   - Uses `JacksonJmsMessageConverter` to convert from object to message structure

The `ProductMsgProducer.java` file is as follows:

```
@Component
public class ProductMsgProducer {

    @Autowired
    JmsTemplate prodUpdtemplate ;
```

```
    @Value("${jms.ProductTopic}")
    private String productTopic ;
@Bean
    public MessageConverter jacksonJmsMessageConverter() {
         MappingJackson2MessageConverter converter = new
MappingJackson2MessageConverter();
         converter.setTargetType(MessageType.TEXT);
         converter.setTypeIdPropertyName("_type");
         return converter;


    public void sendUpdate(Product product, boolean isDelete) {
         ProductUpdMsg msg = new ProductUpdMsg(product, isDelete);
         prodUpdtemplate.convertAndSend(productTopic, msg);
    }
}
```

6. Finally, in your service, declare the `producer` and invoke it after finishing the insert, update, and delete operations and before returning the response. The `DELETE` method is shown in the following, where the flag `isDelete` is true. The other methods will have the flag as false. The `ProductService.java` file is as follows:

```
@Autowired
ProductMsgProducer producer ;

@RequestMapping(value="/product/{id}", method =
RequestMethod.DELETE)
Product deleteProduct(@PathVariable("id") String id) {
    // First fetch an existing product and then delete it.
    Product existingProduct = prodRepo.findOne(id);
    if (existingProduct == null) {
         String errMsg = "Product Not found with code " + id ;
         throw new
BadRequestException(BadRequestException.ID_NOT_FOUND, errMsg);
    }
    // Return the deleted product
    prodRepo.delete(existingProduct);
    producer.sendUpdate(existingProduct, true);
    return existingProduct ;
}
```

This will send the message on the topic, which you can see in the admin console under the topics section.

Query model update

On the `productsearch` project, we will have to make changes to update the records in Elasticsearch.

Insert, update, and delete methods

These methods are very different from the ones we designed in MongoDB. Here are the differences:

1. MongoDB methods had stringent validations. Validations are not required for Elasticsearch as the master (command model or golden source) is assumed to be updated and we have to apply the updates to the query model.

2. Any error in updating the query model has to be alerted, and should not go unnoticed. We will look at that aspect in the chapters ahead.

3. We do not separate the insert and update method. The single save method suffices for both purposes due to our `ProductRepository` class.

4. Also, these methods do not have to be exposed as REST HTTP services, as they might not be called directly other than through message updates. We do that here only for convenience.

5. In the `product-nosql` (MongoDB) project, we called our `ProductMsgProducer` class from the `ProductService` class. In this `productsearch-nosql` project, it will be the other way around, with the `ProductUpdListener` calling the service methods.

Here are the changes:

1. Maven POM—dependency on the ActiveMQ:

```
<dependency>
    <groupId>org.springframework.boot</groupId>
    <artifactId>spring-boot-starter-activemq</artifactId>
</dependency>
```

2. Application properties to include the topic and connection details:

```
spring.activemq.broker-url=tcp://localhost:61616
jms.ProductTopic=ProductT
spring.jms.pub-sub-domain=true
```

3. `Product` service to include calls to repository save and delete methods:

```
@PutMapping("/product/{id}")
public void insertUpdateProduct(@RequestBody Product product) {
    prodRepo.save(product) ;
}
@DeleteMapping("/product/{id}")
public void deleteProduct(@RequestBody Product product) {
    prodRepo.delete(product);
}
```

JMS-related classes and changes as follows:

1. In `ProductSpringApp,` include annotation `EnableJms,` as done in the MongoDB project.
2. Create a `ProductUpdListener` class that calls the service:

```
@Component
public class ProductUpdListener {

    @Autowired
    ProductService prodService ;
    @JmsListener(destination = "${jms.ProductTopic}", subscription =
"productSearchListener")
    public void receiveMessage(ProductUpdMsg msg) {

        Product product = msg.getProduct() ;
        boolean isDelete = msg.isDelete() ;
        if (isDelete) {
            prodService.deleteProduct(product);
            System.out.println("deleted " + product.getId());
        } else {
            prodService.insertUpdateProduct(product);
            System.out.println("upserted " + product.getId());
        }
    }

    @Bean // Serialize message content to json using TextMessage
    public MessageConverter jacksonJmsMessageConverter() {
        MappingJackson2MessageConverter converter = new
        MappingJackson2MessageConverter();
        converter.setTargetType(MessageType.BYTES);
        converter.setTypeIdPropertyName("_type");
        return converter;
    }
}
```

Testing the CQRS update scenario end to end

To test our scenario, perform the following steps:

1. Start the three server processes on a local machine, such as Elasticsearch, MongoDB, and ActiveMQ, as discussed earlier.
2. Start the Eureka server.
3. Start the two applications, one connecting to MongoDB (golden source, command model), listening on `8085` and the other connecting to Elasticsearch (query model), listening on `8086`.
4. Test the `GET` request on Elasticsearch—`http://localhost:8086/products?id=1`, and note the IDs and descriptions.
5. Now, change the product description on the golden source by issuing the following on your Postman, assuming the service is listening on port `8085`:

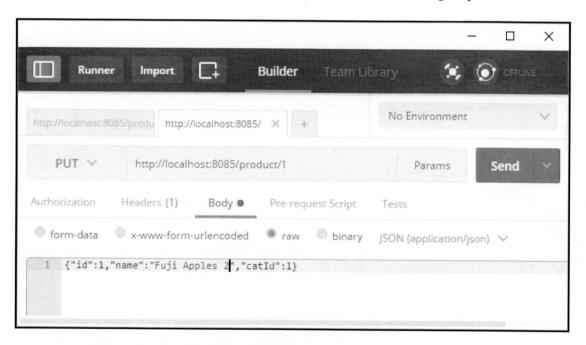

6. Test the `GET` request on Elasticsearch again—`http://localhost:8086/products?id=1`. You will find the product description in Elasticsearch is updated.

Summary

In this chapter, we covered a lot of core concepts, starting with adding a regular relational database to back our get requests. We enhanced its performance with a local cache and then a distributed cache, Hazelcast. We also looked at a CQRS pattern, replacing our relational databases with a MongoDB for flexible schema and Elasticsearch for flexible search and query capabilities.

We added insert, update, and delete operations to our `product` service and ensured that the necessary cache invalidation happens in the case of the relational project. We added input validations and proper error messages to our APIs. We covered eventing to ensure that the query model stays up to date with the command model. This is achieved by command model services sending a broadcast of changes, and query model services listening to the changes and updating their data model.

Up next, we will look at how to make these projects robust enough to work in a runtime environment.

5
Testing Cloud-Native Applications

In this chapter, we take a deep dive into testing cloud-native applications. Testing has matured a lot from manual testing to automated testing, using various testing tools, strategies, and patterns. The benefit of this approach is that the testing can be done frequently in a failsafe fashion that is important for cloud development.

We will cover the following topics in this chapter:

- Testing concepts, such as **behavior-driven development (BDD)** and **test-driven development (TDD)**
- Testing patterns, such as A/B testing and test doubles
- Testing tools, such as JUnit, Cucumber, JaCoCo, and Spring Test
- Types of testing, such as unit, integration, performance, and stress testing
- Applying the concepts of BDD and integration testing to the Product service that we developed in Chapter 2, *Writing Your First Cloud-Native Application*, and enhanced in Chapter 4, *Extending Your Cloud-Native Application*

Writing test cases before development

In this book, we started developing a simple service in Chapter 2, *Writing Your First Cloud-Native Application*, in Spring Boot to get you excited about cloud development. However, real development follows a different style of best practice.

TDD

A project starts with understanding the requirements and writing test cases that validate the requirements. Since the code does not exist at this point, the test case will fail. Then, the code is written that passes the test case. This process iterates till the test cases and the required code are complete to realize the business functionality. Kent Beck has an excellent book on this subject, *Test Driven Development by Example*. In the next section, we will redo the product service from `Chapter 4`, *Extending Your Cloud-Native Application*, using the principles in this chapter. But before that, let's look at another important concept, BDD.

BDD

Taking a leaf out of Agile development principles and user stories, BDD encourages us to think of development as a set of scenarios in which, given certain conditions, the system behaves in a certain, predictable way to the set stimuli. If these scenarios, conditions and actions can be captured in an easy-to-understand common language between the business and IT team, which brings a lot of clarity to development and reduces the chances of committing mistakes. It is a way to write specifications that are easily testable.

Moving ahead in this chapter, we will take our product service and apply BDD to it using the Cucumber tool.

Testing patterns

Testing large internet applications for the cloud requires a disciplined approach where a few patterns come in handy.

A/B testing

The original intent of A/B testing, also called **split testing**, was for experimentation to find out the user response of a few selected users to two different web pages with the same functionality. If the users responded favorably to a certain pattern as compared to the other set, it was selected.

This concept can be expanded to the introduction of new features in a phased manner. The feature, campaign, layout, or new service is introduced to a controlled set of users and the response is measured:

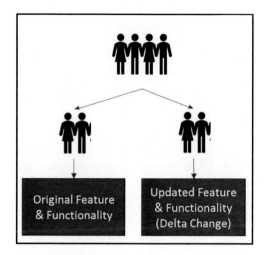

After the test window is over, the results are aggregated to plan the effectiveness of the updated functionality.

The strategy in such testing is that for the selected set of users, an HTTP 302 (temporary redirect) is used to switch the users from the regular website to a newly designed website. This will require running a variation of the website or functional services for the test period. Once the test is successful, the feature is slowly expanded to more users and is merged into the main website/code base.

Test doubles

Often, the functionality under test depends on components and APIs which are independently being developed by other teams, which has the following disadvantages:

- They may not be available for testing at the time of development of your functionality
- They may not be always available and be set up with the data required for testing various cases
- Using the actual components each time may be slower

Hence, the concept of a test double became popular. A test double (like a stunt double in a movie) is a component/API that replaces the actual component and mimics its behavior. The test double component is typically a lightweight and easy-to-change component that is under the control of the team building the functionality, unlike the real components that could be dependencies or external processes.

There are many types of test doubles, such as Dummy, Fakes, Test Stubs, and Mocks.

Test Stubs

Test Stubs are useful when a downstream component returns a response that alters the behavior of the system under test; for example, if our product service was to call a reference data service whose output decides the behavior of the product service. A Test Stub for a reference data service can mimic the various response types that cause change in the behavior of the product service:

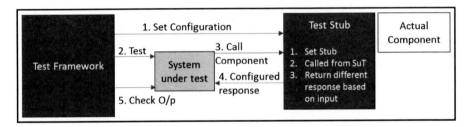

Mock objects

The next type of test double is a Mock object, which records how the system behaves with it and then presents the recording for verification. For example, a Mock database component could check whether it was not being called for a product that was supposed to be answered from a cache layer instead of a database.

Here is a basic diagram representation of the ecosystem around Mocks:

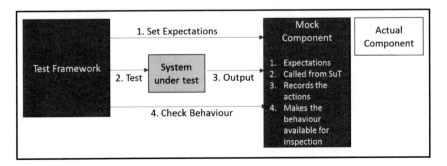

Mock APIs

In cloud development, you will be building a service that depends on other services or mainly the APIs through which the services are accessed. Often, the other services will not be available for testing immediately. But you cannot stop your development. This is where mocking or adding a dummy service is a useful pattern to test your service.

A service Mock emulates all the contracts and behavior of the real service. A few examples such as `WireMock.org` or `Mockable.io` help us to emulate the API and test the main cases, edge cases, and failure conditions.

Types of testing

The various types of testing we discuss later in the chapter were already known even before cloud computing became popular. The principles of Agile development using **continuous integration (CI)** and **continuous development (CD)** make it important to automate these types of testing so that they are executed each time a code check-in and build happens.

Unit testing

The aim of unit testing is to test each class or code component and ensure it is performing as expected. JUnit is the popular Java framework for unit testing.

Using the Mock object pattern and Test Stubs, it is possible to isolate the dependent components of the services being tested so that the testing focuses on the system under test, which is the service.

JUnit is the most popular tool to perform unit testing.

Integration testing

The aim of component testing is to check whether the components, such as the Product service, perform as expected.

Components such as `spring-boot-test` help run the test suites and run the test on whole components. We are going to see this in action in this chapter.

Load testing

Load testing involves pushing a large volume of concurrent requests to the system under test for a period and observing the effect, such as response time and error rates on the system. A system is said to be horizontally scalable if adding more instances of the service enables it to handle additional loads.

JMeter and Gatling are the popular tools to cover this dimension.

Regression testing

In introducing new functionality, the existing functionality should not break. Regression testing covers this.

Selenium is a web browser-based, open source tool popular in this space to perform regression testing.

Ensuring code review and coverage

The manual review of code is augmented by automatic code review tools. This helps to identify any possible errors in the code and ensure the coverage is complete and all paths are tested.

We will look at the code coverage tool JaCoCo later.

Testing the Product service

Let's apply the testing principles we learned to the Product service that we have been building so far. We start from a user point of view and hence with acceptance testing.

BDD through Cucumber

The first step is to recall the specification of our product service. In `Chapter 4`, *Extending Your Cloud-Native Application*, we built a few features on our product service that allowed us to fetch, add, modify, and delete products, and get a list of product IDs given a product category.

Let's represent this as features in Cucumber.

Why Cucumber?

Cucumber allows the expression of behavior in a plain-English-like language called **Gherkin**. This enables a ubiquitous language from the domain-driven design parlance, so that the communication between the business, development, and testing is seamless and well-understood.

How does Cucumber work?

Let's understand how Cucumber works:

1. The first step in Cucumber is to express the user story as features with scenarios, and `Given-When-Then` conditions:
   - `Given`: Sets the preconditions for the behavior
   - `When`: Trigger that changes the state of the system, for example, making a request to the service
   - `Then`: How the service should respond
2. These are translated to automated test cases using the `cucumber-spring` translation layer so that they can be executed.

Let's start with a simple `getProduct` acceptance test case. We will write a simple feature in Gherkin that gets the product if the product ID exists, or returns an error if the product ID is not found.

Let's realize the following feature in a true BDD style. The `get` API on the Product service returns product details such as description and category ID given a product ID. It can also return an error, for example, 404 if the product is not found. Let's represent these two behaviors as two separate scenarios on our Gherkin feature file.

Feature: `getProduct`

Get the product details given a product ID.

Scenario 1: The product ID is valid and exists. The product name and category it belongs to will be returned:

1. `Given` the product service is running
2. `When` the get product service is called with existing product ID 1
3. `Then` we should get a response with HTTP status code `200`
4. `And` return product details with, name `Apples` and category 1

Scenario 2: The product ID is invalid or does not exist. An error should be returned:

1. `Given` product service is running
2. `When` the get product service is called with a non-existing product ID `456`
3. `Then` return a 404 not found status
4. `And` return the error message `No product for ID 456`

Scenario 1 is a successful scenario where a product ID existing in the database is returned and validated against.

Scenario 2 checks for a failure condition of an ID that does not exist in the database.

Each scenario is divided into multiple parts. For the happy-path scenario:

- `Given` sets a precondition. In our case, it is simple enough: that the product service should be running.
- `When` changes the state of the system and, in our case, it is making the request to the service by giving a product ID.
- `Then` and `And` are the results that are expected on the system. In this case, we expect the service to return a `200` success code and the valid description and category codes for the given product.

As you may have noticed, this is the documentation of our service that can be understood by the business and the testing team as well as the developers. It is technology-agnostic; that is, it does not change if the implementation is done through Spring Boot, Ruby, or a .NET microservice.

In the next section, we will map the service to the Spring Boot application that we developed.

Spring Boot Test

Spring Boot Test extends and simplifies the Spring-test module provided by the Spring Framework. Let's look at the essential elements to write our acceptance tests and then we can revisit the details later in the chapter:

1. Copy the project that we created in `Chapter 4`, *Extending Your Cloud-Native Application* with HSQLDB and Hazelcast, as a new project for this chapter.

2. Include the dependency on Spring in the Maven POM file:

```
<dependency>
    <groupId>org.springframework.boot</groupId>
    <artifactId>spring-boot-starter-test</artifactId>
    <scope>test</scope>
</dependency>
```

As you may have noticed, the `scope` is changed to `test`. This means that the dependency we are defining is not required for normal runtime, only for compilation and test execution.

3. Add two more dependencies to Maven. We are downloading the libraries for Cucumber and its Java translation, along with `spring-boot-starter-test`:

```
<dependency>
    <groupId>info.cukes</groupId>
    <artifactId>cucumber-spring</artifactId>
    <version>1.2.5</version>
    <scope>test</scope>
</dependency>
<dependency>
    <groupId>info.cukes</groupId>
    <artifactId>cucumber-junit</artifactId>
    <version>1.2.5</version>
    <scope>test</scope>
</dependency>
```

The `CucumberTest` class is the main class that starts the Cucumber tests:

```
@RunWith(Cucumber.class)
@CucumberOptions(features = "src/test/resources")
public class CucumberTest {
}
```

`RunWith` tells the JUnit to use Spring's testing support, which then uses Cucumber. We give the path to our `.feature` file, which contains the test cases in Gherkin discussed earlier.

The `Productservice.feature` file is the text file containing the scenarios in Gherkin language, as discussed earlier. We will have two test cases featured here. This file is present in the `src/test/resources` folder.

The `CucumberTestSteps` class contains the translation of the steps in Gherkin to the equivalent Java code. Each step corresponds to a method and the methods get called based on the scenario construction in the Gherkin file. Let's discuss all steps related to one use case:

```java
@SpringBootTest(webEnvironment = SpringBootTest.WebEnvironment.RANDOM_PORT)
@ContextConfiguration
public class CucumberTestSteps {
    @Autowired
    private TestRestTemplate restTemplate;
    private ResponseEntity<Product> productResponse;
    private ResponseEntity<String> errResponse;
    @Given("(.*) Service is running")
    public void checkServiceRunning(String serviceName) {
        ResponseEntity<String> healthResponse =
restTemplate.getForEntity("/health",String.class, new HashMap<>());
        Assert.assertEquals(HttpStatus.OK,
healthResponse.getStatusCode());
    }
    @When("get (.*) service is called with existing product id (\d+)$")
    public void callService(String serviceName, int prodId) throws
Throwable {
        productResponse =
this.restTemplate.getForEntity("/"+serviceName+"/" + prodId, Product.class,
new HashMap<>());
    }
    @Then("I should get a response with HTTP status code (.*)")
    public void shouldGetResponseWithHttpStatusCode(int statusCode) {
        Assert.assertEquals(statusCode,
productResponse.getStatusCodeValue());
    }
    @And("return Product details with name (.*) and category (\d+)$")
    public void theResponseShouldContainTheMessage(String prodName, int
categoryId) {
        Product product = productResponse.getBody() ;
        Assert.assertEquals(prodName, product.getName());
        Assert.assertEquals(categoryId, product.getCatId());
    }
```

The `@SpringBootTest` annotation tells the Spring Boot Framework that it is a test class. The `RANDOM_PORT` indicates the test service to start Tomcat on a random port for testing.

We inject an autowired `restTemplate` which will help access the HTTP/REST service and receive the response which will be tested.

Now, note the methods with the annotations @Given, @When, and @Then. Each method uses a regular expression to extract the variable (from the feature file) and uses it for assertions in the method. We have systematically tested this by doing the following:

1. Checking whether the service is running first by accessing the /health (as we did for Spring Boot Actuator in Chapter 2, *Writing Your First Cloud-Native Application*).
2. Calling the service with the product ID.
3. Checking whether the return code is 200 and the description and category of the response match the expected result.
4. Running the tests.
5. Right-clicking the CucumberTest.java file and selecting **Run As | JUnit Test**:

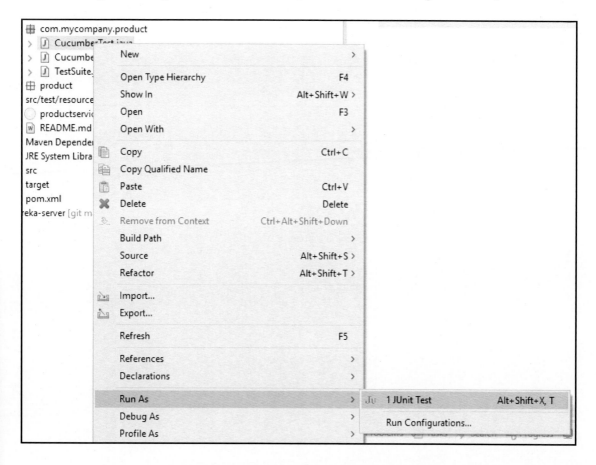

You will see the console fire up with the start-up messages. Finally, the JUnit will reflect the test results as follows:

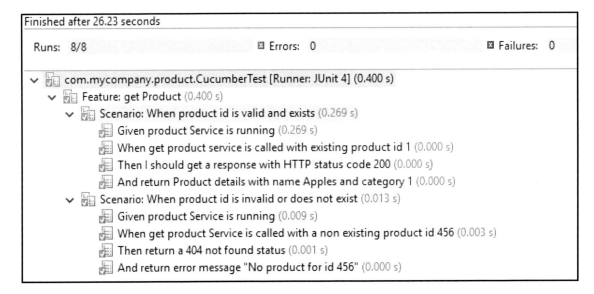

As an exercise, try adding the test cases to the inserting, updating, and deleting a product methods in the `ProductService` class.

Code coverage using JaCoCo

JaCoCo is a code coverage library developed by the EclEmma team. JaCoCo embeds an agent in JVM which scans the code paths traversed and creates a report.

This report can be imported into a wider DevOps code quality tool such as SonarQube. SonarQube is a platform that helps to manage code quality with numerous plugins and integrates nicely with DevOps processes (as we shall see in later chapters). It is open source but also has a commercial edition. It is a platform as it has multiple components, such as server (Compute Engine Server, Web Server, and Elasticsearch), database, and scanners that are language-specific.

Integrating JaCoCo

Let's integrate JaCoCo into our existing project:

1. First, include the plugin that includes JaCoCo in the POM file:

```
<plugin>
    <groupId>org.jacoco</groupId>
    <artifactId>jacoco-maven-plugin</artifactId>
    <version>0.7.9</version>
</plugin>
```

 The second and third step is to include pre-executions and post-executions into the preceding plugin.

2. The pre-execution prepares the agent to be configured and added to the command line.
3. The post-execution ensures that the reports get created in the output folders:

```
<executions>
    <execution>
        <id>pre-unit-test</id>
        <goals>
            <goal>prepare-agent</goal>
        </goals>
        <configuration>
            <destFile>${project.build.directory}/coverage-
reports/jacoco-ut.exec</destFile>
            <propertyName>surefireArgLine</propertyName>
        </configuration>
    </execution>
    <execution>
        <id>post-unit-test</id>
        <phase>test</phase>
        <goals>
```

```
        <goal>report</goal>
    </goals>
    <configuration>
        <dataFile>${project.build.directory}/coverage-
reports/jacoco-ut.exec</dataFile>
    <outputDirectory>${project.reporting.outputDirectory}/jacoco-
ut</outputDirectory>
    </configuration>
    </execution>
</executions>
```

4. Finally, the created command-line change has to be inserted into the `maven-surefire-plugin` as follows:

```
<plugin>
    <groupId>org.apache.maven.plugins</groupId>
    <artifactId>maven-surefire-plugin</artifactId>
    <configuration>
        <!-- Sets the VM argument line used when unit tests are
run. -->
        <argLine>${surefireArgLine}</argLine>
        <excludes>
            <exclude>**/IT*.java</exclude>
        </excludes>
    </configuration>
</plugin>
```

5. Now, we are all set to run the coverage report. Right-click on the project and select **Run As** | **Maven test** to test the program, as shown in the following screenshot:

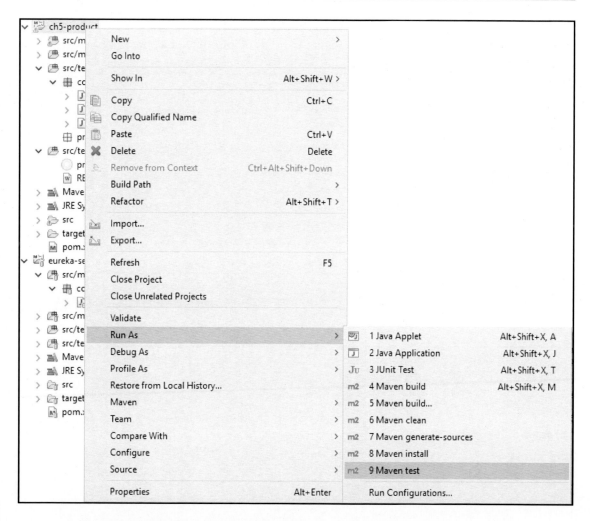

6. As the console gets filled with the Spring Boot initiation, you will find the following lines:

```
2 Scenarios ([32m2 passed[0m)
8 Steps ([32m8 passed[0m)
0m0.723s
```

**Tests run: 10, Failures: 0, Errors: 0, Skipped: 0, Time elapsed: 26.552 sec
- in com.mycompany.product.CucumberTest......Results :Tests run: 10,
Failures: 0, Errors: 0, Skipped: 0[INFO] [INFO] --- jacoco-maven-
plugin:0.7.9:report (post-unit-test) @ product ---[INFO] Loading execution
data file D:AppswkNeonch5-producttargetcoverage-reportsjacoco-ut.exec[INFO]
Analyzed bundle 'product' with 6 classes**

7. This tells us that two scenarios were executed with `8 Steps` (as before). But in addition, `coverage-reports` got generated and placed in the `target` directory:

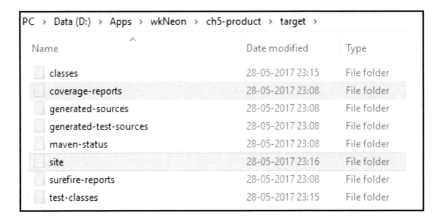

8. In the `site` folder, click on `index.html`; you will see the coverage report as follows:

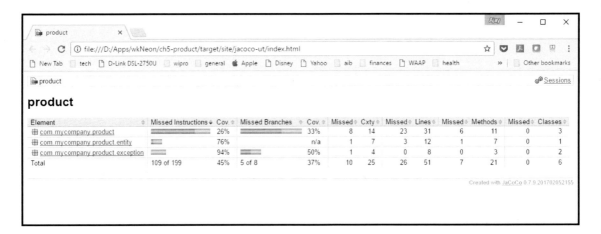

9. On investigation of the `product` package, you can see that the `ProductService` is only `24%` covered, as shown in the following screenshot:

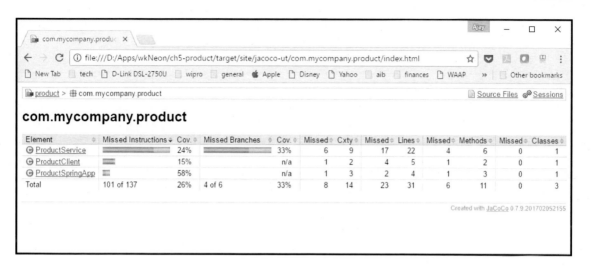

10. The reason for this is that we have covered only the `getProduct` API in the service. The `insertProduct` and `updateProduct` have not been covered. This is showcased in the drill-down report in the following screenshot:

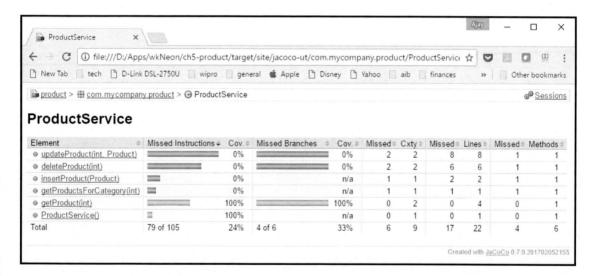

11. On the `getProduct` method, the coverage is complete. This is because, in two scenarios, we have covered the happy path as well as the error condition:

12. On the other hand, you will find that we have missed covering the branches in the `ExceptionHandler` class as follows:

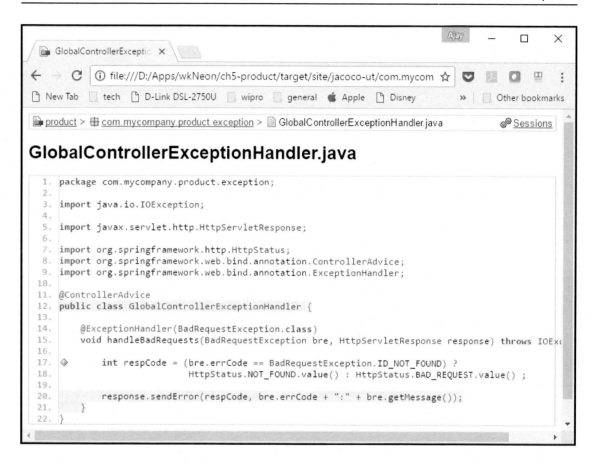

Summary

In the upcoming chapters, we will integrate the coverage report with the DevOps pipeline and see it working during CI and CD. However, first, let's look at the deployment mechanisms.

6
Cloud-Native Application Deployment

One of the most unique things about cloud-native applications is their deployment. In traditional application deployment, teams deploy their applications by logging on to a server and installing the application. But in the cloud there are usually many servers, and logging into each one and installing the application manually is not feasible and can be very error prone. To combat these problems, we use cloud provisioning tools to automate the deployment of cloud-native applications.

In this chapter, we will dive into the deployment model for the microservice—including how to package your application as a Docker container, how to set up the CI/CD pipeline, and how to protect your service from security attacks such as a **distributed denial of service (DDoS)**. We will cover the following:

- Deployment models, packaging, and containerization (using Docker)
- Deployment patterns (blue-green, canary release, and dark release)
- DDoS
- CI/CD

Deployment models

We will cover the deployment models that will be used to deploy our application in the cloud environment.

Virtualization

The fundamental building block of the cloud is a virtual machine (referred to as VM from now on), which is equivalent to a physical server (or host) on which users can log in and install or maintain applications. The difference being that there can be several VMs hosted on a single host thereby increasing the resource utilization. This is achieved by using virtualization, where a hypervisor is installed on the host that can then apportion the resources available on the physical server, such as compute, memory, storage, and networking to the different VMs hosted on it. Cloud-native applications can be deployed on such VMs using the following strategies:

- Several applications per VM
- One application per VM

When running several applications per VM there is the possibility of one application hogging all the resources available on the VM and starving out the other applications. On the other hand, running a single application per VM ensures that the applications are isolated so that they are not affecting each other, but the down side of such a deployment is the waste of resources, as each application might not always be consuming all the resources that are available to it.

PaaS

PaaS or Platform as a Service is another popular option for deploying cloud-native applications. PaaS offers additional services that complement the development, scaling, and maintenance of cloud-native applications. Services such as automated builds and deployments through buildpacks greatly minimize the time spent in setting up additional infrastructure to support these activities. PaaS also provides some basic infrastructure services such as monitoring, log aggregation, secrets management, and load balancing out-of-the-box. Cloud Foundry, Google App Engine, Heroku, and OpenShift are some examples of PaaS.

Containers

The efforts made to provide the level of isolation required for independent operation, while also conserving resource utilization, has resulted in the development of container technology. By leveraging features of the Linux kernel, containers provide CPU, memory, storage, and network isolation at a process level. The following figure demonstrates the difference between virtualizations:

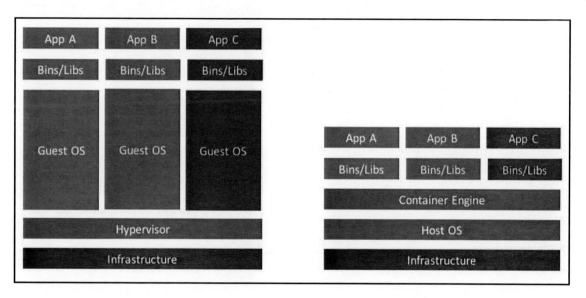

Containers eliminate the need for the guest operating system, thereby greatly increasing the number of containers that can be run versus the number of VMs on the same host. Containers also have a smaller footprint, in the order of MBs, whereas VMs can easily exceed several GBs.

Containers are also very resource efficient in terms of the amount of CPU and memory required, as they do not have to support the many peripheral systems that have to be supported when running a fully fledged operating system:

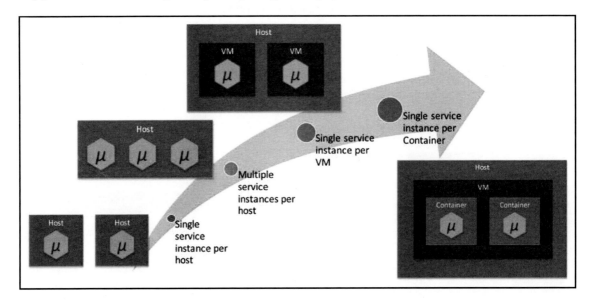

The previous diagram shows the evolution of cloud-native application deployment strategies with the aim of increasing the resource utilization and isolation of the applications. At the top of the stack are running containers within VMs running on a host. This allows the applications to scale by two degrees:

- Increasing the number of containers within a VM
- Increasing the number of VMs running containers

Docker

Docker is a container runtime that has gained popularity, and has proved itself to be a robust platform for deploying cloud-native applications. Docker is available on all major platforms, such as Windows, Mac, and Linux. Since containers require the Linux kernel, it is easier to run the Docker engine in a Linux environment. But, there are several resources available to run Docker containers comfortably in both Windows and Mac environments. We will be demonstrating how to deploy the services that we have been developing so far as Docker containers, including connecting to an external database running in its own container.

In our examples, we will be using Docker Toolbox and using Docker Machine to create a VM, within which the Docker engine will be running. We will connect to this engine using the Docker command-line client and use the various commands provided.

Building Docker images

We will begin to containerize our current projects as a set of Docker containers. We will go through the steps for each of the projects.

Eureka server

1. Add a `.dockerignore` file with the following contents in `$WORKSPACE/eureka-server/.dockerignore`:

   ```
   .*
   target/*
   !target/eureka-server-*.jar
   ```

2. Add a Dockerfile with the following contents in `$WORKSPACE/eureka-server/Dockerfile`:

   ```
   FROM openjdk:8-jdk-alpine

   RUN mkdir -p /app

   ADD target/eureka-server-0.0.1-SNAPSHOT.jar /app/app.jar

   EXPOSE 8761

   ENTRYPOINT [ "/usr/bin/java", "-jar", "/app/app.jar" ]
   ```

3. Build the runnable JAR, which will be available in the target folder:

   ```
   mvn package
   ```

4. Build the Docker container:

   ```
   docker build -t cloudnativejava/eureka-server .
   ```

The output of the preceding command is shown in the following screenshot:

```
$ docker build -t cloudnativejava/eureka-server .
Sending build context to Docker daemon  39.92MB
Step 1/5 : FROM openjdk:8-jdk-alpine
 ---> 478bf389b75b
Step 2/5 : RUN mkdir -p /app
 ---> Using cache
 ---> 9a09e0b0d6f2
Step 3/5 : ADD target/eureka-server-0.0.1-SNAPSHOT.jar /app/app.jar
 ---> 2964965b585e
Removing intermediate container f757ed7f6818
Step 4/5 : EXPOSE 8761
 ---> Running in 848041f9fdee
 ---> d9484343075e
Removing intermediate container 848041f9fdee
Step 5/5 : ENTRYPOINT /usr/bin/java -jar /app/app.jar
 ---> Running in a6ea9f525f56
 ---> 76e53a88d2ce
Removing intermediate container a6ea9f525f56
Successfully built 76e53a88d2ce
Successfully tagged cloudnativejava/eureka-server:latest
```

5. Before running the container, we need to create a network on which the different containers can communicate freely with each other. This can be created by running the following command:

```
docker network create app_nw
```

The output of the preceding command is shown in the following screenshot:

```
$ docker network create app_nw
5828658b7d30f10391c6ce4dcfd7bef0c966873eb6df81c7b6f678fbf62c58f7
```

6. Run the container with the name `eureka` and attach it to the network created earlier:

```
docker run -d --network app_nw --name eureka
cloudnativejava/eureka-server
```

The output of the preceding command is shown in the following screenshot:

```
$ docker run -d --network app_nw --name eureka cloudnativejava/eureka-server
c26a460a4cb384204dde3ff27a07773f0070fc809a9238145b88b34641a6c32c
```

Product API

Next we work on the product API project:

1. Add a new Spring profile, `docker` in the `application.yml` by appending the following contents to the existing file:

   ```
   ---
   spring:
     profiles: docker
   eureka:
     instance:
       preferIpAddress: true
     client:
       serviceUrl:
         defaultZone: http://eureka:8761/eureka/
   ```

2. Build the Spring Boot JAR to reflect changes to `application.yml`:

   mvn clean package

3. Add a `.dockerignore` file with the following contents:

   ```
   .*
   target/*
   !target/product-*.jar
   ```

4. Add a Dockerfile with the following contents:

   ```
   FROM openjdk:8-jdk-alpine

   RUN mkdir -p /app

   ADD target/product-0.0.1-SNAPSHOT.jar /app/app.jar

   EXPOSE 8080

   ENTRYPOINT [ "/usr/bin/java", "-jar", "/app/app.jar", "--
   spring.profiles.active=docker" ]
   ```

5. Build the Docker container:

   docker build -t cloudnativejava/product-api .

The output of the preceding command is shown in the following screenshot:

```
$ docker build -t cloudnativejava/product-api .
Sending build context to Docker daemon  61.06MB
Step 1/5 : FROM openjdk:8-jdk-alpine
 ---> 478bf389b75b
Step 2/5 : RUN mkdir -p /app
 ---> Using cache
 ---> 9a09e0b0d6f2
Step 3/5 : ADD target/product-0.0.1-SNAPSHOT.jar /app/app.jar
 ---> Using cache
 ---> 4facc6546ab1
Step 4/5 : EXPOSE 8080
 ---> Using cache
 ---> 4982d78f6443
Step 5/5 : ENTRYPOINT /usr/bin/java -jar /app/app.jar --spring.profiles.active=docker
 ---> Using cache
 ---> f3fe921a8988
Successfully built f3fe921a8988
Successfully tagged cloudnativejava/product-api:latest
```

6. Start several Docker containers:

```
docker run -d -p 8011:8080 \
    --network app_nw \
    cloudnativejava/product-api

docker run -d -p 8012:8080 \
    --network app_nw \
    cloudnativejava/product-api
```

The output of the preceding commands is shown in the following screenshot:

```
$ docker run -d -p 8011:8080 \
>       --network app_nw \
>       cloudnativejava/product-api
74cc71e3baf4c10df238235c642d3a264d22c03b669b4552821d901b64f33d20
$ docker run -d -p 8012:8080 \
>       --network app_nw \
>       cloudnativejava/product-api
f57adbd3bb3bb0628ef11d90b6ed98457e3290064cc588313e29cecc4e7c3708
```

The product API will be available at the following URLs:

- `http://<docker-host>:8011/product/1`
- `http://<docker-host>:8012/product/1`

Connecting to an external Postgres container

To connect the `product` API to an external database instead of an in-memory database, first create a container image with the data already populated in it:

1. Create a file, `import-postgres.sql`, with the following contents:

```
create table product(id serial primary key, name varchar(20),
cat_id int not null);
begin;
insert into product(name, cat_id) values ('Apples', 1);
insert into product(name, cat_id) values ('Oranges', 1);
insert into product(name, cat_id) values ('Bananas', 1);
insert into product(name, cat_id) values ('Carrots', 2);
insert into product(name, cat_id) values ('Beans', 2);
insert into product(name, cat_id) values ('Peas', 2);
commit;
```

2. Create a `Dockerfile.postgres` with the following contents:

```
FROM postgres:alpine

ENV POSTGRES_USER=dbuser
    POSTGRES_PASSWORD=dbpass
    POSTGRES_DB=product

EXPOSE 5432

RUN mkdir -p /docker-entrypoint-initdb.d

ADD import-postgres.sql /docker-entrypoint-initdb.d/import.sql
```

3. Now build the Postgres container image which will have the database initialized with the contents of `import-postgres.sql`:

```
docker build -t cloudnativejava/datastore -f Dockerfile.postgres .
```

The output of the preceding command is shown in the following screenshot:

```
$ docker build -t cloudnativejava/datastore -f Dockerfile.postgres .
Sending build context to Docker daemon  61.06MB
Step 1/5 : FROM postgres:alpine
 ---> e9e9c4470522
Step 2/5 : ENV POSTGRES_USER dbuser POSTGRES_PASSWORD dbpass POSTGRES_DB product
 ---> Using cache
 ---> 20dcc938b14b
Step 3/5 : EXPOSE 5432
 ---> Using cache
 ---> aba503937193
Step 4/5 : RUN mkdir -p /docker-entrypoint-initdb.d
 ---> Using cache
 ---> b162459a436a
Step 5/5 : ADD import-postgres.sql /docker-entrypoint-initdb.d/import.sql
 ---> Using cache
 ---> d5def9256c7e
Successfully built d5def9256c7e
Successfully tagged cloudnativejava/datastore:latest
```

4. Add a new Spring profile, `postgres` to the `application.yml` by appending the following contents to the existing file:

```
---
spring:
  profiles: postgres
  datasource:
    url: jdbc:postgresql://<docker-host>:5432/product
    username: dbuser
    password: dbpass
    driver-class-name: org.postgresql.Driver
  jpa:
    database-platform: org.hibernate.dialect.PostgreSQLDialect
    hibernate:
      ddl-auto: none
```

Ensure that you replace `<docker-host>` with the value appropriate for your environment.

5. Build the Spring Boot JAR to reflect changes to `application.yml`:

```
mvn clean package
```

6. Build the Docker container:

```
docker build -t cloudnativejava/product-api .
```

The output of the preceding command is shown in the following screenshot:

```
$ docker build -t cloudnativejava/product-api .
Sending build context to Docker daemon  61.06MB
Step 1/5 : FROM openjdk:8-jdk-alpine
 ---> 478bf389b75b
Step 2/5 : RUN mkdir -p /app
 ---> Using cache
 ---> 9a09e0b0d6f2
Step 3/5 : ADD target/product-0.0.1-SNAPSHOT.jar /app/app.jar
 ---> Using cache
 ---> 4facc6546ab1
Step 4/5 : EXPOSE 8080
 ---> Using cache
 ---> 4982d78f6443
Step 5/5 : ENTRYPOINT /usr/bin/java -jar /app/app.jar --spring.profiles.active=docker
 ---> Using cache
 ---> f3fe921a8988
Successfully built f3fe921a8988
Successfully tagged cloudnativejava/product-api:latest
```

7. If you already have containers running off the old image you can stop and remove them:

```
old_ids=$(docker ps -f ancestor=cloudnativejava/product-api -q)
docker stop $old_ids
docker rm $old_ids
```

8. Start the database container:

```
docker run -d -p 5432:5432
    --network app_nw
    --name datastore
    cloudnativejava/datastore
```

The output of the preceding command is shown in the following screenshot:

```
$ docker run -d -p 5432:5432 \
>     --network app_nw \
>     --name datastore \
>     cloudnativejava/datastore
0663e27115b1807b2924903c3996cd0f927c248624cf8f18ef617168fc31a53b
```

9. Start several Docker containers for the product API:

```
docker run -d -p 8011:8080
    --network app_nw
    cloudnativejava/product-api
    --spring.profiles.active=postgres

docker run -d -p 8012:8080
    --network app_nw
    cloudnativejava/product-api
    --spring.profiles.active=postgres
```

The output of the preceding command is shown in the following screenshot:

```
$ docker run -d -p 8011:8080 \
>       --network app_nw \
>       cloudnativejava/product-api \
>       --spring.profiles.active=postgres
a1b5e68cf251f3073961b75f91caf10bb39c321712114836fc474c002bc1d73a

$ docker run -d -p 8012:8080 \
>       --network app_nw \
>       cloudnativejava/product-api \
>       --spring.profiles.active=postgres
6b9081236786544df3012d3d018c6e17003977d3e6b99715ac1eeb3931b1072b
```

The product API will be available at the following URLs:

- `http://<docker-host>:8011/product/1`
- `http://<docker-host>:8012/product/1`

Deployment patterns

Having covered the packaging and deployment models of cloud-native applications, we will now cover the patterns used for deploying cloud-native applications. Traditionally, applications get deployed in several environments such as development, testing, staging, pre-production, and so on, and each of these environments might be a scaled-down version of the final production environment. Applications move through a series of pre-production environments and get deployed finally to the production environment. However, one significant difference is that while downtime is tolerated in all other environments, downtime in a production deployment could lead to serious business consequences.

With cloud-native applications, it is possible to release software with zero downtime. This is achieved by the rigorous application of automation to every aspect of the development, testing, and deployment of the application. We will cover **continuous integration (CI)** / **continuous deployment (CD)** in a later section, but here we will cover some patterns that enable rapid deployment of applications. All of these patterns rely on the presence of a router component, which not unlike a load balancer can route requests to a certain set of application instances. In some cases, the application itself is built with features that are hidden behind feature flags, which can be enabled through changes to the application configuration.

Blue-green deployment

Blue-green deployment is a pattern that happens over three stages. The initial state of the deployment is depicted in the following figure. All the traffic to the application is routed to the existing instances, which are treated as the blue instances. A representation of blue-green deployment is as follows:

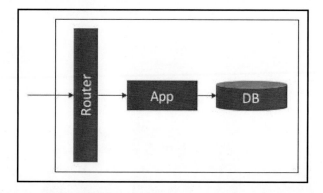

In the first stage of blue-green deployment, a new set of instances with the new release of the application are provisioned and become available. At this stage, the new green application instance is not available to the end users and the deployment is verified internally. This is shown here:

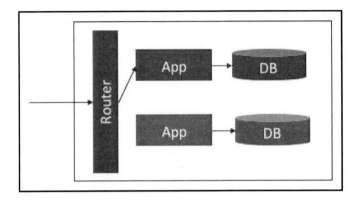

In the next stage of the deployment, a figurative switch is thrown on the router, which now starts routing all the requests to the green instances instead of the old blue instances. The old blue instances are kept around for a period of observation and if any critical issues are detected we can quickly rollback the deployment to the older instance of the application if required:

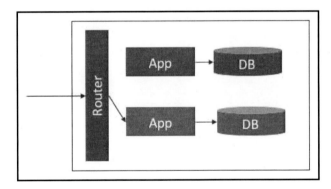

In the last stage of the deployment, the older blue instances of the application are decommissioned and the green instance becomes the next stable production release:

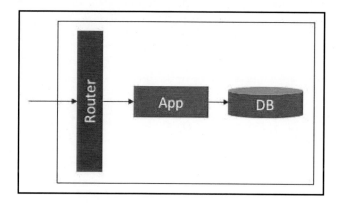

Blue-green deployments are effective when switching between two stable releases of an application and quick recovery is ensured by the availability of a fallback environment.

Canary deployment

Canary deployment is also a variation of the blue-green deployment. Canary deployment addresses the wasted resources that are provisioned when running two production instances simultaneously, albeit for a short duration. In canary deployments, the green environment is a scaled-down version of the blue environment and is relying on the capability of the router to consistently route a small percentage of the requests to the new green environment, while the bulk of the requests are routed to the blue environment. The following figure depicts this:

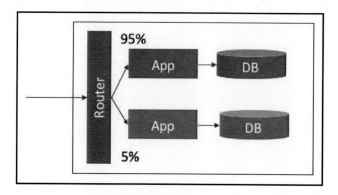

This is particularly useful when releasing new features of an application that need to be tested with a few beta test users, and then based on the feedback of this user group rolled out to all users. Once it is ascertained that the green environment is ready for full rollout, instances in the green environment are ramped up while simultaneously, instances from the blue environment are ramped down. It is best illustrated by the following sequence of diagrams:

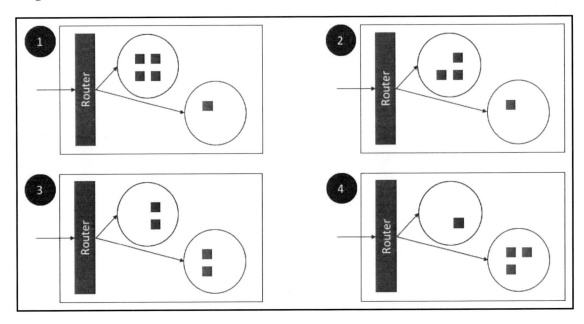

This way the problem of having to run two production level environments is avoided, and there is a smooth transition from one version to the other while also providing an easy fallback to the old version.

Dark release

Another popular deployment pattern that is utilized for deploying cloud-native applications is the dark release pattern. Here, new features are hidden behind feature flags and are enabled for a select group of users, or in some cases the users are totally unaware of the feature while the application mimics the users' behavior and exercises the hidden features of the application. Once the feature is deemed ready and stable for rollout to all users then it is enabled by toggling the feature flags.

Applying CI/CD to automate

One of the central aspects of cloud-native application deployment relies on the ability to effectively automate and build a software delivery pipeline. This is primarily accomplished by using CI/CD tools that can take the source code from the source repositories, run tests, build a deployable artifact, and deploy them to the target environments. Most modern CI/CD tools, such as Jenkins, provide support for configuring build pipelines that can be used to build several artifacts based on a configuration file in the form of a script.

We will take the example of a Jenkins pipeline script to demonstrate how a simple build pipeline can be configured. In our example, we will simply build two artifacts, namely the `eureka-server` and the `product-api` runnable JARs. Add a new file named `Jenkinsfile` with the following contents:

```
node {
  def mvnHome
  stage('Preparation') { // for display purposes
    // Get some code from a GitHub repository
    git 'https://github.com/...'
    // Get the Maven tool.
    // ** NOTE: This 'M3' Maven tool must be configured
    // **       in the global configuration.
    mvnHome = tool 'M3'
  }
  stage('Eureka Server') {
    dir('eureka-server') {
      stage('Build - Eureka Server') {
        // Run the maven build
        if (isUnix()) {
          sh "'${mvnHome}/bin/mvn' -Dmaven.test.failure.ignore clean
package"
        } else {
          bat(/"${mvnHome}binmvn" -Dmaven.test.failure.ignore clean
package/)
```

```
            }
        }
        stage('Results - Eureka Server') {
            archiveArtifacts 'target/*.jar'
        }
    }
}
stage('Product API') {
    dir('product') {
        stage('Build - Product API') {
            // Run the maven build
            if (isUnix()) {
                sh "'${mvnHome}/bin/mvn' -Dmaven.test.failure.ignore clean
package"
            } else {
                bat(/"${mvnHome}binmvn" -Dmaven.test.failure.ignore clean
package/)
            }
        }
        stage('Results - Product API') {
            junit '**/target/surefire-reports/TEST-*.xml'
            archiveArtifacts 'target/*.jar'
        }
    }
}
}
```

The pipeline script does the following:

1. Checks out the source code from GitHub
2. Configures the Maven tool
3. Builds two artifacts by running the Maven build within two directories of the checked-out source repository
4. Stores the test results and the resultant JARs from the build

Create a new pipeline job in Jenkins:

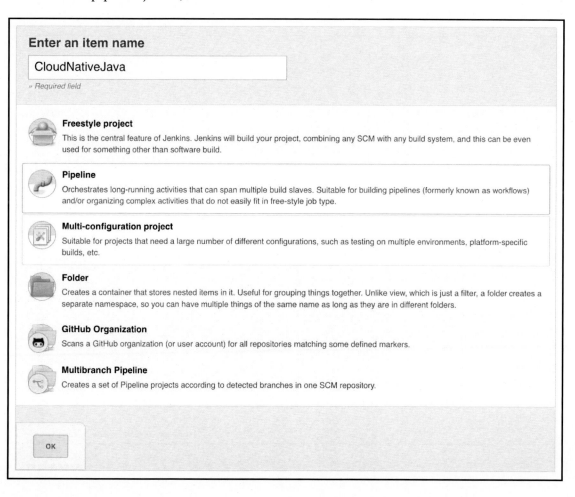

In the pipeline configuration, specify the GitHub repository and the path to the `Jenkinsfile` in that Git repository:

On running the build, it should result in the building of two artifacts:

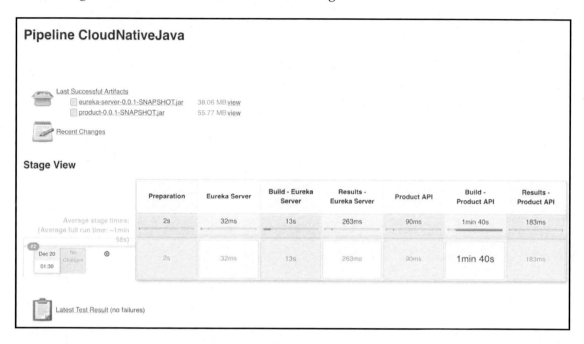

The pipeline script can be extended to build the Docker containers that we built by hand earlier in the chapter using the Docker plugin for Jenkins.

Summary

In this chapter, we learned about the various deployment patterns that can be used for deploying cloud-native applications, and how continuous integration tools such as Jenkins can be used to automate the build and deployment. We also learned how to build and run a sample cloud-native application using Docker containers.

7
Cloud-Native Application Runtime

Having developed, tested, and deployed the applications using a deployment pipeline such as Jenkins, in this chapter, we will look at the runtime ecosystems in which our applications or services run. We will cover the following topics:

- The need for a comprehensive runtime, including a recap of the problems in operating and managing a large number of services
- Implementing the reference runtime architecture, including:
    - Service registry
    - Config server
    - Service frontends, API gateway, reverse proxy, and load balancer
    - A look at Zuul as a reverse proxy
    - Container management and orchestration through Kubernetes and Minikube

- Running on **Platform as a Service (PaaS)**:
    - How the PaaS platforms help realize service runtime reference architecture that we discussed in previous chapter
    - Installing Cloud Foundry and running our `product` service on the Cloud Foundry

The need for a runtime

We have developed our services, written tests for them, automated the continuous integration, and are running them in the container. What else do we need?

Running many services at scale in production is not easy. As more services are released in production, their management starts getting complex. Hence, here is a recap of the problems, discussed in the microservices ecosystem and solved in some code samples in a previous chapter:

- **Service running in the cloud:** A traditional large application was hosted on an application server and ran at an IP address and port. On the other hand, microservices run in multiple containers at various IP addresses and ports so the tracking production service can get complex.
- **Services come up and go down like moles in a Whack-a-Mole game:** There are 100s of services with their loads balanced and failover instances running all over the cloud space. Many teams, thanks to DevOps and agility, are deploying new services and taking down old services. Thus, as we can see, a microservice-driven cloud environment is very dynamic.

  These two issues are addressed by the service registry tracking the services. So, the clients can look up where the services corresponding to a name are running using a client-side load balancing pattern. However, if we want to abstract the clients from the look up, then we use the pattern of server-side load balancing, where a load balancer, such as Nginx, an API gateway like Apigee, or reverse proxy or router, such as Zuul, abstracts the clients from the actual address of the services.

- **Managing my configuration across microservices:** If the deployment unit has broken into multiple services, so has the property file containing the packaged configuration items such as connection addresses, user ID, logging levels, and so on. So, if I have to change a logging level for a set of services or a flow, do I have to change it across all the application's property files? Here, we will see how centralizing the property files in a config server like Spring Config Server or Consul helps to manage the properties in a hierarchical fashion.

- **So many log files to handle:** Each microservice is generating one (or more) log files like `.out` and `.err` and Log4j files. How do we search for log messages across multiple log files from multiple services?

  The pattern to solve this is log aggregation, implemented with commercial tools such as Splunk or open source tools like Logstash or Galaxia. They are also present by default in PaaS offerings like Pivotal Cloud Foundry.

  The other option is to stream logs to the aggregators such as Kafka from where they can be centrally stored.

- **Metrics from each service**: In `Chapter 2`, *Writing Your First Cloud-Native Application*, we added Spring actuator metrics, which are exposed as endpoints. There are many other metrics, such as Dropwizard metrics, that can be captured and exposed.

  Either an agent has to monitor all services actuator metrics, or they can be exported and then aggregated in a monitoring and reporting tool.

  Another option is for application monitoring tools like Dynatrace, AppDynamics to monitor application, and extract metrics at Java level. We will take a look at these in the next chapter.

Implementing runtime reference architecture

The problems discussed in the previous section are addressed by the following reference runtime architecture:

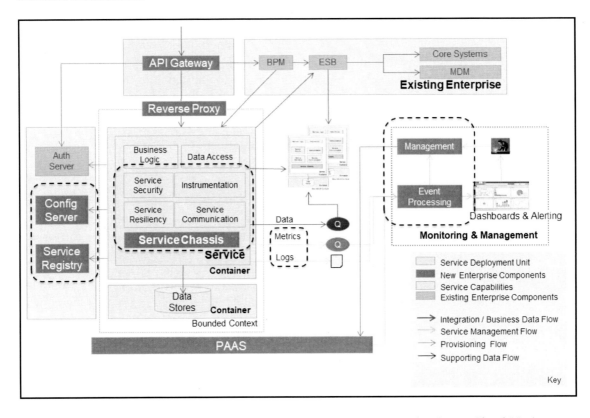

All these components were already discussed in Chapter 1, *Introduction to Cloud-Native*. Now, we proceed to choose technologies and show an implementation.

Service registry

Running the service registry Eureka was discussed in Chapter 2, *Writing Your First Cloud-Native Application*. Please refer to that chapter to refresh your memory on how a product service registers itself with Eureka and how the client uses Ribbon and Eureka to find the product service.

The importance of service registry is slightly diminished if we are using Docker Orchestration, such as Kubernetes. In this case, Kubernetes itself manages the registration of a service, which a proxy looks up and redirects to.

Configuration server

The config server stores configurations in a hierarchical manner. This way, the application only needs to know the address of the config server and then connect to it to get the remaining configurations.

There are two popular config servers. One is Hashicorp's Consul and the other is Spring Config Server. We will use Spring Config Server to keep the stack consistent to Spring.

Let's go over the steps to start using a config server. There are two parts to using externalized configuration: the server (serving the properties) and the client.

The server part of the config server

There are many options to serve the properties over an HTTP connection, Consul and Zookeeper being popular ones. However, for Spring projects, Spring Cloud provides a flexible config server that can connect to multiple backends, including Git, databases, and filesystems. Given that the properties are best stored in a version control, we will use the Git backend for Spring Cloud Config for this example.

The Spring Cloud Config server code, configuration, and runtime is very similar to Eureka and it is easy to fire up an instance like we did for Eureka in Chapter 2, *Writing Your First Cloud-Native Application*.

Follow these steps to get a service registry running:

1. Create a new Maven project with the artifact ID set to `config-server`.
2. Edit the POM file and add the following:

   1. The parent as `spring-boot-starter-parent`

   2. The dependency as `spring-cloud-config-server`

3. The dependency management as `spring-cloud-config`

```xml
M  config-server/pom.xml ⊠

 1  <project xmlns="http://maven.apache.org/POM/4.0.0" xmlns:xsi="http://www.w3.org/2001/XMLSchema-instance"
 2     xsi:schemaLocation="http://maven.apache.org/POM/4.0.0 http://maven.apache.org/xsd/maven-4.0.0.xsd">
 3     <modelVersion>4.0.0</modelVersion>
 4
 5     <groupId>com.mycompany.infra</groupId>
 6     <artifactId>config-server</artifactId>
 7     <version>0.0.1-SNAPSHOT</version>
 8
 9     <parent>
10         <groupId>org.springframework.boot</groupId>
11         <artifactId>spring-boot-starter-parent</artifactId>
12         <version>1.5.9.RELEASE</version>
13     </parent>
14
15     <dependencyManagement>
16         <dependencies>
17             <dependency>
18                 <groupId>org.springframework.cloud</groupId>
19                 <artifactId>spring-cloud-config</artifactId>
20                 <version>1.4.0.RELEASE</version>
21                 <type>pom</type>
22                 <scope>import</scope>
23             </dependency>
24         </dependencies>
25     </dependencyManagement>
26
27     <dependencies>
28         <dependency>
29             <groupId>org.springframework.cloud</groupId>
30             <artifactId>spring-cloud-config-server</artifactId>
31         </dependency>
32     </dependencies>
33
34     <build>
35         <plugins>
36             <plugin>
37                 <groupId>org.springframework.boot</groupId>
38                 <artifactId>spring-boot-maven-plugin</artifactId>
39             </plugin>
40         </plugins>
41     </build>
42 </project>
```

3. Create an `ConfigServiceApplication` class that will have annotation to start the config server:

```
 1  package com.mycompany.infra.configsvr;
 2
 3
 4⊕ import org.springframework.boot.SpringApplication;
 7
 8  @EnableConfigServer
 9  @SpringBootApplication
10  public class ConfigServiceApplication {
11
12⊖     public static void main(String[] args) {
13          SpringApplication.run(ConfigServiceApplication.class, args);
14      }
15  }
```

4. Create an `application.yml` file in the `config-server/src/main/resources` folder of the application and put the following:

```
server:
  port: 8888
spring:
  cloud:
    config:
      server:
        git:
          uri: file:../..
```

The port number is where the config server will listen for configuration requests over an HTTP connection.

The other property of `spring.cloud.config.server.git.uri` is the location of Git, which we have configured a local folder for development. This is where Git should be running on the local machine. If not, run a `git init` command on this folder.

We are not covering Git authentication or encryption here. Please check the Spring Cloud Config manual (`https://spring.io/guides/gs/centralized-configuration/`) for more details.

5. In the `product.properties` file, we will hold the properties that were initially held in the `application.properties` file of the actual `product` project. These properties will be loaded by the config server. We will start with a small property, as follows:

```
testMessage=Hi There
```

This property file should be present in the Git folder we just referenced in the previous step. Please add the property file to the Git folder, using the following command:

git add product.properties and then commit.

6. Create a `bootstrap.yml` file in the `resources` folder of application and input the name of this project:

```
spring:
  application:
    name: configsvr
```

7. Build the Maven project and then run it.

8. You should see a Tomcat started message, as follows:

```
Registering beans for JMX exposure on startup
Bean with name 'configurationPropertiesRebinder' has been autodetected for JMX exposure
Bean with name 'refreshEndpoint' has been autodetected for JMX exposure
Bean with name 'environmentManager' has been autodetected for JMX exposure
Bean with name 'refreshScope' has been autodetected for JMX exposure
Located managed bean 'environmentManager': registering with JMX server as MBean [org.spr
Located managed bean 'refreshScope': registering with JMX server as MBean [org.springfra
Located managed bean 'configurationPropertiesRebinder': registering with JMX server as M
Located managed bean 'refreshEndpoint': registering with JMX server as MBean [org.spring
Starting beans in phase 0
Tomcat started on port(s): 8888 (http)
Started ConfigServiceApplication in 5.666 seconds (JVM running for 6.102)
```

`ConfigurationServiceApplication` has started and is listening on port 8888

Let's check if the property we added is available for consumption.

Fire up a browser and check for `product.properties`. There are two ways you can do this. The first is by viewing the property file as JSON and the second is by viewing it as a text file:

1. `http://localhost:8888/product/default:`

2. `http://localhost:8888/product-default.properties:`

In case you are wondering, the default is the profile name. Spring Boot applications support profile overrides, for example, for test and **user acceptance testing (UAT)** environments, where the production properties can be replaced with the `product-test.properties` file. Hence, the config server supports the following form of URL reads:
`http://configsvrURL/{application}/{profile}` or
`http://configsvrURL/{application-profile}.properties` or `.yml`.

In production, it is highly unlikely that we will access the config server directly, as shown previously. It will be the clients who will access the config server; we shall see this next.

The config client

We will use the `product` service code developed earlier as a baseline to start extracting the properties out of the application into the config server.

1. Copy the `product` service project from eclipse to create a new project for this chapter.
2. Add the `spring-cloud-starter-config` dependency to the list of the dependencies in the POM file:

```xml
<dependencies>
    <dependency>
        <groupId>org.springframework.boot</groupId>
        <artifactId>spring-boot-starter-web</artifactId>
    </dependency>
    <dependency>
        <groupId>org.springframework.boot</groupId>
        <artifactId>spring-boot-starter-actuator</artifactId>
    </dependency>
    <dependency>
        <groupId>org.springframework.cloud</groupId>
        <artifactId>spring-cloud-starter-eureka</artifactId>
    </dependency>
    <dependency>
        <groupId>org.springframework.cloud</groupId>
        <artifactId>spring-cloud-starter-config</artifactId>
    </dependency>
    <dependency>
        <groupId>org.springframework.cloud</groupId>
        <artifactId>spring-cloud-starter-ribbon</artifactId>
    </dependency>
    <dependency>
        <groupId>org.springframework.boot</groupId>
        <artifactId>spring-boot-starter-data-jpa</artifactId>
    </dependency>
</dependencies>
```

3. Our main work will be on the resources. Tell the `product` service to use the config server running at: `http://localhost:8888`.

   The `failFast` flag indicates that we do not want the application loading to continue if we don't find the config server. This is important, as it will ensure that the `product` service should not assume defaults if it does not find the config server:

   ```
   spring:
     application:
       name: product

     cloud:
       config:
         uri: http://localhost:8888
         failFast: true
   ```

4. Shift all properties in the `application.properties` section of the resources folder of the `product` service to the `product.properties` that we had defined as part of the `git` folder loaded by the config server in the previous section. Your `product.properties` file will now have useful configuration, in addition to the `Hi There` message that we had put in for testing:

   ```
   server.port=8082
   eureka.instance.leaseRenewalIntervalInSeconds=15
   logging.level.org.hibernate.tool.hbm2ddl=DEBUG
   logging.level.org.hibernate.SQL=DEBUG
   testMessage=Hi There
   ```

5. We can now delete the `application.properties` file that is present in the `resources` folder of the `product` service.

6. Let's add a test method to our `product` service to check the property being set from the config server:

```
@Value("${testMessage:Hello default}")
private String message;
@RequestMapping("/testMessage")
String getTestMessage() {
     return message ;
}
```

7. Fire up the Eureka server, as done in the previous chapters.
8. Ensure the config server from the previous section is still running.
9. Now, start the `product` service from the `ProductSpringApp` main class. Right at the beginning of the logs, you will see the following statements:

```
: Fetching config from server at: http://localhost:8888
: Located environment: name=product, profiles=[default], label=null,
```

When the ProductSpringApp starts, it first goes and gets the configuration from the external configuration service running on port 8888

The environment with `name=product` is picked as our application name in the `bootstrap.yml` file.

The port number at which `product` service should listen is picked up from this config server, along with the other properties, such as the test message which we will see now:

```
: Discovery Client initialized at timestamp 1518938358612 with initial
Registering application product with eureka with status UP
Saw local status change event StatusChangeEvent [timestamp=1518938358
DiscoveryClient_PRODUCT/localhost:product:8082: registering service..
DiscoveryClient_PRODUCT/localhost:product:8082 - registration status:
Tomcat started on port(s): 8082 (http)
Updating port to 8082
Started ProductSpringApp in 20.527 seconds (JVM running for 21.081)
```

`ProductSpringApp` starts on port `8082` picked up from the externalized configuration.

Test the application with two URLs as follows:

- `http://localhost:8082/testMessage`: This returns `Hi There`, which was our configured message

 Run one of the other REST services, such as product view. You will see the required product information to indicate our services are working fine.

- `http://localhost:8082/product/1`: This will return `{"id":1,"name":"Apples","catId":1}`

Refreshing the properties

Now, what if there is a change in the properties that you want to reflect centrally on all the services?

1. You can change the message in the `product.properties` file to a new message, such as `Hi Spring`.

2. You will notice that the config server picks up this change on the next read, as follows:

However, this property is not picked up by the service immediately, as calling `http://localhost:8082/testMessage` results in the older `Hi There` message. How do we refresh the properties on the command line?

This is where the actuator command `/refresh` comes in handy. We configure the beans to be part of the `@RefreshScope` annotation. These beans will get reloaded when the POST method call to `http://localhost:8082/refresh` is executed from the Postman application. See the following log to check what calling refresh results in reloading of properties looks like:

```
: Refreshing org.springframework.context.annotation.AnnotationConfigApplicationContext@711ddba5: stal
: JSR-330 'javax.inject.Inject' annotation found and supported for autowiring
: Bean 'configurationPropertiesRebinderAutoConfiguration' of type [org.springframework.cloud.autocon1
: Cannot determine local hostname
: Fetching config from server at: http://localhost:8888
```

The first line shows in the logs how product service refreshes its properties on executing `http://localhost:8082/refresh`

You can check how, after the marked line, the property loading started again and the message after calling `http://localhost:8082/testMessage` gets reflected.

The microservice frontend

It is a popular pattern to frontend a microservice with a reverse proxy, a load balancer, an edge gateway or an API gateway, in an increasing order of complexity.

- **Reverse proxy**: A reverse proxy is defined as a process that makes the downstream resource available as though it originated from itself. In that respect, the webserver frontend and the application server also act as reverse proxies. The reverse proxy is useful in cloud-native applications, as it ensures that the clients do not need to look up services and then access them like we did in `Chapter 2`, *Writing Your First Cloud-Native Application*. They have to access the reverse proxy, which looks up the microservices, calls them, and makes the response available to the client.
- **Load balancer**: The load balancer is an extended form of reverse proxy that can balance the request it receives from clients across multiple services. This increases the availability of the services. The load balancer can work with service registry to find out which are the active services and then balance the requests between them. Nginx and HAProxy are good examples of load balancers that can be used to frontend microservices.
- **Edge gateway**: As the name implies, the edge gateway is a higher-order component that is deployed on the edge of the enterprise or division and has more capabilities than a load balancer, such as authentication, authorization, traffic control, and routing functions. Netfix Zuul is a good example of this pattern. We will cover code examples of using Zuul in this section.
- **API gateway**: With the popularity of Mobile and APIs, this component provides more complex capabilities, such as fanning out requests to multiple services doing orchestration between them, intercepting and enhancing the requests or responses or converting their formats, doing sophisticated analysis on the requests. It is also possible to use both an API gateway and a load balancer, reverse proxy, or edge in a single flow. This approach helps with the segregation of responsibilities, but also adds latency due to an additional hop. We will see API gateway in later chapters.

Netflix Zuul

Netflix Zuul is a popular Edge gateway popularized by Netflix and then offered as part of Spring Cloud. Zuul means gatekeeper and performs all those functions, including authentication, traffic control, and most importantly, routing, as discussed earlier. It is well-integrated with Eureka and Hystrix in looking up services and reporting metrics. The services in an enterprise or a domain can be frontended by Zuul.

Let's put a Zuul gateway in front of our `product` service:

1. Create a new Maven project and set its artifact ID as `zuul-server`.
2. Edit the POM file and add the following:

   1. Set the parent as `spring-boot-starter-parent`

   2. Set the dependency on `spring-cloud-starter-zuul`, `-eureka`, and `-web` projects

   3. Set dependency management on `spring-cloud-starter-netflix`:

```xml
 5        <groupId>com.mycompany.infra</groupId>
 6        <artifactId>zuul-server</artifactId>
 7        <version>0.0.1-SNAPSHOT</version>
 8
 9        <parent>
10            <groupId>org.springframework.boot</groupId>
11            <artifactId>spring-boot-starter-parent</artifactId>
12            <version>1.5.9.RELEASE</version>
13        </parent>
14
15        <dependencyManagement>
16            <dependencies>
17                <dependency>
18                    <groupId>org.springframework.cloud</groupId>
19                    <artifactId>spring-cloud-starter-netflix</artifactId>
20                    <version>1.4.0.RELEASE</version>
21                    <type>pom</type>
22                    <scope>import</scope>
23                </dependency>
24            </dependencies>
25        </dependencyManagement>
26
27        <dependencies>
28            <dependency>
29                <groupId>org.springframework.cloud</groupId>
30                <artifactId>spring-cloud-starter-zuul</artifactId>
31            </dependency>
32            <dependency>
33                <groupId>org.springframework.boot</groupId>
34                <artifactId>spring-boot-starter-web</artifactId>
35            </dependency>
36            <dependency>
37                <groupId>org.springframework.cloud</groupId>
38                <artifactId>spring-cloud-starter-eureka</artifactId>
39            </dependency>
40        </dependencies>
```

3. Create an application class with an annotation to enable Zuul Proxy:

```
 ch7-zuul/pom.xml        ZuulProxy.java

 1  package com.mycompany.infra.edge;
 2
 3
 4⊕ import org.springframework.boot.SpringApplication;
 7
 8  @EnableZuulProxy
 9  @SpringBootApplication
10  public class ZuulProxy {
11
12⊖     public static void main(String[] args) {
13             SpringApplication.run(ZuulProxy.class, args);
14     }
15  }
```

The configuration information in `application.yml` is very critical for Zuul. This is where we configure the routing capabilities of Zuul to redirect it to the correct microservice.

1. Since Zuul interacts well with Eureka, we will leverage that to our advantage:

```
eureka:
  client:
    serviceUrl:
defaultZone: http://127.0.0.1:8761/eureka/
```

This tells Zuul to look for services in the Eureka registry running at that port.

2. Configure the port to listen at `8080`.

3. Finally, configure the routes.
   These are the mappings of the URL in the REST request to the respective service that can handle it:

```
zuul:
  routes:
    product:
      path: /product*/**
      stripPrefix: false
```

What happens behind the scenes

Let's have a look at what happens behind the scenes:

1. The `product` section in the route definition tells Zuul that the paths configured after `/product*/**` are to be redirected to the `product` service, if it is present in the Eureka registry configured in the Zuul server.
2. The path is configured to be `/product*/**`. Why three `*` ? If you remember, our `product` service can handle two types of REST services: `/product/1` GET and `/product` PUT, DELETE, POST requests. The `/products?id=1` GET requests that it return a list of products for the given category ID. Hence, the `product*` maps to both `/product` and `/products` in the URL.
3. The `false` setting of `stripPrefix` lets the `/product/` pass on to the `product` service. If the flag is not set, then only the rest of the URL after `/product*/` will be passed on to the microservice. Our `product` microservice has mapping including the `/product`, hence we want the prefix to be preserved when forwarding to the `product` service.

Running them all at once

Let's now try to run our `product` service, along with the rest of the ecosystem:

1. Start the services in the reverse order of dependency.
2. Start the config server and the Eureka server by running the main class of the projects or through Maven.
3. Start the `product` service.
4. Start the Zuul service.
   Watch the log windows and wait till all servers start.
5. Now, run the following requests in your browser:
   - `http://localhost:8080/product/3`
   - `http://localhost:8080/products?id=1`

You should see product 3 listed in the first request and the products corresponding to category 1 in the second request.

Let's have a look at the logs of Zuul and `product` service:

- In Zuul, you can see that the mapping of the `/product*/**` was resolved and the endpoint to the `product` service was fetched from the Eureka registry:

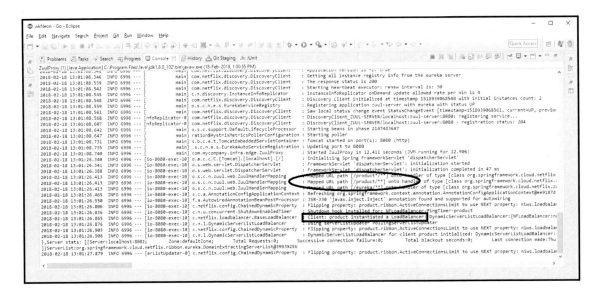

Zuul edge is now registered to map requests for product service, and forward it to the service address pointed by Eureka

- In the `product` service, the service execution has happened by running the queries on the database:

```
: FrameworkServlet 'dispatcherServlet': initialization started
: FrameworkServlet 'dispatcherServlet': initialization completed in 39 ms
: [172.21.185.129]:5701 [ProductCluster] [3.7.8] Initializing cluster partition table arrangement...
: HHH000397: Using ASTQueryTranslatorFactory
: select product0_.id as id1_0_, product0_.cat_id as cat_id2_0_, product0_.name as name3_0_ from product product0_ where product0_.cat_id=?
: Resolving eureka endpoints via configuration
: select product0_.id as id1_0_0_, product0_.cat_id as cat_id2_0_0_, product0_.name as name3_0_0_ from product product0_ where product0_.id=?
```

Kubernetes – container orchestration

So far, we have been individually deploying the services such as Eureka, the config server, the `product` service, and Zuul.

Recollecting from the previous chapter, we can automate their deployment through CI, such as Jenkins. We also saw how the deployment could be done with Docker containers.

However, during runtime, the containers still run independently of each other. There is no mechanism to scale the containers, or to restart them if one has failed. Also, the decision on which service to deploy on which VM is manual, which means that the services always get deployed onto the static VMs that are designated for the services to run, instead of being mixed and matched intelligently. In short, the orchestration layer managing our application services is missing.

Kubernetes is a popular orchestration mechanism that makes deployment and runtime management an easier task.

Kubernetes architecture and services

Kubernetes is an open source project spearheaded by Google. It attempts to implement some of the tried-and-tested ideas that were implemented in its own internal container orchestration system called Borg. Kubernetes architecture is composed of two components: the master and minion nodes. The master nodes have the following components:

- **Controller**: To manage the nodes, replicas, and services
- **API Server**: To provide REST endpoints used by the `kubectl` client and the minion nodes
- **Scheduler**: To decide where a particular container must be spawned
- **Etcd**: To store the state of the cluster and configurations

The minion nodes contain two components:

- **Kubelet**: An agent to communicate resource availability to the master and launch the containers specified by the scheduler

- **Proxy**: To route network requests to the kubernetes services

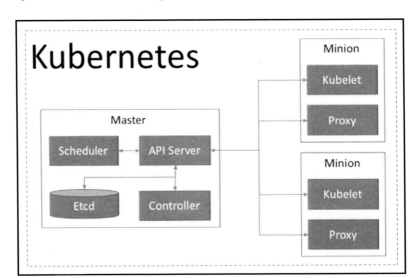

Kubernetes is a container scheduler which uses two primitives, namely Pod and Service. A Pod is a collection of related containers which may be tagged with certain Labels; a service can target Pods using these Labels and expose endpoints. The following diagram illustrates the concept:

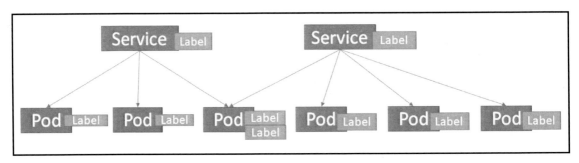

Pods are considered ephemeral in kubernetes and may be killed. However, if the Pods were created using a `ReplicaSet`, where we can specify how many replicas or instances of a certain Pod have to be present in the system, then the kubernetes scheduler will automatically schedule new instances of the Pod and once the Pod becomes available, the service will start routing traffic to it. As you may notice that a Pod may be targeted by multiple services provided the labels match, this feature is useful to do rolling deployments.

We will now look at how to deploy a simple API on kubernetes and do a rolling upgrade.

Minikube

Minikube is a project that helps in running a working, single-node Kubernetes on a virtual machine.

You can install Minikube by following the instructions at: `https://github.com/kubernetes/minikube`.

For Windows, ensure that the following steps have been completed:

- The kubectl binary also needs to be downloaded and placed in the path so that once Minikube gets kubernetes running, we can communicate and manage the kubernetes resources from the command prompt. You can download it from: `https://storage.googleapis.com/kubernetes-release/release/v1.9.0/bin/windows/amd64/kubectl.exe`.
- You have to run Minikube from the same drive (say, `C:`) where your `Users` directory is present.

Running product service in Kubernetes

Let's change our existing `product` service to run through Kubernetes container orchestration:

```
$ minikube start
Starting local Kubernetes v1.9.0 cluster...
Starting VM...
Downloading Minikube ISO
 142.22 MB / 142.22 MB [============================================] 100.00% 0s
Getting VM IP address...
Moving files into cluster...
Downloading localkube binary
 162.41 MB / 162.41 MB [============================================] 100.00% 0s
 0 B / 65 B [--------------------------------------------------------]   0.00%
 65 B / 65 B [=======================================================] 100.00% 0sSetting up certs...
Connecting to cluster...
Setting up kubeconfig...
Starting cluster components...
Kubectl is now configured to use the cluster.
Loading cached images from config file.
$
```

1. You can test if the configuration is working by running it, as shown in the following screenshot:

```
$ kubectl get svc
NAME         TYPE        CLUSTER-IP   EXTERNAL-IP   PORT(S)   AGE
kubernetes   ClusterIP   10.96.0.1    <none>        443/TCP   1m
```

2. Set up the Docker client to connect to the Docker daemon running within the Minikube VM as follows:

```
$ eval $(minikube docker-env)
```

3. Build the Docker image from the instructions in the previous chapters where we created a Docker image as follows:

```
$ docker build -t cnj/product-api .
Sending build context to Docker daemon  58.55MB
Step 1/5 : FROM openjdk:8-jdk-alpine
 ---> 224765a6bdbe
Step 2/5 : RUN mkdir -p /app
 ---> Using cache
 ---> b77b32c3d77b
Step 3/5 : ADD target/product-0.0.1-SNAPSHOT.jar /app/app.jar
 ---> aa5d22ada069
Step 4/5 : EXPOSE 8080
 ---> Running in 497306e36f52
 ---> 147b0640c16b
Removing intermediate container 497306e36f52
Step 5/5 : ENTRYPOINT /usr/bin/java -jar /app/app.jar --spring.profiles.active=docker
 ---> Running in 19d66666d16c
 ---> 5b294eb92199
Removing intermediate container 19d66666d16c
Successfully built 5b294eb92199
Successfully tagged cnj/product-api:latest
$
```

4. Create a `deployment` file (note that the `imagePullPolicy` is set to `never`, because otherwise, the default behavior of Kubernetes is to pull from the Docker registry):

```yaml
apiVersion: apps/v1beta2
kind: Deployment
metadata:
  name: product-api
  labels:
    app: product-api
spec:
  replicas: 3
  selector:
    matchLabels:
      app: product-api
  template:
    metadata:
      labels:
        app: product-api
    spec:
      containers:
      - name: product-api
        image: cnj/product-api:latest
        imagePullPolicy: Never
        ports:
        - containerPort: 8080
```

5. Verify that the three instances are running:

```
[$ kubectl get deployment
NAME            DESIRED    CURRENT    UP-TO-DATE    AVAILABLE    AGE
product-api     3          3          3             3            15m

[$ kubectl get pod
NAME                             READY     STATUS     RESTARTS    AGE
product-api-7dcbbbf9b6-h2bjs     1/1       Running    0           13m
product-api-7dcbbbf9b6-mttcb     1/1       Running    0           13m
product-api-7dcbbbf9b6-qdbvq     1/1       Running    0           13m
```

6. Create a `service.yml` file, so that we can access the Pods:

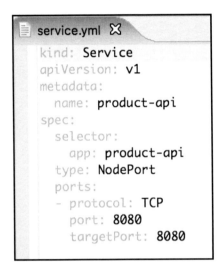

Now, run the `service.yml` file as follows:

```
$ kubectl create -f service.yml
service "product-api" created
$ kubectl get service
NAME          TYPE        CLUSTER-IP       EXTERNAL-IP   PORT(S)          AGE
kubernetes    ClusterIP   10.96.0.1        <none>        443/TCP          2h
product-api   NodePort    10.108.166.132   <none>        8080:31709/TCP   5s
$
```

Now, you can get the address of the service:

```
$ minikube service --url product-api
http://192.168.99.100:31709
$
```

You can now access the API, which will route requests to all three Pods:

```
$ curl http://192.168.99.100:31709/product/1
{"id":1,"name":"Apples","catId":1}
$ curl http://192.168.99.100:31709/products?id=1
[{"id":1,"name":"Apples","catId":1},{"id":2,"name":"Oranges","catId":1},{"id":3,"name":"Bananas","catId":1}]
$ curl -XDELETE http://192.168.99.100:31709/product/1
{"id":1,"name":"Apples","catId":1}
$ curl -v http://192.168.99.100:31709/product/1
*   Trying 192.168.99.100...
* TCP_NODELAY set
* Connected to 192.168.99.100 (192.168.99.100) port 31709 (#0)
> GET /product/1 HTTP/1.1
> Host: 192.168.99.100:31709
> User-Agent: curl/7.54.0
> Accept: */*
>
< HTTP/1.1 200
< X-Application-Context: product:docker
< Content-Type: application/json;charset=UTF-8
< Transfer-Encoding: chunked
< Date: Fri, 19 Jan 2018 21:00:45 GMT
<
* Connection #0 to host 192.168.99.100 left intact
{"id":1,"name":"Apples","catId":1}
$
```

You may use -v for individual commands to get the following details:

```
$ curl -v http://192.168.99.100:31709/product/1
*   Trying 192.168.99.100...
* TCP_NODELAY set
* Connected to 192.168.99.100 (192.168.99.100) port 31709 (#0)
> GET /product/1 HTTP/1.1
> Host: 192.168.99.100:31709
> User-Agent: curl/7.54.0
> Accept: */*
>
< HTTP/1.1 200
< X-Application-Context: product:docker
< Content-Type: application/json;charset=UTF-8
< Transfer-Encoding: chunked
< Date: Fri, 19 Jan 2018 21:00:45 GMT
<
* Connection #0 to host 192.168.99.100 left intact
{"id":1,"name":"Apples","catId":1}
$
```

7. Change the code, as follows:

```
J ProductService.java ⊠

    package com.mycompany.product;

⊕ import java.util.List;▢

  @RestController
  public class ProductService {

⊖     @Value("${version:v0.0.0}")
      String version;

⊖     @Autowired
      ProductRepository prodRepo ;

⊖     @RequestMapping(value="/product/{id}", method = RequestMethod.GET )
      ResponseEntity<Product> getProduct(@PathVariable("id") int id) {
          Product prod = prodRepo.findOne(id);
          if (prod == null)
              throw new BadRequestException(BadRequestException.ID_NOT_FOUND, "No product for id " + id) ;
          else {
              HttpHeaders responseHeaders = new HttpHeaders();
              responseHeaders.set("X-Application-Version", version);
              return new ResponseEntity<>(prod, responseHeaders, HttpStatus.OK);
          }
      }
  }
```

8. Build Docker image with a new tag:

```
$ docker build -t cnj/product-api:v1.0.1 .
Sending build context to Docker daemon  58.55MB
Step 1/5 : FROM openjdk:8-jdk-alpine
 ---> 224765a6bdbe
Step 2/5 : RUN mkdir -p /app
 ---> Using cache
 ---> b77b32c3d77b
Step 3/5 : ADD target/product-0.0.1-SNAPSHOT.jar /app/app.jar
 ---> 41625a85e526
Step 4/5 : EXPOSE 8080
 ---> Running in ab7936f82d38
 ---> 18e8b967a8f7
Removing intermediate container ab7936f82d38
Step 5/5 : ENTRYPOINT /usr/bin/java -jar /app/app.jar --spring.profiles.active=docker
 ---> Running in 5a84379a5912
 ---> 2a6c03bd5a15
Removing intermediate container 5a84379a5912
Successfully built 2a6c03bd5a15
Successfully tagged cnj/product-api:v1.0.1
$
```

9. Update the `deployment.yml` file:

10. Apply the change:

```
$ kubectl apply -f deployment.yml
deployment "product-api" configured

$ kubectl rollout status deployment/product-api
deployment "product-api" successfully rolled out

$ kubectl get pods
NAME                           READY   STATUS        RESTARTS   AGE
product-api-55946666bc-2qddd   1/1     Running       0          14s
product-api-55946666bc-5bgrc   1/1     Running       0          11s
product-api-55946666bc-hd2fw   1/1     Running       0          8s
product-api-7dcbbbf9b6-6h7n4   0/1     Terminating   0          1m
product-api-7dcbbbf9b6-d79kk   0/1     Terminating   0          1m
product-api-7dcbbbf9b6-g7hm2   0/1     Terminating   0          1m

$ curl -v http://192.168.99.100:31709/product/1
*   Trying 192.168.99.100...
* TCP_NODELAY set
* Connected to 192.168.99.100 (192.168.99.100) port 31709 (#0)
> GET /product/1 HTTP/1.1
> Host: 192.168.99.100:31709
> User-Agent: curl/7.54.0
> Accept: */*
>
< HTTP/1.1 200
< X-Application-Context: product:docker
< X-Application-Version: v1.0.1
< Content-Type: application/json;charset=UTF-8
< Transfer-Encoding: chunked
< Date: Fri, 19 Jan 2018 21:17:49 GMT
<
* Connection #0 to host 192.168.99.100 left intact
{"id":1,"name":"Apples","catId":1}
$
```

Platform as a Service (PaaS)

Another popular runtime for cloud-native applications is to use a PaaS platform, specifically, application PaaS platforms. PaaS provides an easy way to deploy cloud-native applications. They provide additional services like file storage, encryption, key-value storage, and databases which can be easily bound to the applications. PaaS platforms also provide an easy mechanism to scale cloud-native applications. Let's now understand why PaaS platforms provide an excellent runtime for cloud-native applications.

The case for PaaS

In the runtime architecture realization, we saw that a number of components, such as the config server, the service registry, the reverse proxy, monitoring, log aggregation, and metrics have to come together to realize a scalable microservices architecture. With the exception of the business logic in `ProductService`, the rest of the services and components were pure supporting components, thus involving a lot of platform building and engineering.

What if all the components we built came out of the box in a platform which was provided as a service? Thus, PaaS is a higher level of abstraction over container orchestration. PaaS provides all the basic infrastructure services which we discussed in container orchestration, such as restarting services, scaling them, and load balancing, out of the box. In addition, PaaS offers additional services that complement the development, scaling, and maintenance of cloud-native applications. This approach has a trade-off that it reduces the choices in the selection and fine-tuning of the components. However, for most enterprises focusing on the business problem, this will be a fine trade-off to have.

Thus, with PaaS, the developer can now concentrate on writing the code and not worrying about the infrastructure he/she is going to deploy on. All the engineering now becomes configuration that the developers and operations team can configure.

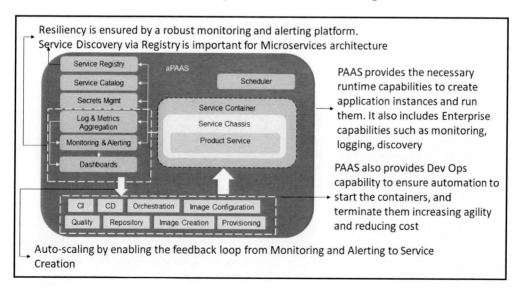

Another few advantages of the PaaS include:

- **Runtimes**: Providing various runtimes for developer to develop services, such as Java, Go, Node.js, or .NET. Thus, the developer focuses on generating a deployment, which can run in the various runtimes provided by the PaaS environment.
- **Services**: PaaS provides application services, such as databases and messaging out of the box for the applications to use. This is beneficial, as the developers and the operations do not have to install or manage them separately.
- **Multi-cloud**: PaaS abstracts the developer from the underlying infrastructure (or IaaS). Thus, the developer can develop for the PaaS environment, without worrying about deploying it in a data center or to various cloud providers such as AWS, Azure, or the Google Cloud Platform, if the PaaS runs on these infrastructures. This avoids lock-in to an infrastructure or cloud environment.

The trade-off of the PaaS environment is that they can be restrictive and reduce flexibility. The default services and runtime selected may not be suitable for all use cases. However, most PaaS providers provide plug points and APIs to include more services and configurations, and policies to fine tune the runtime behaviors, which can mitigate the trade-offs.

Cloud Foundry

Cloud Foundry is one of the most mature open source PaaS owned by the Cloud Foundry foundation.

It is primarily composed of, following parts:

- **Application runtime**: The foundation platform, where the developer deploys the application workloads like Java or Node.js applications. Application runtime provides for capabilities like application life cycle, application execution, and supporting functions, such as routing, authentication, platform services, including messaging, metrics, and logging.
- **Container runtime**: The runtime abstraction where the containers run. This provides deployment, management, and integration of the containers on which the applications run, using Kubernetes as the base platform. It is based on project Kubo.

- **Application services**: These are services like databases that the application binds to. Typically, they are provided by third-party providers.
- **Cloud Foundry components**: There are a lot of them, such as BOSH (for container runtime), Diego (for application runtime), **Bulletin Board System** (**BBS**), NATS, Cloud Controller, and so on. However, these are responsible for providing various capabilities of PaaS and can be abstracted from the developers. They are of relevance and interest to the operations and infrastructure.

The concept of org, account, and space

Cloud Foundry has an elaborate **role-based access control** (**RBAC**) for managing the applications and its various resources:

- **Org**: This represents an organization, to which multiple users can be bound. An org shares the applications, service availability, resource quota, and plans.
- **User account**: The user account represents an individual login that can act on the applications or operations in cloud foundry.
- **Space**: Every application or service runs in a space that is bound to org and managed by a user account. An org has at least one space.
- **Roles and permissions**: The users belonging to org have roles which can do restricted actions (or permissions). The details are documented at: `https://docs.cloudfoundry.org/concepts/roles.html`.

The need for implementations of Cloud Foundry

There is a lot of engineering involved in getting the vanilla Cloud Foundry installed and running. Hence, there are many PaaS implementations that use Cloud Foundry as a foundation and provide additional features, the most popular ones being Bluemix from IBM, OpenShift from Redhat, and **Pivotal Cloud Foundry** (**PCF**) from Pivotal.

Pivotal Cloud Foundry (PCF)

Pivotal's Cloud Foundry aims to increase developer productivity and operator efficiency and to provide security and availability.

Though readers of this book are free to choose the PaaS implementations that are based on Cloud Foundry, we have chosen Pivotal for a few reasons:

- Pivotal has been behind Spring Framework, which we have used amply in the book. Pivotal's Cloud Foundry implementation has native support of the Spring Framework and its components, such as Spring Boot and Spring Cloud. Hence, the Spring Boot deployable that we create can be directly deployed to the application runtime of the Cloud Foundry and managed.
- Pivotal's service marketplace is rich, covering most of the platform components by partners including MongoDB, PostgreSQL, Redis, and native support (Pivotal developed) services for MySQL and Cloud Cache.
- Pivotal has been doing a number of releases in this space and hence the service offerings are updated frequently.

PCF components

The Pivotal website `pivotal.io/platform` gives a very simple diagram for the implementation of Cloud Foundry, which maps to our earlier discussion:

- **Pivotal Application Service (PAS)**: This is an abstraction for applications that map to application runtime in Cloud Foundry. Internally, it uses Diego, but that is hidden from the developer. PAS has excellent support for Spring Boot and Spring Cloud, but can run other Java, .NET, and Node apps as well. It is suitable for running custom written application workloads.
- **Pivotal Container Service (PKS)**: This is an abstraction for containers and maps to container runtime in Cloud Foundry. It uses BOSH internally. It is suitable for running workloads that are provided as containers, that is, **independent service vendor (ISV)** applications like Elasticsearch.
- **Pivotal Function Service (PFS)**: This is a new offering of Pivotal outside of the Cloud Foundry platform. It provides abstraction for functions. It promotes serverless computing. The functions are invoked on a HTTP request (synchronous) or when messages arrive (asynchronous).
- **Marketplace**: This maps to the application services in Cloud Foundry. Given the popularity of the PCF, there are a lot of services available in the marketplace.

- **Shared components**: These include the supporting services to run functions, applications, and containers, such as authentication, authorization, logging, monitoring (PCF watch), scaling, networking, and so on.

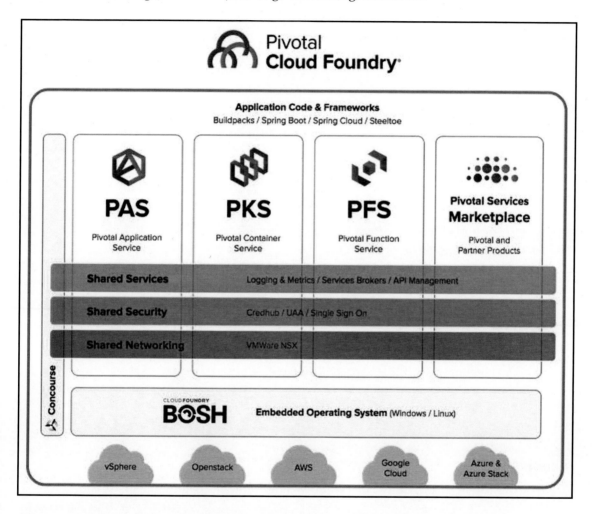

PCF can be run on most of the popular clouds, including Google Compute Platform, Azure, AWS, and Open Stack (IaaS), hosted on a data center.

While PCF and its components are great for the server-side loads, it might be cumbersome for developers who are building software on their local machines. We are at that stage now. We have developed `product` service and matured through various stages to reach cloud-native runtime.

The entire PCF with its runtime components is difficult to fit on a laptop for development.

PCF Dev

PCF Dev is a condensed PCF distribution that can run locally on a VM on a desktop or laptop. It promises to enable the same environment that the developers would have on the main PCF environment, so that there is no difference when an application meant for PCF Dev runs on the main PCF environment. Refer to the table in `https://docs.pivotal.io/pcf-dev/index.html` for an exact comparison of the size and capabilities provided by PCF Dev vis-à-vis the full PCF and **Cloud Foundry** (**CF**):

- It supports the application runtime for Java, Ruby, PHP, and Python.
- It has a mini version of PAS that gives the essential capabilities for our service development that we have discussed so far, such as logging and metrics, routing, Diego (Docker) support, application services, scaling, monitoring, and failure recovery.
- It also comes with four application services built-in, these are: **Spring Cloud Services** (**SCS**), Redis, RabbitMQ, and MySQL.
- However, it is not meant for production. It does not have BOSH, which orchestrates over the infrastructure layer.

If your desktop/laptop has over 8 GB of memory and disk space over 25 GB, let's get started.

Installation

PCF Dev can run in a Mac, Linux, or Windows environment. Follow the instructions, for example, `https://docs.pivotal.io/pcf-dev/install-windows.html` for Windows, to get PCF Dev running on your machine. This essentially is in three steps:

- Getting Virtual Box
- CF command line interface
- Finally, the PCF Dev

Starting PCF Dev

The first time we start using **cf dev start**, it will take a long time to download the VM image (4 GB), extract it (20 GB), and then start the various services of the PCF. Hence, once the VM is downloaded and running, we would just suspend and resume the VM with the Cloud Foundry services running.

Command line options for starting PCF Dev are as follows:

1. Assuming you have a multi-core machine, you can allocate half the cores for this VM, such as -c 2 for a four core machine.
2. The SCS version will use 8 GB of memory; to keep the buffer, let's use 10 GB of memory which is expressed in terms of MB on the command line.
3. We will need the services of MySQL and SCS for the next chapter. Internally, SCS needs RabbitMQ to run. Hence, let's include all servers while running the instance.
4. It is optional to give the domain and IP address, and hence, we will skip -d and -i options.
5. Set the environment variable PCFDEV_HOME to a specific folder on a drive that has a good amount of space, so that it does not default to the home folder on the home drive. We would recommend the home folder to be a fast drive like SSD, as the Cloud Foundry start and stop operations are very I/O intensive.

So, our start command will be as follows:

```
cf dev start -c 2 -s all -m 10000
```

This will take a long time till finally your PCF Dev environment is ready.

Speeding up development time

It is difficult to wait 20 minutes while the entire PCF Dev environment is started each time. Once you finish working for the day or before shutting down your laptop, you can suspend the PCF Dev by using cf dev suspend and resume it the next day by using the cf dev resume command.

Other useful commands include:

- A default PCF Dev creates two users—admin and user. To install or manage the applications, you should login as one of the users. The command `cf dev target` logs you in as a default user.
- The `cf dev trust` command installs a certificate to enable SSL communication, so that you don't need to use parameter `-skip ssl` every time you log in on the command line or on an application manager in the browser.
- The `cf marketplace` command (once you have logged in as a user) shows the various services that can be installed in the org and space.

Let's see the output of the commands discussed so far:

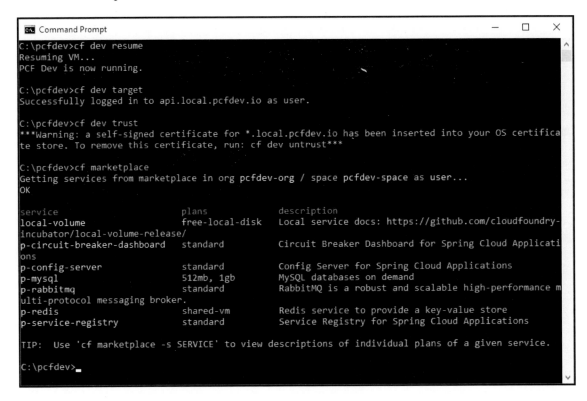

As we can see in the marketplace, since we started the PCF Dev with the all services option, we can see the marketplace ready with the seven services.

Creating the MySQL service on PCF

From the list, in this chapter, we will configure our `product` service to work with the MySQL database and look at Spring Cloud services, such as the circuit breaker dashboard and other services in the next chapter.

Run the following command:

```
cf create-service p-mysql 512mb prod-db
```

Check whether the services are running:

```
Select Command Prompt

D:\Apps\wkNeon\ch7-pcf-product>cf services
Getting services in org pcfdev-org / space pcfdev-space as user...
OK

name        service    plan     bound apps      last operation
prod-db     p-mysql    512mb    pcf-product     create succeeded

D:\Apps\wkNeon\ch7-pcf-product>
```

Running the product service on PCF Dev

Let's create a simplified version of the `product` service that just connects to a MySQL service that we created earlier to run queries.

You can write the practice code from `Chapter 3`, *Designing Your Cloud-Native Application* or download the file from Git to your Eclipse environment. The artifacts worth noting are:

- In the Maven file:
  - Note that, in the following screenshot, we have renamed our artifact to `pcf-product`.
  - A new dependency worth noting is the `spring-cloud-cloudfoundry-connector`. This discovers the services bound to the Cloud Foundry application, such as MySQL configuration, and uses them.

- We have included a MySQL connector for the JPA to connect to the MySQL database:

```xml
<artifactId>pcf-product</artifactId>
<version>0.1-SNAPSHOT</version>

<dependencyManagement>
    <dependencies>
        <dependency>
            <groupId>org.springframework.cloud</groupId>
            <artifactId>spring-cloud-dependencies</artifactId>
            <version>Edgware.RELEASE</version>
            <type>pom</type>
            <scope>import</scope>
        </dependency>
    </dependencies>
</dependencyManagement>

<dependencies>
    <dependency>
        <groupId>org.springframework.boot</groupId>
        <artifactId>spring-boot-starter-web</artifactId>
    </dependency>
    <dependency>
        <groupId>org.springframework.boot</groupId>
        <artifactId>spring-boot-starter-actuator</artifactId>
    </dependency>
    <dependency>
        <groupId>org.springframework.boot</groupId>
        <artifactId>spring-boot-starter-data-jpa</artifactId>
    </dependency>
    <dependency>
        <groupId>mysql</groupId>
        <artifactId>mysql-connector-java</artifactId>
    </dependency>
    <dependency>
        <groupId>org.springframework.cloud</groupId>
        <artifactId>spring-cloud-cloudfoundry-connector</artifactId>
    </dependency>
</dependencies>
```

- In the `application.properties` file:
    - Notice that we have not given any MySQL connection properties, such as database, user, or password. These are picked up automatically by the Spring application, when the application is uploaded into Cloud Foundry and binds with the MySQL database service.

- The auto create setting in case of MySQL should be `true` only for development purposes as it will recreate the database on every application deploy. In the UAT or production profile, this setting will be `none`:

```
management.security.enabled=false
logging.level.org.hibernate.tool.hbm2ddl=DEBUG
logging.level.org.hibernate.SQL=DEBUG
spring.jpa.hibernate.ddl-auto=create
```

- The `ProductSpringApp` class is simplified to a plain Spring Boot start up application. We will enhance this in the next chapter for metrics, lookup, load balancing, monitoring, and management:

```java
@SpringBootApplication
public class ProductSpringApp {

    public static void main(String[] args) throws Exception {
        SpringApplication.run(ProductSpringApp.class, args);
    }

    @Bean
    public RestTemplate restTemplate() {
        return new RestTemplate();
    }

}
```

- The `ProductRepository` class only has one method, called `findByCatId`, listed. The rest of the methods, such as `get`, `save`, `delete`, and `update` are automatically derived in the repository.
- The `ProductService`, `product`, and other classes are unchanged from those in Chapter 3, *Designing Your Cloud-Native Application*.
- In the `manifest.yml` file:
    - This is the new file containing instructions for deploying into cloud foundry
    - We will write the most basic version that has the application name, allotment of 1 GB of memory space, and the binding to the MySQL service from CloudFoundry

- The random route lets the application take a route to reach the URL without having collisions in case of multiple versions:

```
manifest.yml
1 ---
2 applications:
3 - name: pcf-product
4   memory: 1G
5   random-route: true
6   path: target/pcf-product-0.1-SNAPSHOT.jar
7   services:
8   - prod-db
9   |
10
11
```

Once your project is ready, run `mvn install` to create the comprehensive `.jar` file in the `target` directory. Its name should match the name of the `.jar` in the `manifest.yml` file.

Deploying to Cloud Foundry

Deploying to Cloud Floundry is simple, use the command `cf push pcf-product`, as follows:

```
D:\Apps\wkNeon\ch7-pcf-product>cf push pcf-product
Using manifest file D:\Apps\wkNeon\ch7-pcf-product\manifest.yml

Creating app pcf-product in org pcfdev-org / space pcfdev-space as user...
OK

Creating route pcf-product-undedicated-spirketting.local.pcfdev.io...
OK

Binding pcf-product-undedicated-spirketting.local.pcfdev.io to pcf-product...
OK

Uploading pcf-product...
Uploading app files from: C:\Users\ajay\AppData\Local\Temp\unzipped-app422286615
Uploading 496.4K, 105 files
Done uploading
OK
Binding service prod-db to app pcf-product in org pcfdev-org / space pcfdev-space as user...
OK

Starting app pcf-product in org pcfdev-org / space pcfdev-space as user...
```

Cloud Foundry does a lot of work creating the application in the space, creating routes to reach the application, and then binding the various services with the application. You should perhaps read more on Cloud Foundry if you are interested in what happens under the hood.

Once the deployment is complete, you will see the success method, as follows:

```
Staging complete
Uploading droplet, build artifacts cache...
Uploading build artifacts cache...
Uploading droplet...
Uploaded build artifacts cache (109B)
Uploaded droplet (71M)
Uploading complete
Destroying container
Successfully destroyed container

0 of 1 instances running, 1 starting
0 of 1 instances running, 1 starting
0 of 1 instances running, 1 starting
1 of 1 instances running

App started
```

Note the URL which is generated in the preceding screenshot.

It is `http://pcf-product-undedicated-spirketting.local.pcfdev.io`. We will see how to make this URL shorter in the next chapter.

In case you got an error on startup, for example, with a wrong configuration or missing a few steps, you can always check the logs by giving the following command in the command line:

```
cf logs pcf-product --recent
```

Now, it is time to test our service. In the browser window, run the two services that we generally run:

- `http://pcf-product-undedicated-spirketting.local.pcfdev.io/product/1`
- `http://pcf-product-undedicated-spirketting.local.pcfdev.io/products?id=1`

You will see the response coming from the database, that is, the output and logs, as follows:

This completes deploying our simple `product` service into PCF on PCF Dev.

Summary

In this chapter, we saw the various runtime components supporting cloud-native applications and ran our application on various runtimes, such as Kubernetes and Cloud Foundry.

In the next chapter, we will deploy our service on AWS Cloud.

Platform Deployment – AWS

8

In this chapter, we will cover some of the deployment options available in the Amazon AWS platform. The AWS platform is one of the oldest and most mature of the cloud service providers. It was introduced in 2002 and has been a leader in the space since then. AWS has also been constantly innovating and has introduced several new services that have found wide adoption among a broad variety of customers, from single person start-ups to enterprises.

In this chapter, we will cover the following topics:

- The AWS platform
- AWS platform deployment options

AWS platform

Amazon AWS was the pioneer of cloud computing, and has been expanding its cloud offerings ever since to maintain its leadership position. The following diagram gives an indicative list of services offered by the AWS platform for application developers:

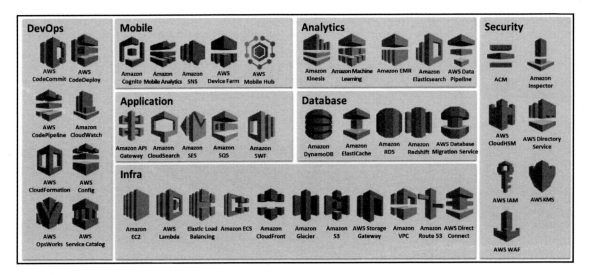

This is just an indicative list and by no means an exhaustive list; refer to the Amazon AWS portal for a complete list.

The categories are as follows:

- **Infrastructure**: This is probably the core of the AWS platform that enables it to provide a plethora of other services. These can be further classified into:
    - **Compute**: Services such as EC2, Lambda, ECS, and ELB. We will be demonstrating the deployment of our sample application using primarily compute services, but it is relatively easy to tie them up with the other services offered by AWS.
    - **Storage**: Services such as S3, EBS, and CloudFront.
    - **Networking**: Services such as VPC, Route53, and DirectConnect.
- **Application**: These services can be used as components to build and support applications.
- **Database**: These services target databases, providing access to different **relational database management system** (**RDBMS**) and NoSQL data stores.

- **DevOps**: These services provide the ability to construct build pipelines and enable continuous delivery. These include source code hosting, continuous integration tools, and cloud and software provisioning tools.
- **Security**: These services provide **role-based access control** (**RBAC**) to the various services offered by AWS, and provide a mechanism to specify quotas and enforce them, key management, and secret storage.
- **Mobile**: These services are targeted at providing backends for mobile applications and services such as notification.
- **Analytics**: These services include batch systems such as MapReduce, and stream processing systems such as Spark are available for building analytics platforms.

AWS platform deployment options

Of the various services offered by the AWS platform, we will be focusing this chapter on covering some deployment options specifically targeted for the kind of web APIs that we have been using as an example. We will therefore cover the deployment into:

- AWS Elastic Beanstalk
- AWS Elastic Container Service
- AWS Lambda

Since we will be running our application in the cloud environment, where we will not be required to manage the infrastructure directly, that is, we will not be launching virtual machines and installing the application within them, we will not require service discovery, as elastic load balancers will automatically route to all the instances of the application that are up. So, we will use a version of the product API that does not use the Eureka discovery client:

```
package com.mycompany.product;

import org.springframework.boot.SpringApplication;
import org.springframework.boot.autoconfigure.SpringBootApplication;

@SpringBootApplication
public class ProductSpringApp {

    public static void main(String[] args) throws Exception {
        SpringApplication.run(ProductSpringApp.class, args);
    }

}
```

Deploying Spring Boot API to Beanstalk

AWS Elastic Beanstalk (**AEB**) is a service offered by AWS to host web applications on AWS without having to provision or manage the IaaS layer directly. AEB supports popular languages such as Java, .NET, Python, Ruby, Go, and PHP. Recently, it has also offered support for running Docker containers. We will take a simplified version of the `product` service that we have built so far in our journey, and deploy it in AEB as a runnable JAR and also as a Docker container.

Deploying a runnable JAR

Log in to the AWS console, select the Elastic Beanstalk service under the **Compute** category, and click on the **Get started** button:

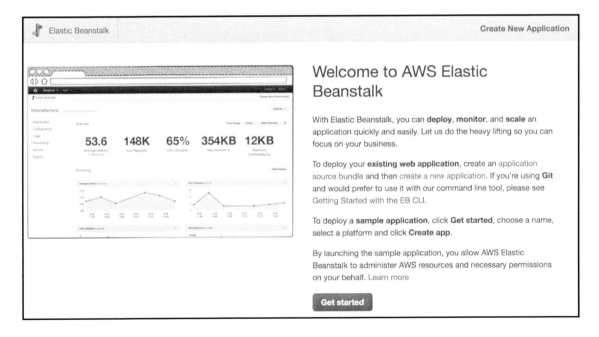

Fill in the application details in the next screen:

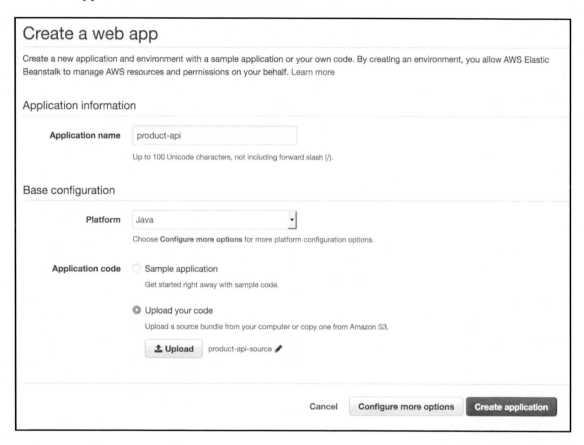

Upload the `product.jar` from the `target` folder and click on the **Configure more options** button. You will be presented with the different categories which you can configure by selecting **Software,** and under that, in the **Environment properties,** add a new environment variable called `SERVER_PORT` and set the value to `5000`. This is necessary, because by default the NGINX server that is created by the AEB environment will proxy all requests to this port, and by setting the variable we are making sure that our Spring Boot application will run on port `5000`:

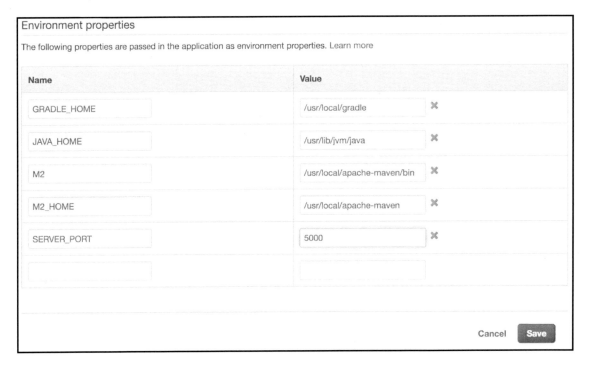

Now, a new environment with our application running will be provisioned by AWS:

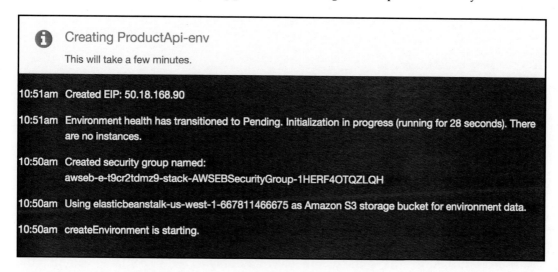

Once the environment is provisioned, AEB will generate a **URL** for the application:

We can use this URL to access the API endpoint:

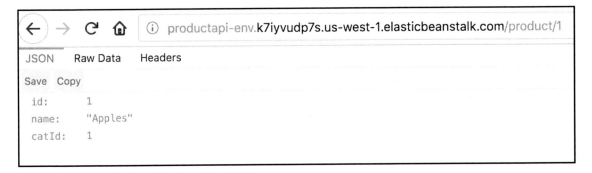

Deploying Docker containers

Now that we have learned how to deploy a runnable JAR to the Elastic Beanstalk service, let's also see a variation of the same where we will deploy a Docker container running the same application. The advantage offered by using a Docker container is that we can use languages and platforms not already supported by the AWS Elastic Beanstalk service and still deploy them in the cloud, reaping the benefits offered by the service.

For this deployment, we will be using the Docker registry available within the **Elastic Container Service** (**ECS**) offering to store the Docker container that we build from our application. We will cover how we can push our local Docker containers to the ECS repository, when we are deploying to ECS. For now, let's assume that the Docker container that we want to deploy is available in a repository called `<aws-account-id>.dkr.ecr.us-west-2.amazonaws.com/product-api`. Since we need to access this repository, we need to add the **AmazonEC2ContainerRegistryReadOnly** policy to the default Elastic Beanstalk role, **aws-elasticbeanstalk-ec2-role**.

This can be done from the **IAM** console under the **Roles** section:

Create a file called `Dockerfile.aws.json` with the following contents:

```
{
  "AWSEBDockerrunVersion": "1",
  "Image": {
    "Name": "<aws-account-id>.dkr.ecr.us-west-2.amazonaws.com/product-api",
    "Update": "true"
  },
  "Ports": [
    {
      "ContainerPort": "8080"
    }
  ]
}
```

Now we are ready to deploy our Docker container. In the Elastic Beanstalk console, instead of choosing **Java**, we will choose a single **Docker** container and create a new application:

Select and upload the `Dockerfile.aws.json` to create the environment:

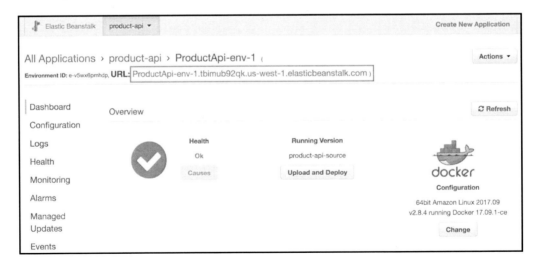

We can test our API endpoints to verify if our Docker container is running correctly. We can also configure the container to use Amazon CloudWatch logging and monitoring to better monitor our application:

```
$ curl  http://ProductApi-env-1.tbimub92qk.us-west-1.elasticbeanstalk.com/product/1 | jq .
{
  "id": 1,
  "name": "Apples",
  "catId": 1
}
$ curl  http://ProductApi-env-1.tbimub92qk.us-west-1.elasticbeanstalk.com/products?id=1 | jq .
[
  {
    "id": 1,
    "name": "Apples",
    "catId": 1
  },
  {
    "id": 2,
    "name": "Oranges",
    "catId": 1
  },
  {
    "id": 3,
    "name": "Bananas",
    "catId": 1
  }
]
$
```

Deploying Spring Boot App to the Elastic Container Service

AWS **Elastic Container Service** (**ECS**) is a service that allows a user to deploy applications using a managed Docker instance. Here, the AWS ECS service is responsible for provisioning the virtual machine and the Docker installation. We can deploy our application by doing the following:

1. Start ECS, click on **Continue**:

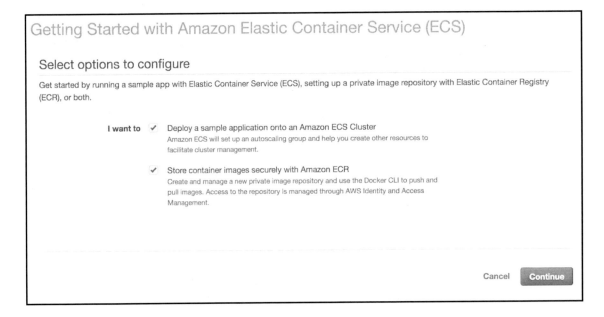

2. Create the ECS repository with name `product-api` and click on **Next step**:

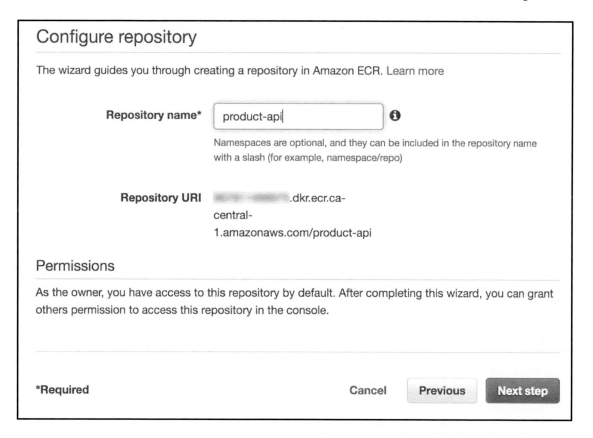

3. Build and push a Docker container to the repository, following the instructions given on the screen:

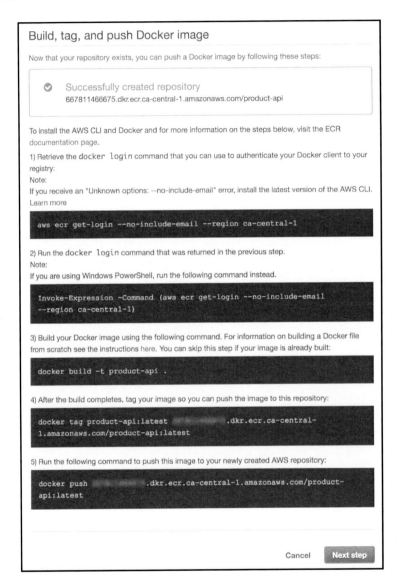

4. The Docker login command generated by the GUI has an extra `http://` which should be excluded for:

```
$ cmd=$(aws ecr get-login --no-include-email --region ca-central-1)
$ docker_cmd=$(echo $cmd | sed 's/https:\/\///')
$ eval $docker_cmd
Login Succeeded
```

5. We can now build and push the Docker container to the created repository:

```
$ docker build -t product-api .
Sending build context to Docker daemon  29.14MB
Step 1/5 : FROM openjdk:8-jdk-alpine
 ---> 224765a6bdbe
Step 2/5 : RUN mkdir -p /app
 ---> Using cache
 ---> e06b3e1d15c2
Step 3/5 : ADD target/product.jar /app/app.jar
 ---> Using cache
 ---> 759113de40f8
Step 4/5 : EXPOSE 8080
 ---> Using cache
 ---> d57360fdfe1b
Step 5/5 : ENTRYPOINT [ "/usr/bin/java", "-jar", "/app/app.jar", "--spring.profiles.active=docker" ]
 ---> Using cache
 ---> a71d17d9fb63
Successfully built a71d17d9fb63
Successfully tagged product-api:latest
$ docker tag product-api:latest          .dkr.ecr.ca-central-1.amazonaws.com/product-api:latest
$ docker push 667811466675.dkr.ecr.ca-central-1.amazonaws.com/product-api:latest
The push refers to a repository [          .dkr.ecr.ca-central-1.amazonaws.com/product-api]
b1139def75d5: Pushed
879a1a62c6c6: Pushed
685fdd7e6770: Pushed
c9b26f41504c: Pushed
cd7100a72410: Pushed
latest: digest: sha256:2eeba844bb82cd904e2b597029a8701a4a0ade7cc033ea3925e0afc45b01dc7f size: 1365
$
```

6. We will use this container repository when configuring our task definition:

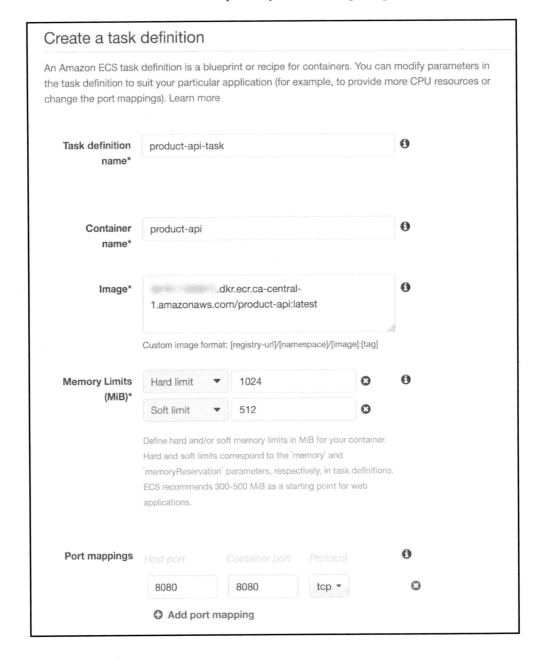

7. In the advanced options, we can configure AWS CloudWatch logging to capture the logs from the Docker container, under the **STORAGE AND LOGGING** section:

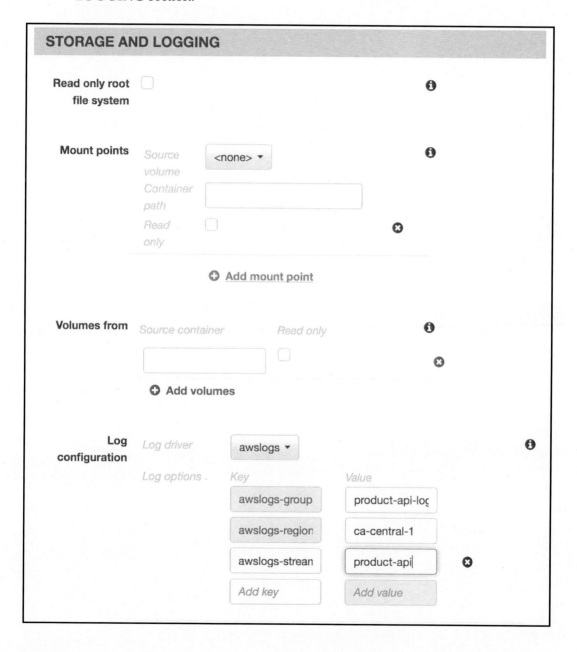

8. We need to create a corresponding log group in the CloudWatch console to capture the logs created from our application:

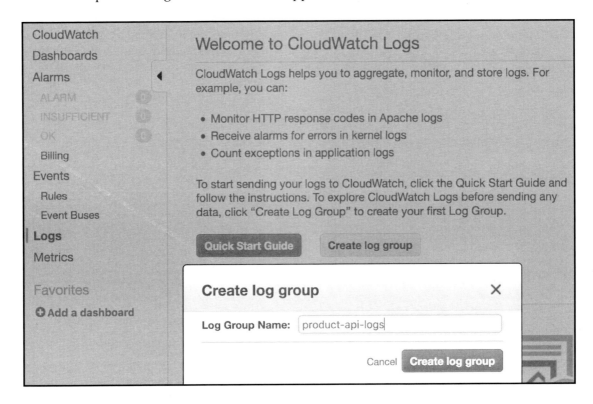

9. We can create a service mapping to the port exposed from the container, which is
`8080`:

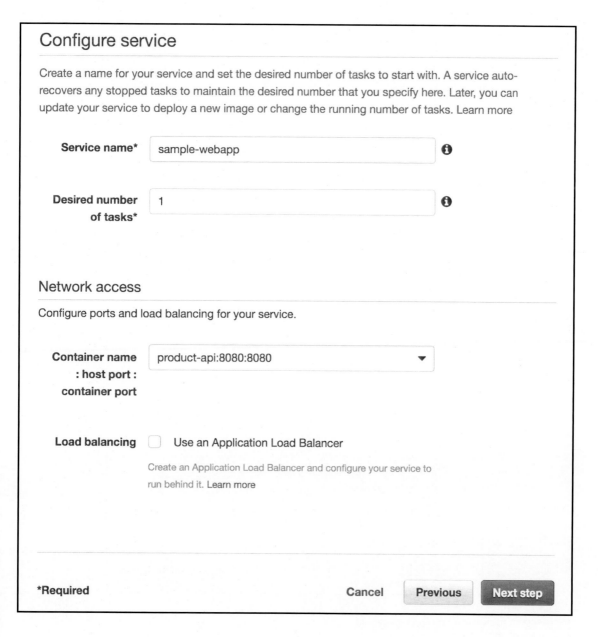

10. Optionally, we can picture the **EC2 instance type** and configure a **Key pair** so that we will be able to log in to the EC2 instance that ECS will create for our application:

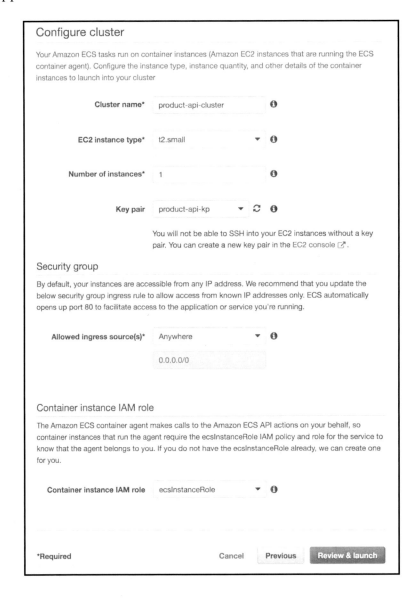

11. Once we review the configurations and submit, ECS will begin creating the EC2 instance and deploying our application into it:

Amazon ECS status - 2 of 4 complete

Create cluster: product-api-cluster

> ✓ Amazon ECS cluster created
>   **Amazon ECS cluster** product-api-cluster

Create task definition: product-api-cluster product-api-task

> ✓ Task definition created
>   **Task definition** product-api-task:3

Create instances for:product-api-cluster

> ℹ Waiting for Amazon EC2 setup to complete...
>   **Amazon ECS instances** Pending; see status below

Create service: sample-webapp

> **Service** Pending

---

12. We can click on **Auto Scaling group** and find the instance that was launched:

13. Find the instance:

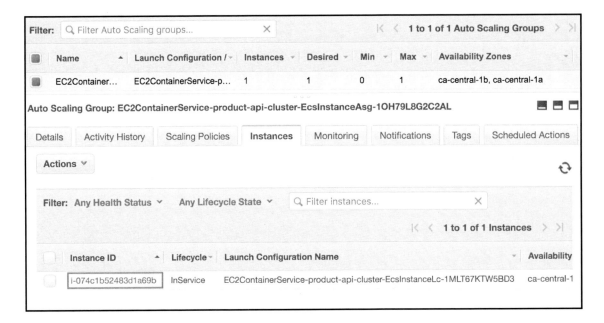

14. Find the instance hostname:

15. Access the application through the instance hostname:

```
$ curl ec2-35-183-28-76.ca-central-1.compute.amazonaws.com:8080/product/1 | jq .
{
  "id": 1,
  "name": "Apples",
  "catId": 1
}
$ curl ec2-35-183-28-76.ca-central-1.compute.amazonaws.com:8080/products?id=1 | jq .
[
  {
    "id": 1,
    "name": "Apples",
    "catId": 1
  },
  {
    "id": 2,
    "name": "Oranges",
    "catId": 1
  },
  {
    "id": 3,
    "name": "Bananas",
    "catId": 1
  }
]
$
```

But it is not feasible to access applications individually by their hostnames, so, instead, we will create an Elastic load balancer, which will route requests to the instances, thereby allowing us to have a stable endpoint while scaling up or down:

1. We will go to the EC2 console and select **Create** under **Application Load Balancer**:

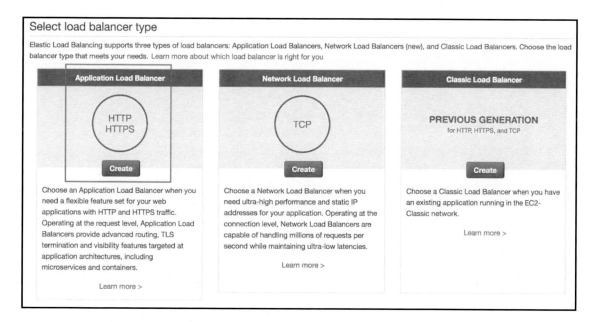

2. Configure the **Load Balancer Port**:

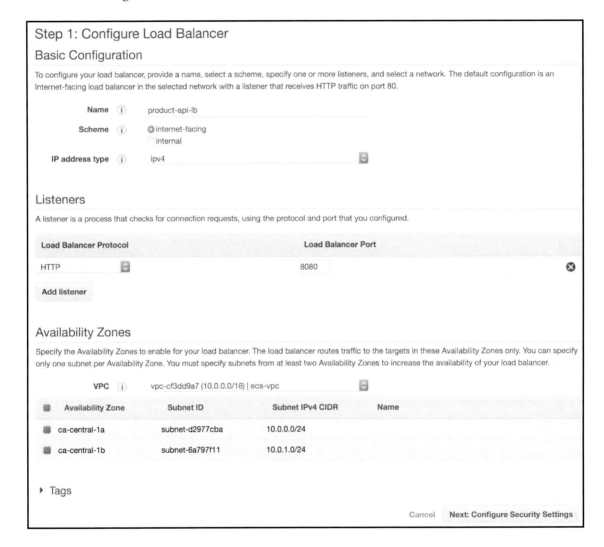

3. Configure the **Target group** and the **Health checks** endpoint:

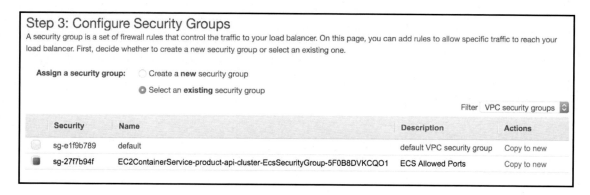

4. Register the target instances to the instance that was created by our cluster definition:

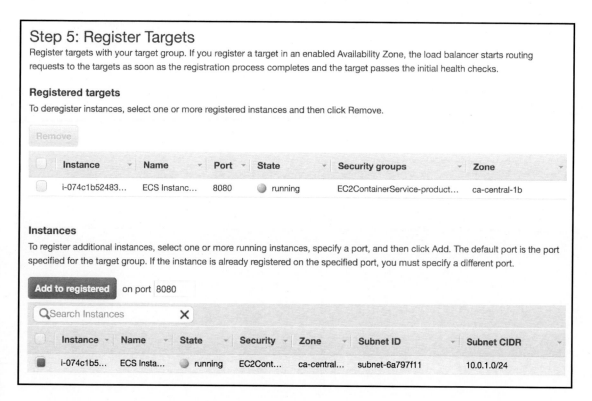

5. Find the DNS record for the **Load balancer**:

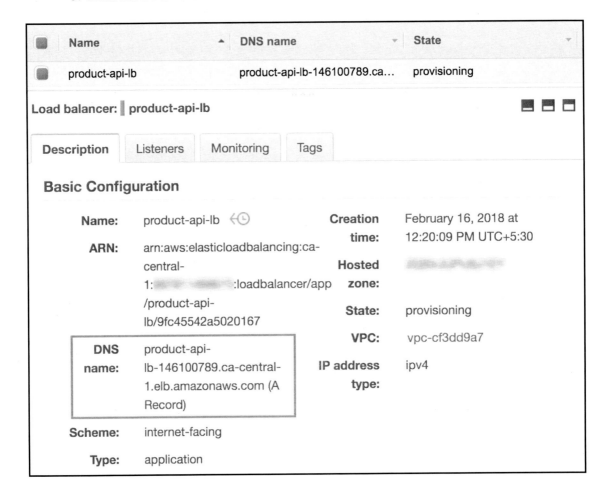

6. Connect to the load balancer endpoint and verify the application is working:

```
$ curl http://product-api-lb-146100789.ca-central-1.elb.amazonaws.com:8080/product/1 | jq .
{
  "id": 1,
  "name": "Apples",
  "catId": 1
}
$ curl http://product-api-lb-146100789.ca-central-1.elb.amazonaws.com:8080/products?id=1 | jq .
[
  {
    "id": 1,
    "name": "Apples",
    "catId": 1
  },
  {
    "id": 2,
    "name": "Oranges",
    "catId": 1
  },
  {
    "id": 3,
    "name": "Bananas",
    "catId": 1
  }
]
$
```

Deploying to AWS Lambda

The AWS Lambda service allows the deployment of simple functions to be invoked on event triggers. These event triggers can be classified into four types, namely:

- Data Store (for example, AWS DyanmoDB)
- Queues and Streams (for example, AWS Kinesis)
- Blob Store (for example, AWS S3)

- API Dateways:

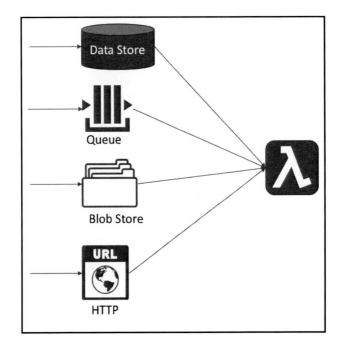

The complete list of event sources supported by AWS Lamda can be found at `https://docs.aws.amazon.com/lambda/latest/dg/invoking-lambda-function.html#api-gateway-with-lambda`.

Unlike the other deployment options discussed earlier, AWS Lambda provides the most transparent scaling option where the AWS platform scales the instances required, based on the demand. We are freed from configuring instances, load balancers, and so on, and instead can focus on the application logic.

We will now build a simple AWS Lambda function and bind it to an API endpoint to invoke it.

We will begin by creating a new Spring Boot application with the following dependencies. We will also be using the `maven-shade-plugin` to create a runnable JAR:

```
<project xmlns="http://maven.apache.org/POM/4.0.0"
xmlns:xsi="http://www.w3.org/2001/XMLSchema-instance"
         xsi:schemaLocation="http://maven.apache.org/POM/4.0.0
http://maven.apache.org/xsd/maven-4.0.0.xsd">
   <modelVersion>4.0.0</modelVersion>
   <groupId>com.mycompany</groupId>
```

```xml
<artifactId>hello-lambda</artifactId>
<version>0.0.1-SNAPSHOT</version>

<dependencies>
  <dependency>
    <groupId>junit</groupId>
    <artifactId>junit</artifactId>
    <version>4.12</version>
    <scope>test</scope>
  </dependency>
  <dependency>
    <groupId>com.amazonaws</groupId>
    <artifactId>aws-lambda-java-core</artifactId>
    <version>1.1.0</version>
  </dependency>
  <dependency>
    <groupId>com.amazonaws</groupId>
    <artifactId>aws-lambda-java-events</artifactId>
    <version>2.0.1</version>
  </dependency>
  <dependency>
    <groupId>com.amazonaws</groupId>
    <artifactId>aws-lambda-java-log4j2</artifactId>
    <version>1.0.0</version>
  </dependency>
</dependencies>

<build>
  <finalName>hello-lambda</finalName>
  <plugins>
    <plugin>
      <groupId>org.apache.maven.plugins</groupId>
      <artifactId>maven-compiler-plugin</artifactId>
      <configuration>
        <source>1.8</source>
        <target>1.8</target>
      </configuration>
    </plugin>
    <plugin>
      <groupId>org.apache.maven.plugins</groupId>
      <artifactId>maven-shade-plugin</artifactId>
      <version>3.0.0</version>
      <configuration>
        <createDependencyReducedPom>false</createDependencyReducedPom>
      </configuration>
      <executions>
        <execution>
          <phase>package</phase>
```

```
            <goals>
              <goal>shade</goal>
            </goals>
          </execution>
        </executions>
      </plugin>
    </plugins>
  </build>

</project>
```

Now create `HelloHandler.java` with the following contents:

```java
package com.mycompany;

import com.amazonaws.services.lambda.runtime.Context;
import com.amazonaws.services.lambda.runtime.RequestHandler;
import
com.amazonaws.services.lambda.runtime.events.APIGatewayProxyRequestEvent;
import
com.amazonaws.services.lambda.runtime.events.APIGatewayProxyResponseEvent;

import java.net.HttpURLConnection;

public class HelloHandler implements
RequestHandler<APIGatewayProxyRequestEvent, APIGatewayProxyResponseEvent> {

    @Override
    public APIGatewayProxyResponseEvent
handleRequest(APIGatewayProxyRequestEvent request, Context context) {
        String who = "World";
        if ( request.getPathParameters() != null ) {
          String name  = request.getPathParameters().get("name");
          if ( name != null && !"".equals(name.trim()) ) {
            who = name;
          }
        }
        return new
APIGatewayProxyResponseEvent().withStatusCode(HttpURLConnection.HTTP_OK).wi
thBody(String.format("Hello %s!", who));
    }

}
```

Since lambda functions are simple functions, we can test them quite easily just by using the inputs and outputs of the functions. For example, a sample test case could be:

```
package com.mycompany;

import
com.amazonaws.services.lambda.runtime.events.APIGatewayProxyRequestEvent;
import
com.amazonaws.services.lambda.runtime.events.APIGatewayProxyResponseEvent;
import org.junit.Before;
import org.junit.Test;
import org.junit.runner.RunWith;
import org.junit.runners.BlockJUnit4ClassRunner;

import java.util.Collections;
import java.util.HashMap;
import java.util.Map;

import static org.junit.Assert.*;

@RunWith(BlockJUnit4ClassRunner.class)
public class HelloHandlerTest {

    HelloHandler handler;
    APIGatewayProxyRequestEvent input;
    @Before
    public void setUp() throws Exception {
        handler = new HelloHandler();
        Map<String, String> pathParams = new HashMap<>();
        pathParams.put("name", "Universe");
        input = new
APIGatewayProxyRequestEvent().withPath("/hello").withPathParamters(pathPara
ms);
    }

    @Test
    public void handleRequest() {
        APIGatewayProxyResponseEvent res = handler.handleRequest(input, null);
        assertNotNull(res);
        assertEquals("Hello Universe!", res.getBody());
    }
    @Test
    public void handleEmptyRequest() {
        input.withPathParamters(Collections.emptyMap());
        APIGatewayProxyResponseEvent res = handler.handleRequest(input, null);
        assertNotNull(res);
        assertEquals("Hello World!", res.getBody());
```

```
        }
    }
```

Now we can build the lambda function using Maven:

```
$ mvn clean package
[INFO] Scanning for projects...
[WARNING]
[WARNING] Some problems were encountered while building the effective model
for com.mycompany:hello-lambda:jar:0.0.1-SNAPSHOT
[WARNING] 'build.plugins.plugin.version' for
org.apache.maven.plugins:maven-compiler-plugin is missing. @ line 35,
column 15
[WARNING]
[WARNING] It is highly recommended to fix these problems because they
threaten the stability of your build.
[WARNING]
[WARNING] For this reason, future Maven versions might no longer support
building such malformed projects.
[WARNING]
[INFO]
[INFO] ------------------------------------------------------------------
----
[INFO] Building hello-lambda 0.0.1-SNAPSHOT
[INFO] ------------------------------------------------------------------
----
[INFO]
[INFO] --- maven-clean-plugin:2.5:clean (default-clean) @ hello-lambda ---
[INFO] Deleting /Users/shyam/workspaces/msa-
wsp/CloudNativeJava/chapter-09/hello-lambda/target
[INFO]
[INFO] --- maven-resources-plugin:2.6:resources (default-resources) @
hello-lambda ---
[WARNING] Using platform encoding (UTF-8 actually) to copy filtered
resources, i.e. build is platform dependent!
[INFO] skip non existing resourceDirectory /Users/shyam/workspaces/msa-
wsp/CloudNativeJava/chapter-09/hello-lambda/src/main/resources
[INFO]
[INFO] --- maven-compiler-plugin:3.1:compile (default-compile) @ hello-
lambda ---
[INFO] Changes detected - recompiling the module!
[WARNING] File encoding has not been set, using platform encoding UTF-8,
i.e. build is platform dependent!
[INFO] Compiling 1 source file to /Users/shyam/workspaces/msa-
wsp/CloudNativeJava/chapter-09/hello-lambda/target/classes
[INFO]
[INFO] --- maven-resources-plugin:2.6:testResources (default-testResources)
@ hello-lambda ---
```

```
[WARNING] Using platform encoding (UTF-8 actually) to copy filtered
resources, i.e. build is platform dependent!
[INFO] skip non existing resourceDirectory /Users/shyam/workspaces/msa-
wsp/CloudNativeJava/chapter-09/hello-lambda/src/test/resources
[INFO]
[INFO] --- maven-compiler-plugin:3.1:testCompile (default-testCompile) @
hello-lambda ---
[INFO] Changes detected - recompiling the module!
[WARNING] File encoding has not been set, using platform encoding UTF-8,
i.e. build is platform dependent!
[INFO] Compiling 1 source file to /Users/shyam/workspaces/msa-
wsp/CloudNativeJava/chapter-09/hello-lambda/target/test-classes
[INFO]
[INFO] --- maven-surefire-plugin:2.12.4:test (default-test) @ hello-lambda
---
[INFO] Surefire report directory: /Users/shyam/workspaces/msa-
wsp/CloudNativeJava/chapter-09/hello-lambda/target/surefire-reports


-------------------------------------------------------
 T E S T S
-------------------------------------------------------
Running com.mycompany.HelloHandlerTest
Tests run: 2, Failures: 0, Errors: 0, Skipped: 0, Time elapsed: 0.055 sec

Results :

Tests run: 2, Failures: 0, Errors: 0, Skipped: 0

[INFO]
[INFO] --- maven-jar-plugin:2.4:jar (default-jar) @ hello-lambda ---
[INFO] Building jar: /Users/shyam/workspaces/msa-
wsp/CloudNativeJava/chapter-09/hello-lambda/target/hello-lambda.jar
[INFO]
[INFO] --- maven-shade-plugin:3.0.0:shade (default) @ hello-lambda ---
[INFO] Including com.amazonaws:aws-lambda-java-core:jar:1.1.0 in the shaded
jar.
[INFO] Including com.amazonaws:aws-lambda-java-events:jar:2.0.1 in the
shaded jar.
[INFO] Including joda-time:joda-time:jar:2.6 in the shaded jar.
[INFO] Including com.amazonaws:aws-lambda-java-log4j2:jar:1.0.0 in the
shaded jar.
[INFO] Including org.apache.logging.log4j:log4j-core:jar:2.8.2 in the
shaded jar.
[INFO] Including org.apache.logging.log4j:log4j-api:jar:2.8.2 in the shaded
jar.
[INFO] Replacing original artifact with shaded artifact.
[INFO] Replacing /Users/shyam/workspaces/msa-
wsp/CloudNativeJava/chapter-09/hello-lambda/target/hello-lambda.jar with
```

```
/Users/shyam/workspaces/msa-wsp/CloudNativeJava/chapter-09/hello-
lambda/target/hello-lambda-0.0.1-SNAPSHOT-shaded.jar
[INFO] -------------------------------------------------------------
----
[INFO] BUILD SUCCESS
[INFO] -------------------------------------------------------------
----
[INFO] Total time: 2.549 s
[INFO] Finished at: 2018-02-12T13:52:14+05:30
[INFO] Final Memory: 25M/300M
[INFO] -------------------------------------------------------------
----
```

We have now built the `hello-lambda.jar`, which we will upload to the AWS Lambda function that we will create from the AWS console.

1. We will begin by going to the API Gateway console, which appears in the **Network and Content Delivery** category of the AWS console, and create a new API:

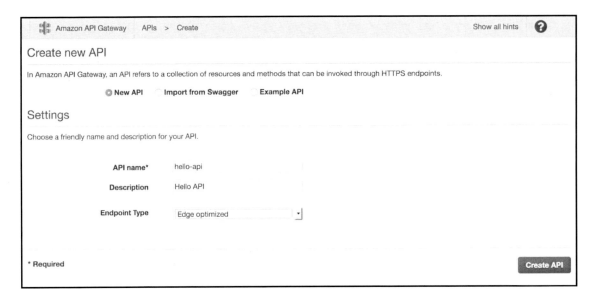

2. We will add a new resource called `hello` for the path `/hello`:

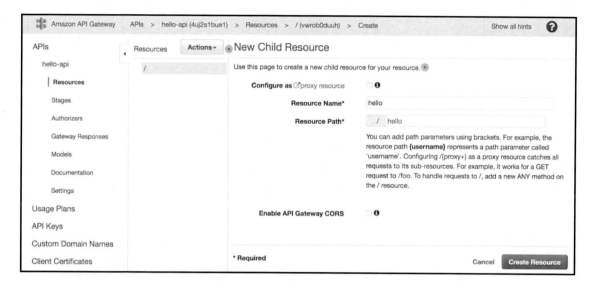

3. We will also create a child resource with a path parameter:

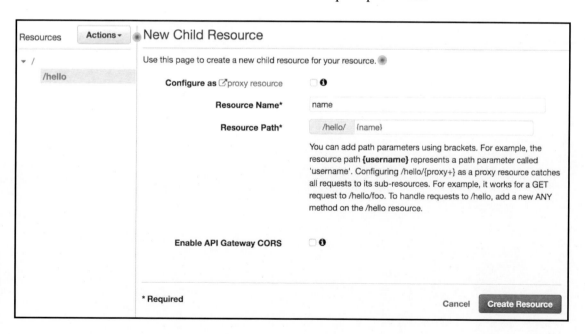

4. Now, we will attach the HTTP GET method:

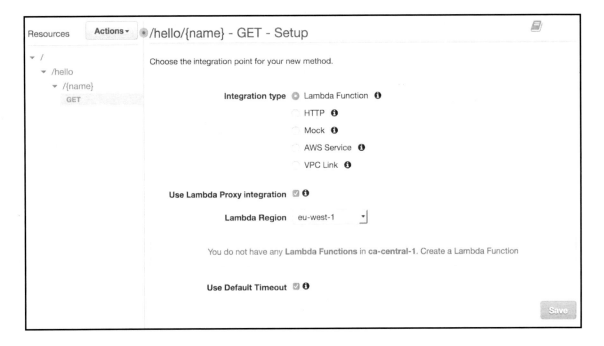

5. Create a lambda function with the details shown as follows:

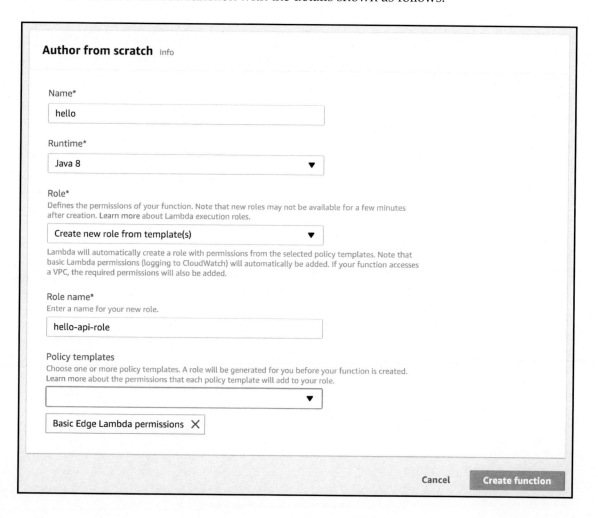

6. Upload the runnable JAR and set the handler method:

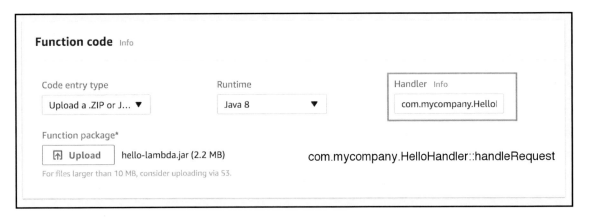

7. Now add this lambda function to the API method:

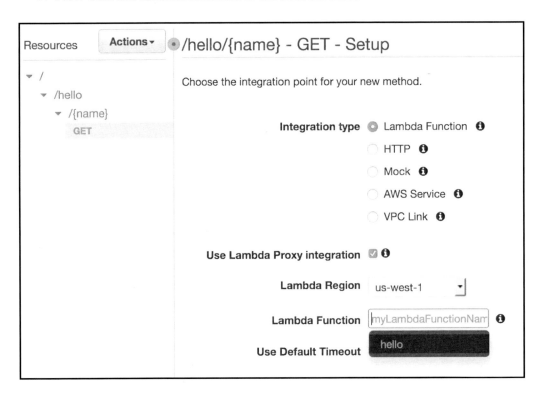

8. Make sure you select **Use Lambda Proxy Integration** so that we can use the specific `RequestHandler` interface, instead of using the generic `RequestStreamHandler`. This will also give API Gateway permission to the lambda function:

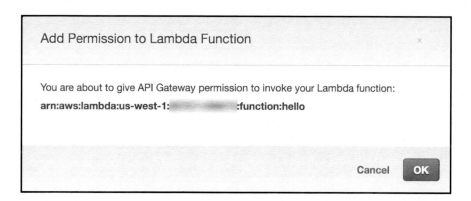

9. Complete the API definition with the lambda function invocation:

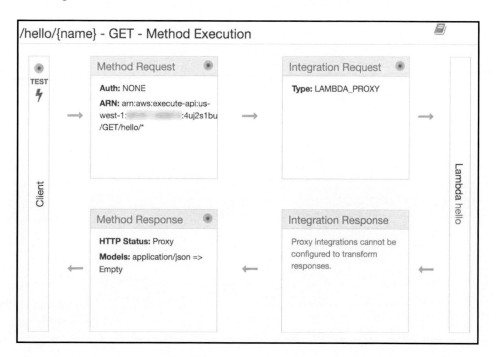

10. We can test the API endpoint from the console:

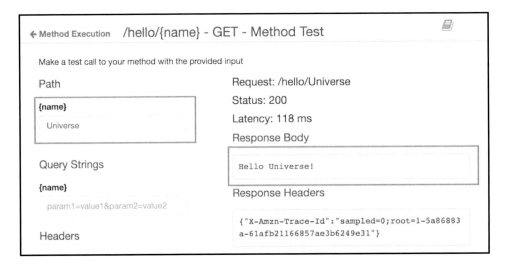

11. Now we can deploy the API:

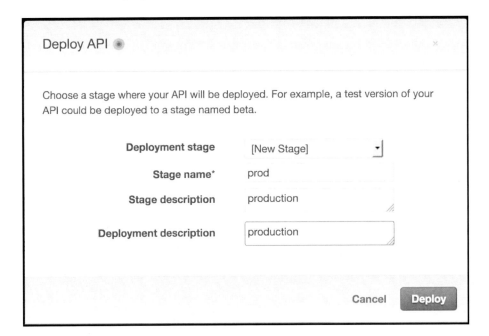

12. Successful deployment of the API will result in the API endpoint:

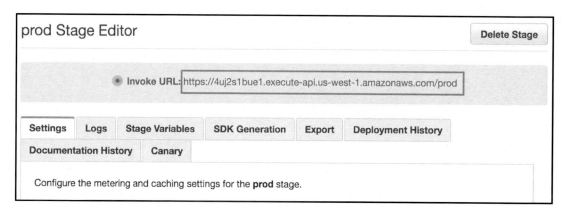

13. Now we can use this API endpoint, generated for this deployment environment, to access the application:

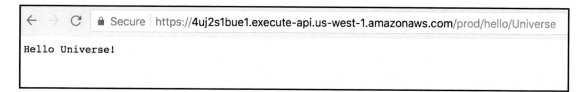

Summary

In this chapter, we covered some options offered by the AWS platform, and how we can deploy our application from Elastic Beanstalk, which is for web applications. We deployed to ECS, which is for deploying containerized workloads and is not restricted to web application workloads. We then deployed an AWS Lambda function without any need for configuring the underlying hardware. We will look at deployment using Azure in the following chapter to see some of the services that it offers for deploying cloud-native applications.

9
Platform Deployment – Azure

This chapter discusses application design and deployment for Azure—a Microsoft public cloud platform. The essence of cloud-native development is the ability to integrate your application with PaaS platforms provided by the cloud provider. You, as a developer, focus on creating value (solving customer problems), and allow the cloud provider to do the heavy lifting for your application's infrastructure.

In this chapter, we will learn the following:

- Different categories of PaaS services provided by Azure. We will delve a little deeper into services that will be used by our sample applications.
- Migrate our sample application to Azure and understand the various options available. We will also evaluate all the options and understand the pros and cons for each option.

We are covering the Azure platform with the intention of showing how to build and deploy applications. We are not going to cover Azure in depth, and we expect the reader to use the Azure documentation (https://docs.microsoft.com/en-us/azure/) to explore additional options.

Azure supports multiple programming languages, but for the purpose of this book we are looking at support for Java applications in Azure.

Azure platform

Azure provides an ever-increasing set of PaaS and IaaS across a spectrum of technology areas. For our purpose, we will look at the subset of areas and services that are directly applicable and used by our application.

For ease of use, I have created this service categorization model across technology areas that are most relevant to typical business applications:

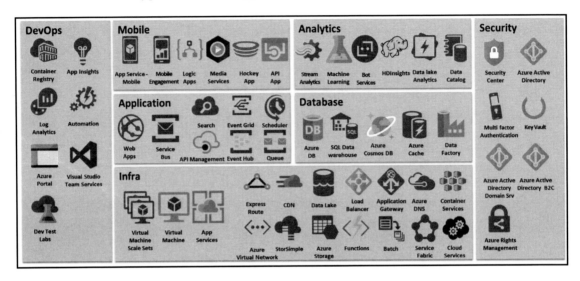

This is just an indicative list and by no means an exhaustive list. Refer to the Azure portal for a complete list.

In the preceding categorization models, we have divided the services into the following areas:

- **Infrastructure**: This is an all-encompassing list of services provided by Azure to deploy and host our applications. We have combined services across compute, storage, and networking in this category. We will be looking at the following set of services for the purpose of our sample Java applications.
    - **App Services**: How can we take the existing Spring Boot applications and deploy them in our Azure platform? This is more of a lift and shift scenario. Here the application is not refactored, but the dependencies are deployed on App Services. Using one of the database services, the application can be deployed and hosted. Azure provides PostgreSQL and MySQL as hosted database models among a variety of other options.
    - **Container Services**: For applications packaged as Docker containers, we can explore how to deploy Docker containers to the platform.

- **Functions**: This is the serverless platform model, where you need not worry about application hosting and deployment. You create a function and let the platform do the heavy lifting for you. As of now, Java-based Azure cloud functions are in beta. We will explore how to create one in a development environment and test locally.
- **Service Fabric**: Service Fabric is a distributed systems platform for deploying and managing microservices and container applications. We will explore how we can deploy our sample `product` API in Service Fabric.

- **Application**: This is a list of services that help build distributed applications. As we move to a distributed microservices model, we need to decouple our application component and services. Features such as Queue, EventHub, EventGrid, and API management help build a cohesive set of robust APIs and services.
- **Database**: This is a list of data store options provided by the Azure platform. This includes relational, key value, redis cache, and data warehouse among others.
- **DevOps**: For building and deploying applications in the cloud, we need the support of robust CI/CD toolsets. Visual Studio team services are provided for hosting code, issue tracking, and automated builds. Again, open source tools are still not first-class citizens in the Azure portal. You can always use hosted versions of the required software.
- **Security**: Another key factor for cloud applications are security services. Active directory, rights management, key vault, and multi-factor authentication are some of the key services provided in this area.
- **Mobile**: If you are building mobile applications, the platform provides key services such as application services for mobile, media services, and mobile engagement services, among others in this area.
- **Analytics**: In the area of analytics, the platform provides robust services in the areas of MapReduce, Storm, Spark through HDInsight and Data Lake services for analytics and a data repository.

In addition, there are multiple other technology areas where Azure provides services—**internet of things (IoT)**, monitoring, management, **artificial intelligence (AI)**, and cognitive and enterprise integration areas.

Azure platform deployment options

As we saw in the previous section, Azure provides a number of options to build and deploy applications on the platform. We will use our example of the `product` API REST service to examine the various options provided by Azure to deploy and run our application.

Before we begin, I am assuming you are familiar with the Azure platform and have already signed up in the portal.

Azure supports multiple programming languages and provides SDKs to support development in the respective areas. For our purpose, we are primarily exploring support for Java applications within the Azure platform.

We will explore application hosting services in the following four areas:

- App Services
- Container Services
- Service Fabric
- Functions

Refer to the following link for more details and getting started: `https://azure.microsoft.com/en-in/downloads/`.

Deploying Spring Boot API to Azure App Service

In this section, we are taking our `product` API service and migrating it to an Azure App Service. We will look at the additional changes made to the application to adhere to the requirements of the Azure App Service.

I have taken the `product` API REST service that we built in Chapter 3, *Designing Your Cloud-Native Application*. In the service, we make the following changes:

Add a file `web.config` in the root folder of the project:

```
<?xml version="1.0" encoding="UTF-8"?>
<configuration>
  <system.webServer>
    <handlers>
      <add name="httpPlatformHandler" path="*" verb="*"
        modules="httpPlatformHandler" resourceType="Unspecified"/>
    </handlers>
    <httpPlatform processPath="%JAVA_HOME%binjava.exe"
```

```
            arguments="-Djava.net.preferIPv4Stack=true -
            Dserver.port=%HTTP_PLATFORM_PORT% -jar &quot;
            %HOME%sitewwwrootproduct-0.0.1-SNAPSHOT.jar&quot;">
        </httpPlatform>
    </system.webServer>
</configuration>
```

The file is added with the following change, `product-0.0.1-SNAPSHOT.jar`, which is the package name of our application. In case your application name differs, you will need to make that change.

We start with checking out the `product` API code here: `https://azure.microsoft.com/en-in/downloads/`.

```
Munish-Guptas-iMac:ch10-product admin$ ls -l
total 16
-rw-r--r--  1 admin  staff  3148 Jan 15 13:13 pom.xml
drwxr-xr-x  5 admin  staff   170 Jan 15 10:31 src
-rw-r--r--  1 admin  staff   530 Jan 15 13:48 web.config
Munish-Guptas-iMac:ch10-product admin$ 
```

We run the `mvn clean package` command to package the project as a fat JAR:

```
[INFO] Scanning for projects...
[INFO]
[INFO] --------------------------------------------------------------------
----
[INFO] Building product 0.0.1-SNAPSHOT
[INFO] --------------------------------------------------------------------
----
[INFO]
[INFO] ......
[INFO]
[INFO] --- maven-jar-plugin:2.6:jar (default-jar) @ product ---
[INFO] Building jar: /Users/admin/Documents/workspace/CloudNativeJava/ch10-
product/target/product-0.0.1-SNAPSHOT.jar
[INFO]
[INFO] --- spring-boot-maven-plugin:1.4.3.RELEASE:repackage (default) @
product ---
[INFO] --------------------------------------------------------------------
----
[INFO] BUILD SUCCESS
[INFO] --------------------------------------------------------------------
----
[INFO] Total time: 14.182 s
[INFO] Finished at: 2018-01-15T15:06:56+05:30
```

```
[INFO] Final Memory: 40M/353M
[INFO] -----------------------------------------------------------------
----
```

Next, we log in to the Azure portal (`https://portal.azure.com/`).

1. Click on the **App Services** menu item in the left-hand column as shown in the following screenshot:

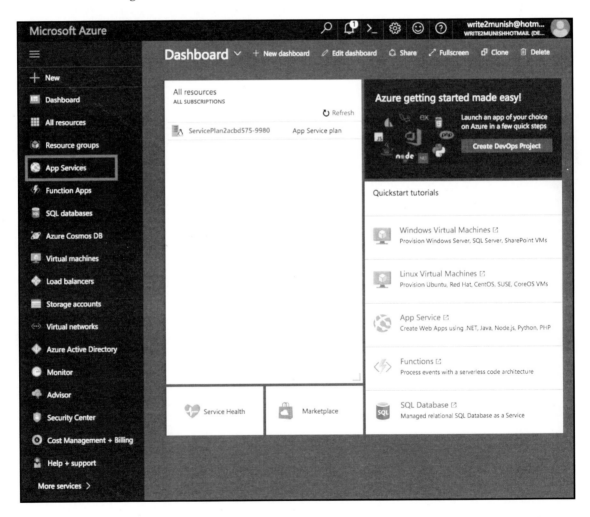

Select **App Services** in Azure portal

2. Click on the **Add** link:

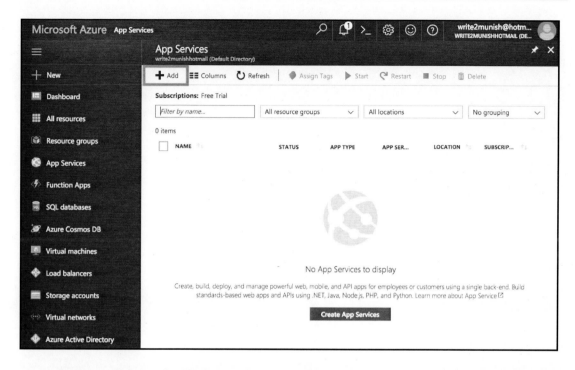

3. Next, click on the **Web App** link as indicated:

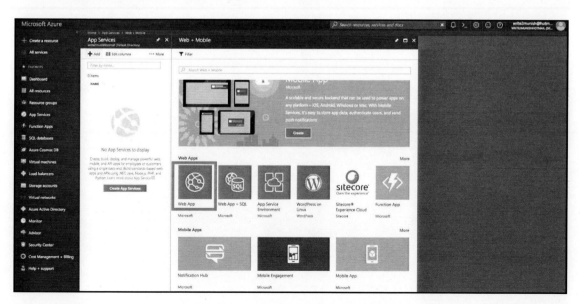

Select Web App by navigating through Azure Portal I App Services I Add.

4. Click on the **Create** button link and you should see the following page

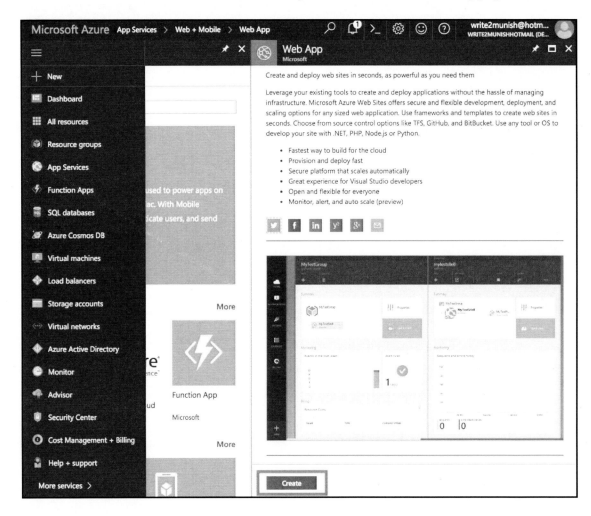

5. We fill in the details for our `product` API. I have filled in **App name** as `ch10product` and left the other options at the default.

6. Next, click the **Create** button at the bottom of the page.

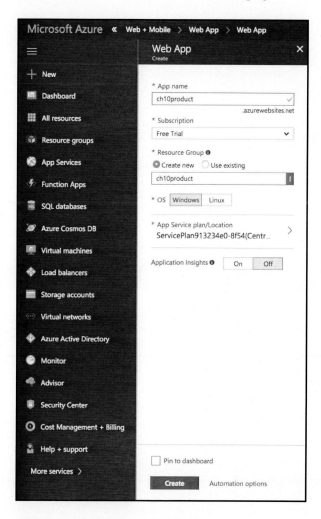

This leads to the creation of the App Service.

7. We click on the `ch10product` under **App Services**, which takes us to the menu:

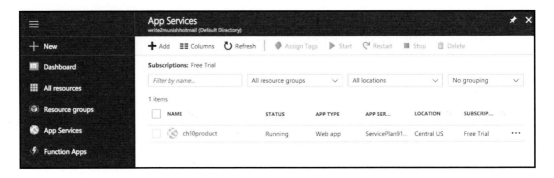

8. Notice the **URL** and the **FTP hostname** where the application is deployed. We need to make changes in two places—**Application settings** and **Deployment credentials**:

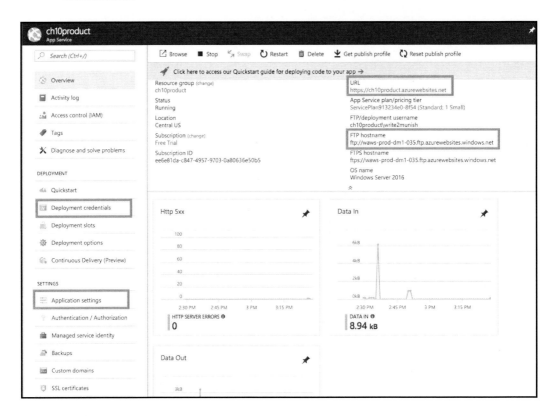

9. We click on the **Application settings** link and select the following options in the drop-down menu:
    1. Choose **Java 8** for the **Java version**
    2. Choose **Newest** for the **Java Minor version**
    3. Choose **Newest Tomcat 9.0** for the **Web container**(This container will not actually be used; Azure uses the container bundled as part of the Spring Boot application.)
    4. Click **Save**

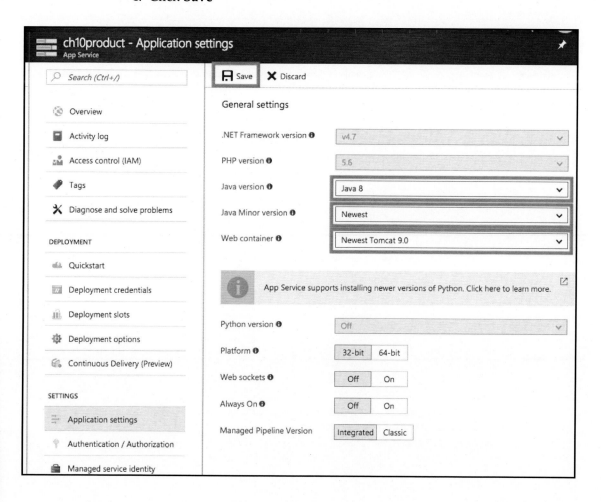

10. Next, we click on the **Deployment credentials** link on the left-hand side. Here we capture the **FTP/deployment username** and **Password** in order to be able to push our application to the host and click on **Save** as shown in the following screenshot:

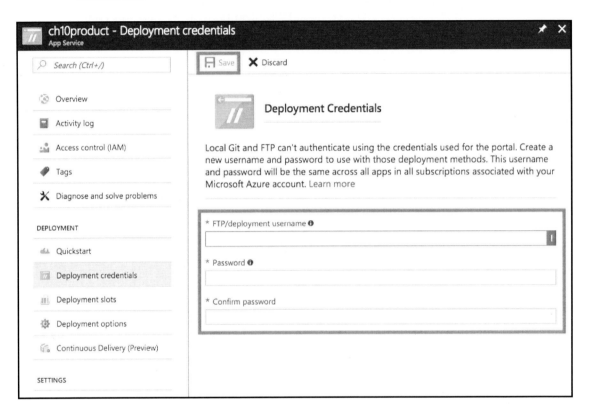

11. Connect to the FTP hostname we saw in *Step 8* and use your credentials saved in *Step 10* to log in:

```
ftp
open ftp://waws-prod-dm1-035.ftp.azurewebsites.windows.net
user ch10productwrite2munish
password *******
```

12. Next, we change directory to `site/wwwroot` on the remote server and transfer the fat JAR and `web.config` to the folder:

```
cd site/wwwroot
put product-0.0.1-SNAPSHOT.jar
put web.config
```

13. We go back to the overview section and restart the application. We should be able to start the application and see our REST API working.

In this section, we saw how to take an existing REST API application and deploy it in Azure. It is not the easiest and best way to deploy. This option is more of a lift and shift, where we take existing applications and try to move the workloads to the cloud. For deploying web applications, Azure provides a Maven plugin that can push your application directly to the cloud. Refer to the following link for more details: `https://docs.microsoft.com/en-in/java/azure/spring-framework/deploy-spring-boot-java-app-with-maven-plugin`.

The REST API is deployed on a Windows Server VM. Azure is adding support for Java applications, but their forte remains .NET applications.

If you want to make use of Linux and deploy your REST API applications, you have the option of using Docker-based deployments. We will cover Docker-based deployment in the next section.

Deploying Docker containers to Azure Container Service

Let's deploy our Docker container applications. I have created Docker images for the `product` API example used in the previous section. The Docker image can be pulled from the Docker hub through the following command:

```
docker pull cloudnativejava/ch10productapi
```

Let's get started and log into the Azure portal. We should see the following:

1. Click on the **App Services** menu item in the left-hand column. We should see the following screen. Click on **New** as indicated in the screenshot:

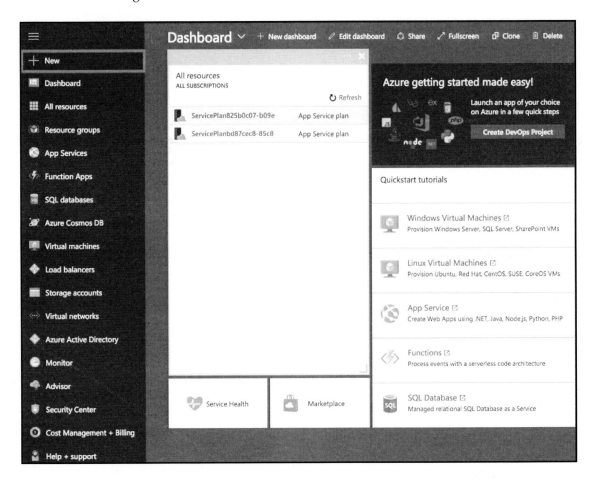

2. Under **New** search for `Web App for Containers`:

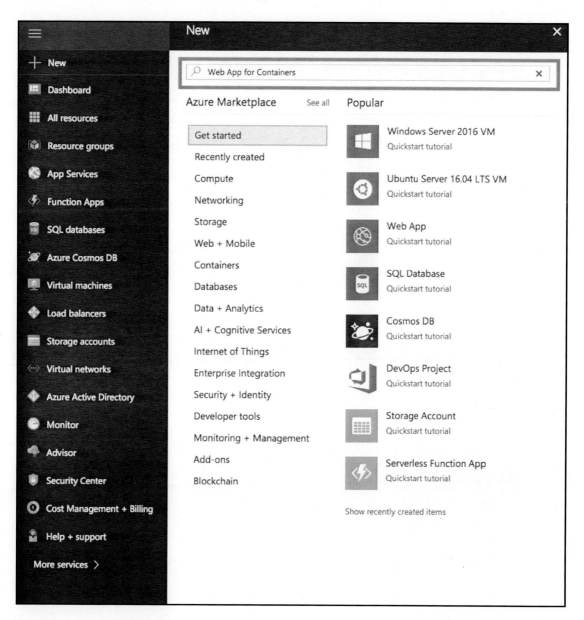

3. Once the **Web App for Containers** is selected, click on **Create** as indicated:

Select **Create** by navigating through **App Services** I **Add** I **Web App**

4. We will fill in the details for our `product` API container:
   1. I have filled in the **App Name** and **Resource Group** as `ch10productContainer` and left the other options at the default.
   2. In the **Configure container** section, we select the container repository. If there is already a Docker image in Docker hub, provide the image pull tag, `cloudnativejava/ch10productapi`.
   3. Click **OK** at the bottom of the page. It validates the image.
   4. Next, we click **Create** at the bottom of the page:

Select Create by navigating through Azure portal I **New** I search for Web App for Containers

5. This leads to the creation of the App Service:

Select Newly created app container by navigating through Azure portal | **App Services**

6. We click on `ch10productcontainer` under **App Services**, which takes us to the menu where we can see the marked URL, `https://ch10productcontainer.azurewebsites.net`, where the container is available.

The URL where the host docker application can be accessed

7. We can see our `product` API running in the browser:

This is an easy way to deploy your application to the cloud platform. In both the previous scenarios we have not used any of the specialized applications or data store services. For a true cloud-native application, we need to make use of the platform services provided by the provider. The whole idea is that the heavy lifting in terms of application scalability and availability is handled by the native platform. We, as developers, focus on building the key business functionality and integration with other components.

Deploying Spring Boot API to Azure Service Fabric

Building and deploying applications to the underlying IaaS platform is how most organizations start working with public cloud providers. As the level of comfort and maturity of cloud processes increases, the application starts getting built with PaaS features. So, applications start consisting of queuing, eventing, hosted data stores, security, and other features of the platform services.

But a key question remains with regards to non-functional requirements. Who will think of the abilities of the application?

- How do I make sure there are enough application instances running?
- What happens when an instance goes down?
- How does the application scale up/down depending on the incoming traffic?
- How do we monitor all the running instances?
- How do we manage distributed stateful services?
- How do we perform rolling upgrades to the deployed services?

In comes the orchestration engines. Products such as Kubernetes, Mesos, and the Docker swarm provide the ability to manage the application containers. Azure has released Service Fabric, which is application/container management software for your application. It can be run on-premises or in the cloud.

Service Fabric provides the following key functions:

- Allows you to deploy applications that can scale massively and provide a self-healing platform
- Allows you to install/deploy both stateful and stateless microservice-based applications
- Provides dashboards to monitor and diagnose the health of applications
- Defines policies for automatic repair and upgrades

In the current version, Service Fabric supports two underlying operating systems—flavors of Windows Server and Ubuntu 16.04 only. Your best bet is a Windows Server cluster, as the support, tooling, and documentation is the best.

For demoing the features and usage of the Service Fabric, I will make use of an Ubuntu image for local testing, and Service Fabric party cluster for online deployment of our `product` API example in the Service Fabric cluster. We will also examine how to scale the application instances, and self-healing features of the Service Fabric.

Basic environment setup

For the environment, I am using a macOS machine. We need to set up the following:

1. Local Service Fabric cluster setup—pull a Docker image:

   ```
   docker pull servicefabricoss/service-fabric-onebox
   ```

2. Update the Docker daemon configuration on your host with the following additional settings and restart the Docker daemon:

   ```
   {
       "ipv6": true,
       "fixed-cidr-v6": "fd00::/64"
   }
   ```

3. Start the Docker image pulled down from Docker hub:

```
docker run -itd -p 19080:19080 servicefabricoss/service-fabric-
onebox bash
```

4. Add the following commands within the container shell:

```
./setup.sh
./run.sh
```

After the last step is complete, a development Service Fabric cluster is started that can be accessed at `http://localhost:19080` from the browser.

Now we need to set up Yeoman generators for containers and guest executables:

1. First, we need to make sure Node.js and **Node Package Manager** (**NPM**) are installed. The software can be installed by using HomeBrew, as follows:

```
brew install node
node -v
npm -v
```

2. Next, we install the Yeoman template generator from NPM:

```
npm install -g yo
```

3. Next, we install the Yeoman generator that will be used to create Service Fabric applications by using Yeoman. Follow these steps:

```
# for Service Fabric Java Applications
npm install -g generator-azuresfjava
# for Service Fabric Guest executables
npm install -g generator-azuresfguest
# for Service Fabric Container Applications
npm install -g generator-azuresfcontainer
```

4. To build a Service Fabric Java application on macOS, JDK version 1.8, and Gradle, the software must be installed on the host machine. The software can be installed by using Homebrew, as follows:

```
brew update
brew cask install java
brew install gradle
```

That completes the environment setup. Next, we will package our product API application as a Service Fabric application to enable deployment in the cluster.

Packaging the product API application

We log into the product API project (full code available at: https://github.com/ PacktPublishing/Cloud-Native-Applications-in-Java) and run the following command:

```
yo azuresfguest
```

We should get the following screen:

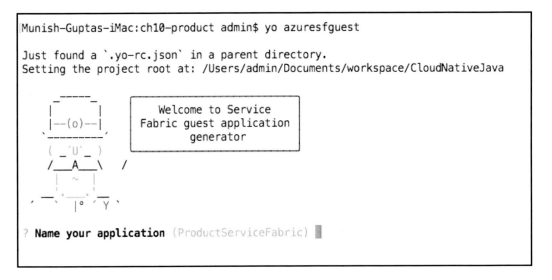

We enter the following values:

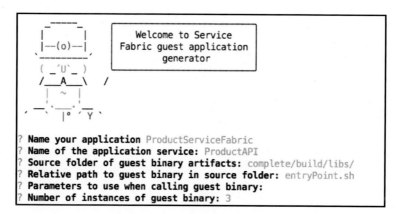

```
              Welcome to Service
 |--(o)--|    Fabric guest application
               generator
 ( _'U`_ )
 /__A__\  /
 |  ~  |
   | o ` Y `

? Name your application ProductServiceFabric
? Name of the application service: ProductAPI
? Source folder of guest binary artifacts: complete/build/libs/
? Relative path to guest binary in source folder: entryPoint.sh
? Parameters to use when calling guest binary:
? Number of instances of guest binary: 3
```

This will create an application package with a set of files:

```
ProductServiceFabric/ProductServiceFabric/ApplicationManifest.xml
ProductServiceFabric/ProductServiceFabric/ProductAPIPkg/ServiceManifest.xml
ProductServiceFabric/ProductServiceFabric/ProductAPIPkg/config/Settings.xml
ProductServiceFabric/install.sh
ProductServiceFabric/uninstall.sh
```

Next, we go to the /ProductServiceFabric/ProductServiceFabric/ProductAPIPkg folder.

Create a directory code and in it, create a file called entryPoint.sh with the following content:

```
#!/bin/bash
BASEDIR=$(dirname $0)
cd $BASEDIR
java -jar product-0.0.1-SNAPSHOT.jar
```

Also, make sure we copy our packaged JAR (product-0.0.1-SNAPSHOT.jar) in this folder.

The value of Number of instances of guest binary should be 1 for local environment developments and can be a higher number for Service Fabric clusters in the cloud.

Next, we will host our application in the Service Fabric cluster. We will make use of the Service Fabric party cluster.

Starting the Service Fabric cluster

We will log into `http://try.servicefabric.azure.com` using our Facebook or GitHub ID:

Join a Linux cluster:

We will be directed to the page with the cluster details. The cluster is available for one hour.

By default, there are certain ports that are open. When we deploy our `product` API application, we can access the same on port `8080`:

> # Your secure Service Fabric cluster is ready!
>
> **ReadMe:** How to connect to a secure Party cluster?
>
> **Certificate required to connect:**
> PFX
>
> **Service Fabric Explorer**
> https://zlnxyngsvzoe.westus.cloudapp.azure.com:19080/Explorer/index.html
>
> **Connection endpoint**
> zlnxyngsvzoe.westus.cloudapp.azure.com:19000
>
> **Expires on:**
> January 27 at 6:50:54 UTC
>
> **Time remaining**
> 0 hours, 59 minutes, and 59 seconds
>
> **Available ports**
> 80, 8081, 8080, 20000, 20001, 20002, 20003, 20004, 20005

The Service Fabric cluster explorer is available at the previously mentioned URL. Since the cluster uses certificate-based authentication, you will need to import the PFX file to your keychain.

If you visit the URL, you can see the Service Fabric cluster explorer. The cluster, by default, comes up with three nodes. You can deploy multiple applications to the cluster. Based on the application settings, the cluster will manage your application availability.

Azure Party Cluster default view

Deploying the product API application to the Service Fabric cluster

For deploying our application to the cluster, we need to log into the ProductServiceFabric folder for the Service Fabric scaffolding created for the application.

Connecting to the local cluster

We can connect to the local cluster here by using the following command:

```
sfctl cluster select --endpoint http://localhost:19080
```

This will connect with the Service Fabric cluster running within the Docker container.

Connecting to the Service Fabric party cluster

Since the Service Fabric party cluster uses certificate-based authentication, we need to download the PFX file in our working folder in /ProductServiceFabric.

Run the following commands:

```
openssl pkcs12 -in party-cluster-1496019028-client-cert.pfx -out party-cluster-1496019028-client-cert.pem -nodes -passin pass:
```

Next, we make use of the **Privacy Enhanced Mail** (**PEM**) file to connect to the Service Fabric party cluster:

```
sfctl cluster select --endpoint
https://zlnxyngsvzoe.westus.cloudapp.azure.com:19080 --pem ./party-cluster-1496019028-client-cert.pem --no-verify
```

Once we are connected to the Service Fabric cluster, we need to install our application by running the following command:

```
./install.sh
```

We should see our application getting uploaded and deployed in the cluster:

Install and start the Service Fabric Cluster within Docker container

Once the application is uploaded, we can see the application in the Service Fabric explorer and the functionality of the application can be accessed:

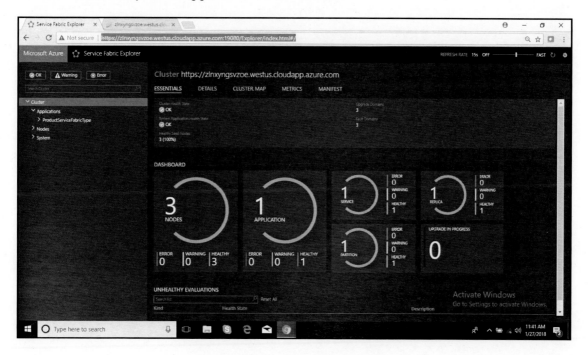

Observe the application deployed in the Azure Party Cluster

The API functionality is available
at: `http://zlnxyngsvzoe.westus.cloudapp.azure.com:8080/product/2`.

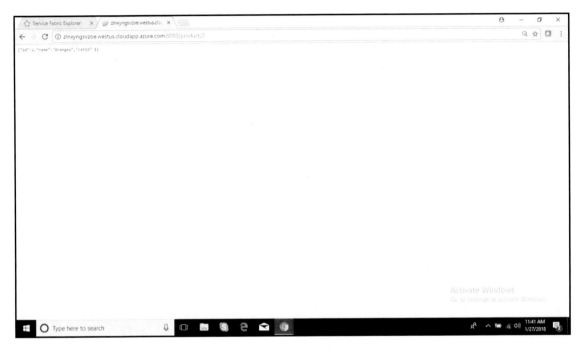

Verify if the API is working

We can see how the application is deployed on one node (_lnxvm_2) currently. If we bring down that node, the application instance is automatically deployed on another node instance:

Observe the application deployed on single node out of the available three hosts

Bring down the node (_lnxvm_2) by selecting the option in the node menu (highlighted in the following screenshot):

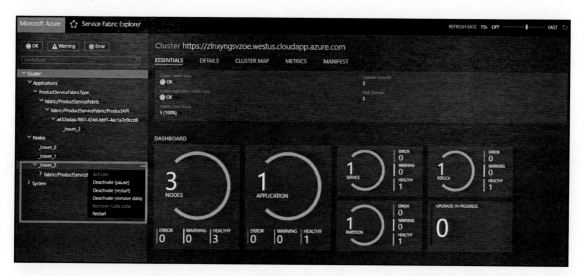

Observe the options available to disable application on the host in the Azure Party Cluster

Immediately, we can see the application getting deployed on node `_lnxvm_0` as a self-healing model of the **Cluster**:

Application getting disabled on one mode is brought up on another node with Service Fabric Cluster

Again, I hope the reader is intrigued enough to go ahead and explore the capabilities of the cluster. The support for Java applications and multiple versions of Linux is limited. Azure is working toward adding additional support to the platform to support all kinds of applications.

Azure cloud functions

As we move applications to the cloud, we are using platform services to improve our focus on business functionality, and not worrying about application scalability. Serverless applications are the next frontier. The developer focus is on building applications, without worrying about server provisioning, availability, and scalability.

Java functions are currently in beta and are not available on the Azure portal.

We can download and try to create Java functions on our local machines. We will see a brief preview of the functionality.

Environment setup

The Azure Functions Core Tools SDK provides a local development environment for writing, running, and debugging your Java Azure Functions:

```
npm install -g azure-functions-core-tools@core
```

Creating a new Java functions project

Let's create a sample Java functions project. We will make use of the following Maven archetype to generate the dummy project structure:

```
mvn archetype:generate -DarchetypeGroupId=com.microsoft.azure -
DarchetypeArtifactId=azure-functions-archetype
```

We run the mvn command to provide the requisite inputs:

```
Define value for property 'groupId': : com.mycompany.product
Define value for property 'artifactId': : mycompany-product
Define value for property 'version':  1.0-SNAPSHOT: :
Define value for property 'package':  com.mycompany.product: :
Define value for property 'appName':  ${artifactId.toLowerCase()}-
${package.getClass().forName("java.time.LocalDateTime").getMethod("now").in
voke(null).format($package.Class.forName("java.time.format.DateTimeFormatte
r").getMethod("ofPattern", $package.Class).invoke(null,
"yyyyMMddHHmmssSSS"))}: : productAPI
Define value for property 'appRegion':
${package.getClass().forName("java.lang.StringBuilder").getConstructor($pac
kage.getClass().forName("java.lang.String")).newInstance("westus").toString
()}: : westus
Confirm properties configuration:
groupId: com.mycompany.product
artifactId: mycompany-product
version: 1.0-SNAPSHOT
package: com.mycompany.product
appName: productAPI
appRegion: westus
 Y: : y
```

Building and running the Java function

Let's go ahead and build the package:

```
mvn clean package
```

Next, we can run the function as follows:

```
mvn azure-functions:run
```

We can see the function getting started in the following image:

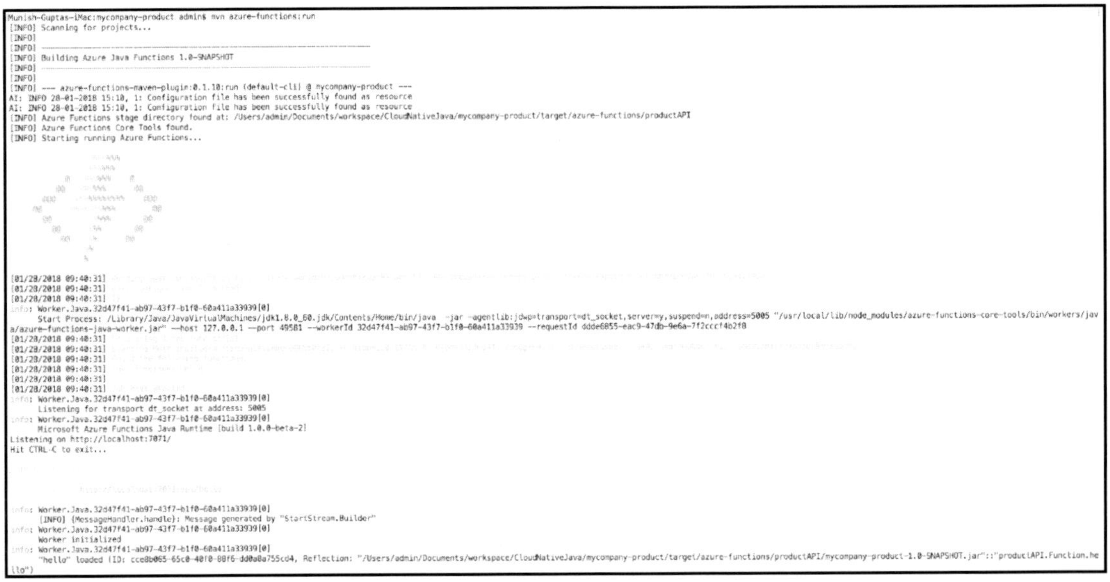

Building your Java cloud function

The default function is available at the following URL:

```
http://localhost:7071/api/hello
```

If we go to `http://localhost:7071/api/hello?name=cloudnative` we can see the output from the function:

Diving into code

If we delve into the code, we can see the main code file where the default function `hello` is defined:

```java
package productAPI;

import java.util.*;

/**
 * Azure Functions with HTTP Trigger.
 */
public class Function {

    @FunctionName("hello")
    public HttpResponseMessage<String> hello(
            @HttpTrigger(name = "req", methods = { "get",
                    "post" }, authLevel = AuthorizationLevel.ANONYMOUS) HttpRequestMessage<Optional<String>> request,
            final ExecutionContext context) {
        context.getLogger().info("Java HTTP trigger processed a request.");

        // Parse query parameter
        String query = request.getQueryParameters().get("name");
        String name = request.getBody().orElse(query);

        if (name == null) {
            return request.createResponse(400, "Please pass a name on the query string or in the request body");
        } else {
            return request.createResponse(200, "Hello, " + name);
        }
    }
}
```

The method is annotated with `@HttpTrigger`, where we have defined the name of the trigger, methods allowed, authorization model used, and so on.

When the function is compiled, it results in a `function.json` where the function bindings are defined:

```
{
  "scriptFile" : "../mycompany-product-1.0-SNAPSHOT.jar",
  "entryPoint" : "productAPI.Function.hello",
  "bindings" : [ {
    "type" : "httpTrigger",
    "name" : "req",
    "direction" : "in",
    "authLevel" : "anonymous",
    "methods" : [ "get", "post" ]
  }, {
    "type" : "http",
    "name" : "$return",
    "direction" : "out"
  } ],
  "disabled" : false
}
```

You can see both input and output data bindings. Functions have exactly one trigger. Triggers are fired with some associated data, which is usually the payload that triggers the function.

Input and output bindings are a declarative way to connect to data from within your code. Bindings are optional and a function can have multiple input and output bindings.

You can develop functions by using the Azure portal. Triggers and bindings are directly configured in a `function.json` file.

Java functions are still a preview feature. The feature set is still under beta and documentation is scant. We will need to wait for Java to become a first-class citizen in the world of Azure Functions.

That brings us to the end of platform development using Azure.

Summary

In this chapter, we saw the various features and services provided by the Azure cloud platform. As we take our applications into a cloud-native model, we move from App Service | Container Service | Service Fabric | serverless model (Cloud Functions). When we build greenfield applications, we skip the initial steps and directly adopt platform services, allowing automatic application scalability and availability management.

In the next chapter, we will cover the various types of XaaS APIs, which includes IaaS, PaaS, iPaaS, and DBaaS. We will cover the architecture and design concerns when building your own XaaS.

10
As a Service Integration

This chapter discusses various types of **Anything as a Service (XaaS)**, which includes **Infrastructure as a Service (IaaS)**, **Platform as a Service (PaaS)**, **Integration Platform as a Service (iPaaS)**, and **Database as a service (DBaaS)**, and everything you need to factor in when exposing infrastructure or platform elements as services. In cloud-native mode, your application might be integrating with social media APIs or PaaS APIs, or you could be hosting services that will be used by other applications. This chapter covers the concerns you need to deal with when building your own XaaS model.

This chapter will cover the following topics:

- Architecture and design concerns when building your own XaaS
- Architecture and design concerns when building your mobile application
- Various backend as a service providers—database, authorization, cloud storage, analytics, and so on

XaaS

Cloud computing has pioneered the distribution model for elastic, pay-as-you-go, on-demand IT hosted services. Any part of the IT delivered as a service is loosely covered under the broad theme of cloud computing.

Within the cloud computing theme, depending on the type of IT service, there are various terms for specific services of the cloud. Most of the terms are different variations of the term XaaS, where X is a placeholder that can be changed to represent multiple things.

Let's see the most common delivery models for cloud computing:

- **IaaS**: When the computing resources (compute, network, and storage) are provided as a service to deploy and run operating systems and applications, it is termed as IaaS. If the organization does not want to invest in building data centers and buying servers and storage, this is a right choice of service to take advantage of. **Amazon Web Services** (**AWS**), Azure, and **Google Cloud Platform** (**GCP**) are leading examples of IaaS providers. In this model, you are responsible for the following:
  - Managing, patching, and upgrading all operating systems, applications, and related tools, database systems, and so on.
  - From a cost optimization perspective, you will be responsible for the bringing the environment up and down.
  - Provisioning of compute resources is almost instantaneous. The elasticity of the compute resources is one of the biggest selling factors for IaaS vendors.
  - Typically, the server images can be backed up by the cloud provider, so backup and restore is easily managed when using a cloud provider.

- **PaaS**: Once the compute, network, and storage have been sorted out, next comes the requirement for a development platform and related environment to build applications. A PaaS platform provides services across the **software development life cycle** (**SDLC**). Services such as runtime (such as Java and .NET), database (MySQL and Oracle), and web servers (such as Tomcat and Apache web server) are considered to be PaaS services. The notion is that the cloud computing vendor will still manage the underlying operational aspects of runtime, middleware, OS, virtualization, servers, storage, and networking. In this model, you will be responsible for the following:
  - The developer's concern will be limited to managing applications and the associated data. Any change/updates to the application need to be managed by you.
  - Abstraction of the PaaS is at a high level (messaging, Lambda, container, and so on), allowing the team to focus on the core competency of working for customer needs.

- **SaaS**: Next comes the model where you rent the entire application. You are not required to build, deploy, or maintain anything. You subscribe to the application, and the provider will provide an instance of the application for you or your organization for use. You can access the application over the browser or can integrate with the public APIs provided by the provider. Services such as Gmail, Office 365, and Salesforce are examples of SaaS services. In this model, the provider provides a standard version of the feature/functionality for all the tenants with very limited customization capabilities. The SaaS vendor might provide a security model where you can integrate your **Lightweight Directory Access Protocol (LDAP)** repository with the vendor using **Security Assertion Markup Language (SAML)** or OAuth models. This model works very well for standard software where the need for customization is low. Office365 and Salesforce are some of the biggest poster children of SaaS vendors:

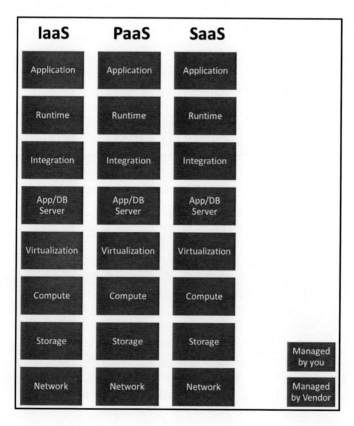

When you are building your organization and its application portfolio, you might subscribe to different vendors for various types of services. Now, if you are trying to build the next Facebook or Instagram or Uber, you will need to address specific architecture concerns to tackle the varied needs of the billions of users out there.

Key design concerns when building XaaS

Let's review the key design concerns that need to be addressed when building XaaS and providing those services for consumption:

- **Multi-tenancy**: When you start designing your service for public consumption, one of the first requirements is the ability to support multiple tenants or customers. As people start signing up to use your service, the service needs to support be able to provide a secure boundary for customer data. Typically, SaaS is a good candidate for the multi-tenancy design concerns. For every tenant, the data and application workload might need to be partitioned. Tenant requests are within the confines of the tenant data. To design multi-tenancy within your application, you will need to look at the following:

    - **Isolation**: Data should be isolated between the tenants. One tenant should not be able to access any other tenant's data. This isolation is not only restricted to the data, but can be extended to underlying resources (including compute, storage, network, and so on) and operational processes (backup, restore, DevOps, admin functionality, application properties, and so on) marked for each tenant.

    - **Cost optimization**: The next big concern is how to optimize the design to lower the overall cost of the cloud resources and still address all kinds of customers. You can look at multiple techniques to manage your costs. For example, for free-tier customers, you can have a tenancy model based on the tenant ID. This model allows you to optimize the database licenses, overall compute and storage costs, DevOps processes, and so on. Similarly, for large customers, you can even look at dedicated infrastructure to provide a guaranteed **service-level agreement (SLA)**. There are a number of small companies that do millions worth of business from a handful of large customers. On the other hand, you have large companies that cater to millions of small customers.

- **DevOps pipeline**: If you end up building multiple instances of the same service for customers, you will encounter problems when customers demand specific features for them. This soon leads to code fragmentation and becomes an unmanageable code problem. The question becomes how to balance the ability to roll out new features/functionality for all customers and still able to provide the level of customization or individuality required by each of them. The DevOps process needs to support multi-tenancy isolation and maintain/monitor each tenant process and database schema to roll out the changes across all the service instances. Unless DevOps is streamlined, rolling out changes across the service can become very complex and daunting. This all leads to increased cost and lower customer satisfaction.

- **Scalability**: One of the basic requirements is to be able to sign up new customers and scale up the services. As the scale of customers grows, the expectation is cost/service or overall service cost should fall. Unless our service is built keeping in mind the preceding three types of tenants, the service will not be able to scale and provide an artificial moat around your business model.

Next, when you get down to the task of designing your multi-tenancy service, you have the following design options:

- **Database per tenant**: Every tenant has its own database. This model provides complete isolation to tenant data.
- **Shared database (single)**: All tenants are hosted within a single database and identified by a tenant ID.

- **Shared database (sharded)**: In this model, a single database is sharded into multiple databases. Typically, the shard key is derived from hash, range, or list partitioning. The tenants are spread across the shard and are accessible by a combination of tenant ID and shard:

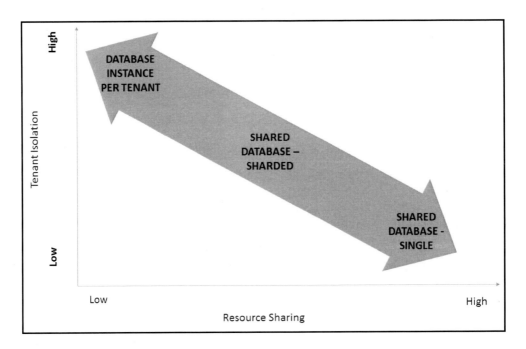

- **Faster provisioning**: When building an XaaS model, another key concern is the ability to provision new customers, meaning customer onboarding should be self-service. Upon signing up, the customer should be immediately able to start making use of the service. All this requires a model where a new tenant can be provisioned effortlessly and very quickly. The ability to provide the underlying compute resources, any database schema creation, and/or specific DevOps pipelines should be very efficient and fully automated. From a customer experience point of view also, the ability to provide a running version of the application to the user helps. For any service that is aiming to be mass market, faster provisioning is given. But if you are providing a very specific service and that requires integration with enterprise customer on-premises data centers, then it may not be possible to provide split-second provisioning. In that case, we should build tools/scripts that can address some of the common integration scenarios to onboard the customer as soon as possible.

- **Auditing**: Another key concern around security is the ability to audit for the access and changes to the service and underlying data store. All of the audit trail needs to be stored for any breaches or security issues or compliance purposes. There will be the requirement for a centralized audit repository that keeps track of the events being generated across the system. You should be able to run analysis on top of the audit repository to flag up any abnormal behavior and take preventive or corrective actions:

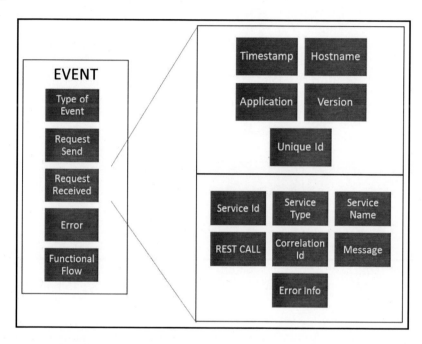

  You can make use of Lamda architecture that uses both real-time streaming coupled with models generated from historical data to flag abnormal behavior. Some of the public cloud providers provide this as a service.

- **Security**: Depending on the nature of the service, the tenants need to have secure access to their data. The service needs to incorporate the basic requirement of authentication and authorization. All the customers have a secure key and passphrase to connect and access their information. There might be requirements for enterprise access and multiple users. In that case, you might have to build a delegated administration model for enterprise(s). You can also use a security mechanism such as OAuth (through Google, Facebook, and so on) to enable access to the service.

- **Data storage**: Your service might require storage of different types of data; depending on the type of the data, the storage requirements will be different. The storage requirement typically falls into the following areas:

    - **Relational data storage**: Tenant data might be relational and we talked of the various multi-tenant strategies to store that data. Tenant-specific application configuration data might need to be stored in a relational model.

    - **NoSQL storage**: Tenant data might not be relational all the time; it might be a columnar, key value, graph, or document-oriented model. In that case, appropriate data storage needs to be designed and then constructed.

    - **Blob storage**: If your service requires Blob storage or storage of binary data, then you will require access to object file storage. You can make use of Blob storage from the likes of AWS or Azure to store your binary files:

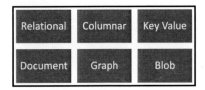

- **Monitoring**: The entire application stack needs to be monitored. You might sign up customers and guarantee them stringent SLAs. In that scenario, monitoring is not just about service or system availability but also about any cost penalty and loss of reputation. At times, individual components might have redundancy and high availability but at a stack level, all the failure rates can be compounded to reduce the overall availability of the stack. Monitoring resources across the stack becomes important and key to managing the availability and defined SLAs. Monitoring encompasses both hardware and software. There is a need to detect any abnormal behavior and automate the corrective response. Typically, the ability to monitor and automate the healing takes multiple iterations to mature.

- **Error handling**: One of the key aspects of the service will be the ability to handle failures and how to respond to the service consumer. Failures can occur at multiple levels; a data store not being available, tables getting locked, queries getting timed out, service instances going down, session data being lost, and so on are some of the issues you will encounter. Your service needs to be robust to handle all these and then some more failure scenarios. Patterns such as CQRS, circuit breaker, bulkheading, reactive, and so on will need to be incorporated into your service design.

- **Automated build/deployment**: As the number of service consumers goes up, the ability to roll out new features and fix bugs will require an automated build and deployment models. This is akin to changing the tires of a car while it is moving. The ability to upgrade the software and release patches / security fixes without any impact on the calls from the consumer is a delicate art and takes time to master. Earlier, we could look for some system downtime during the night when the traffic comes down, but with customers from around the world, there is no longer such a time. Blue-green deployment is a technique that can help in releasing new changes with minimum impact to the customers and reduction of overall risk:

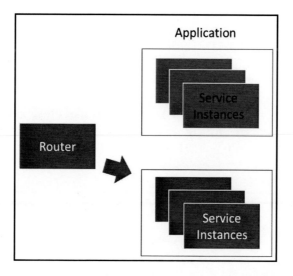

- **Customer tiers**: Another key concern is how to build and price your service for different sets of customers. Companies have been creating multiple tiers to address the needs of myriad customers. These needs help the companies decide the customer tier and then start pricing the service cost. These factors are as follows:
  - **Compute**: Limiting the number of calls made by hour/day/month. This allows you to predict the capacity required by the tenant along with the networking bandwidth requirements.
  - **Storage**: Another parameter is the storage required for the underlying data store. This allows you to balance database shards appropriately.

- **Security**: For enterprise customers, there might be separate requirements for integration with enterprise security models using SAML. This might require additional hardware and support.
- **SLAs/support model**: This is another area which needs to be accounted for when deciding the customer tiers. Support models—community, on-call, dedicated, and so on—come with different cost structures. Depending on the target market—consumer or enterprise—you can evaluate which of the support models will work best for your service.

- **Feature flags**: When building an XaaS model, one of the key questions is how to deal with code changes, feature releases, and so on for multiple tenants. Should I have multiple code branches for each customer or should I use one code base across all the customers? If I use one code base, how do I release features/functionality that are specific to one tenant? If your target market is 8-10 customers, then having specific code branches for each customer is a potential viable option. But if the target market is hundreds of customers, then code branching is a bad option. Code branching is usually a bad idea. To handle differences in features/functionality for different customers or manage new upcoming features not ready for release, a feature flag is a great way to handle such requirements:

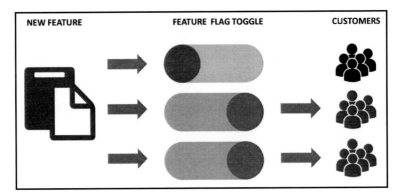

Feature flags allow you to release code in production without immediately releasing the feature for the users. You can use feature flags to provide/restrict certain functionalities of your application to different customers based on what level of services they have bought. You can also use feature flags in conjunction with A/B testing to release new features/functionality to a part of user to check their response and functional correctness before rolling out to the wider audience.

- **Self-service portal**: A key aspect of your service will be a self-service portal where the users can sign up, provision the service, and manage all aspects of the application data and service. The portal allows users to manage enterprise aspects such as authentication/authorization (using a delegated admin model), monitor the provisioned service for availability, set up custom alarms/alerts on the key metrics of the service, and decipher any issues that might be cropping on the server side. A well-crafted portal helps increase overall customer confidence in the service performance. You can also build advanced monitoring and analytics services for your paid customers based on the customer tiers. Remember, anybody can copy the features/functionality your service provides, but building additional value-added features around your service becomes a distinct differentiator for your service.

- **Software development kits (SDKs)**: As one of the key measures of enabling user adoptability of your service, you might want to build and provide SDKs for your consumers. This is not a must-have, but a desirable feature, especially when a customer integrates with your service at an application code level on their side. In this case, SDKs should provide support for multiple languages and come with good examples and documentation to help onboard the developers on the customer side. If your application or service is complex, having an SDK that explains how to invoke your services or integrate within existing services (such as SAML, OAuth, and so on) becomes key to faster adoptability of your service.

- **Documentation and community support**: One more aspect of service adoptability is the level of documentation available along with community support for the product/service. Documentation should minimally cover the following points:
    - How to sign up for the service
    - How to invoke and use the service
    - How to integrate the service within the customer landscape and the SDKs available for integration
    - How to bulk import or bulk export your data
    - How to securely integrate for authentication/authorization with enterprise LDAP / **Active Directory (AD)** servers

The next thing you need to think of is building an active community support. You need to provide appropriate forums for people to interact. You need to have active **subject matter expert** (**SME**) to answer questions from people across forums (internal and external). The likes of Stack Overflow get lots of questions; you should set up alerts, monitor threads, and help answer questions/queries from users. An active community is a sign of interest in your product. Lots of organizations also use this forum to identify early adopters and seek their feedback in the product roadmap.

- **Product roadmap**: A good product might start with a **minimum viable product** (**MVP**) but it usually backed a solid vision and product roadmap. As you receive feedback from the customer, you can keep on updating the product roadmap and reprioritizing the backlog items. A good roadmap indicates the strength of the product vision. When you meet external stakeholders—customers, partners, **venture capitalists** (**VCs**), and so on—the first thing they ask for is a product roadmap.

  A roadmap typically consists of strategic priorities and planned releases along with high-level features and plans for maintenance/bug-fixing releases, among others:

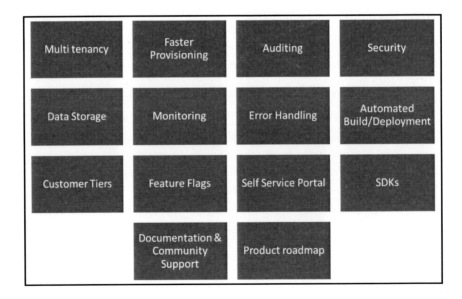

We have covered some of the design concerns that need to accounted for when trying to build your XaaS model. We have covered the basics for each of the concerns. Each of the concerns warrants a minimum of one chapter of its own. Hopefully, it gives you a view into various other non-service aspects that need to be accounted for when you are trying to build your business model around XaaS. The actual design and development of the service is based on the concerns we have covered from `Chapter 2`, *Writing Your First Cloud-Native Application*, onward.

Integration with third-party APIs

In the previous section, we saw the design concerns when building your own service provider. In this section, we will see how, if you are trying to build a consumer application, to take advantage of the REST services provided by third-party companies. For example, you are trying a build a beautiful mobile application, your core competency is building visual design and creating mobile applications. You do not want to get burdened with managing all the complexities that go with hosting/managing the application data. The application will require services that include storage, notifications, location, social integration, user management, chat functions, and analytics, among others. All these providers are bunched together under the umbrella of **Backend as a Service (BaaS)** providers. There is no need to sign up with a single vendor for these services; you can pick and choose which providers fit your business needs and budgets. Each of the providers typically runs a freemium model, that provides a certain number of API calls free per month, and a commercial model, where you are charged. This also falls under the umbrella of building serverless applications, where you, as a developer, do not maintain any servers running any software.

In this regard, we will look at the third-party services that will be required to build a full-fledged serverless application:

- **Authentication services**: One of the first things any application requires is the ability to sign up or register users. A registered user allows the opportunity for application developer to provide personalized services and know his likes/dislikes. This data allows him to optimize the user experience and provide the necessary support to get maximum value out of the application. Authentication as a service focuses on the encapsulation of business functionality around user authentication. Authentication requires an identity provider. This provider can be mapped to your application or enterprise or you can use some of the consumer companies such as Google, Facebook, Twitter, and so on. There are multiple authentication service providers available, such as Auth0, Back&, AuthRocket, and so on. These providers should provide, as a minimum, the following features:

  - **Multi-factor authentication** (**MFA**) (including support for social identity providers): One of the primary requirements, the provider should provide identity provider instance where the application can manage the users. The functionality includes user registration, two-factor authentication either by SMS or by email, and integration with social identity providers. Most of the providers make use of OAuth2/OpenID model.

  - **User management**: Along with the MFA, the authentication provider should provide user interface that allows for user management that has signed up for the application. You should be able to extract the emails and phone numbers for sending push notifications to the customers. You should be able to reset the user credentials and protect resources either by using security realms or adding users to certain predefined roles based on the needs of the application.

- **Plugins/widgets**: Last but not least, the provider should provide widgets/plugins that can be embedded in the application code to provide user authentication as a seamless service:

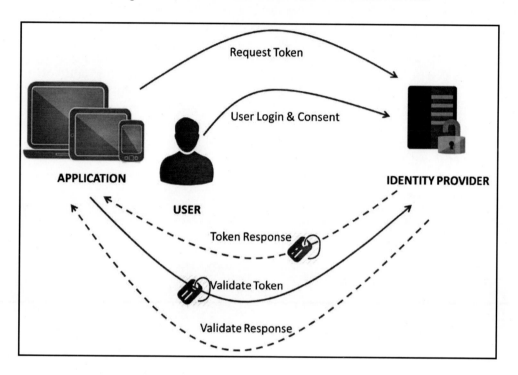

- **Serverless services**: Gone are the days when you needed to manage application servers and the underlying VM to deploy your code. The level of abstraction has moved to what is called the business function. You write a function that takes as input a request, processes the same, and outputs the response. There is no runtime, no application server, no web server, nothing. Just a function! The provider will automatically provision the runtime to run that function, along with the server. You, as developer, need not worry about anything. You are charged on a combination of the number of calls to the function and how long the functions ran, meaning, during lean times, you are incurring zero cost.
From the function, you can access the data store and manage user- and application-specific data. Two functions can talk to each other using a queue model. Functions can be exposed as APIs using the API gateway of the provider. All the public cloud vendors have a version of the serverless model—AWS has Lamda, Azure has Azure Functions, Google has Cloud Functions, Bluemix has Openwhisk, and so on:

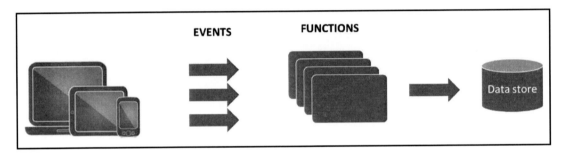

- **Database/storage services**: An application typically requires storage to manage the customer data. This can be as simple as user profile information (such as photo, name, email ID, password, and application preferences) or user-specific data (such as messages, emails, and application data). Depending on the type of data and the format in which it is stored, an appropriate database/storage service can be chosen. For binary storage, we have services such as AWS S3 and Azure Blob Storage for all kind of binary files. For storing data in JSON format directly from the mobile application, you have cloud providers such as Google Firebase, or you can use MongoDB as a service (www.mlab.com). Multiple database models are provided by AWS, Azure, and GCP that can be used to manage all kinds of different storage needs.

- You might need to use AWS Lambda or Google Cloud Functions to be able to access the store the data. For example, if the application request needs to do some validation or processing before storing the data, you can write a Lambda function, that can be exposed as an API. The mobile application accesses the API that invokes the Lambda function, where, after request processing, data gets stored in the data store.
- **Notification services**: An application typically registers the user and device to be able to send notifications to the device. AWS provides a service called Amazon **Simple Notification Service** (**SNS**) that can be used to register and send notifications from your mobile application. AWS service supports push notifications to iOS, Android, Fire OS, Windows, and Baidu-based devices. You can also send push notifications to macOS desktops and **voice over IP** (**VoIP**) applications on iOS devices, emails, and SMS messages to users across over 200 countries.
- **Analytics services**: Once customers start adopting the application, you will want to know what features of the application are being used, where the users are facing issues or challenges and where are the users dropping off. To understand all this, you will need to subscribe to an analytics service that allows you to track the user actions which are then collated to a central server. You can go to that central repository and get an insight into the user activities. You can use this insight into customer behavior to improve the overall customer experience. Google Analytics is a popular service in this area. You track users' overall multiple parameters including location, browser used, device used, time, session details, and so on. You can also enhance it by adding custom parameters. The tools typically provide a certain amount of canned reports. You can also add/design your own reporting templates.
- **Location services**: Another service used by applications is the location service. Your application might require features that require the functionality to be curated for a given context (in this case, location can be one of the context attributes). Context-aware functionality allows you to personalize the features/services to the needs of the end customer and help to improve the overall customer experience. The Google Play service location API provides such a functionality. There is a complete set of services/applications around the location services. For example, companies such as Uber, Lyft, and Ola (India) are great examples of business cases that are built around location services. Most logistics businesses (especially the last mile) make use of location services for route optimization and delivery, among other things.

- **Social integration services**: Your application might warrant social integration with popular social networks (Facebook, Twitter, Instagram, and so on). You will need to be able to access the social feeds of the logged-in user, post on their behalf, and/or get access to their social network. There are multiple ways to access these social networks. Most of these networks provide access for other applications and expose a set of APIs to connect to them. Then there are aggregators that will allow you to provide integration with a set of social networks out of the box.

- **Advertisement services**: Another key service used by applications, especially mobile applications, is to serve advertisements to the user. Based on the application model (free/paid), you need to decide the model for monetization of your application. To serve advertisements (called in-app advertising) to your users, you will need to sign up with the advertising network providers and invoke their API service. Google's AdMob service is one of the pioneers in this area.

There are numerous other service providers you may want to look at when building your application. We have covered the key prominent categories. Based on the needs of your application, you may want to search for providers in that particular area of requirement. I am sure there will be someone already providing the service. There are some comprehensive providers called BaaS. These BaaS providers typically provide multiple services for usage and reduce the overall integration effort from the application side. You do not have to deal with multiple providers; instead, you work with one. This one provider takes care of your multiple needs.

BaaS as a market segment is highly competitive. With multiple providers competing, you will find lots of mergers and acquisitions also in this segment. In recent times, the following have occurred:

- **Parse**: Acquired by Facebook. Parse provides a backend to store your data, the ability to push notifications to multiple devices, and a social layer to integrate your application.

- **GoInstant**: Acquired by Salesforce. GoInstant provides a JavaScript API for integrating real-time, multi-user experiences into any web or mobile application. It's easy to use and provides the full stack needed, from client-side widgets to publish/subscribe messaging to a real-time data store.

There are both vertical and horizontal BaaS providers that provide services or APIs around a specific domain. There are providers in the e-commerce area, gaming domain, analytics domain, and so on.

Remember to check the credibility of the provider before you sign up. Remember, if the provider folds, your application will also be in trouble. Make sure you understand their business model, their product roadmap, their funding model (especially for start-ups), and how much they listen to the customers. You want to hitch a ride with partners who will take you all the way.

Summary

In this chapter, we covered some of the key concerns when trying to build your XaaS provider. We also covered the other side of the spectrum, where we saw the typical services that are available to build an application.

In the next chapter, we will cover API best practices, where we will see how to design consumer-centric APIs that are granular and functionality-oriented. We will also discuss the best practices in API design concerns, such as how to identify the resources that will be used to form the API, how to categorize the APIs, API error handling, API versioning, and so on.

11
API Design Best Practices

This chapter discusses how to design consumer-centric APIs that are granular and functionality-oriented. It also discusses the various best practices for API design concerns, such as how to identify the resources that will be used to form the API, how to categorize the APIs, API error handling, API versioning, and so on. We will cover models for describing the API through Open API and RAML.

We will cover the following topics:

- API design concerns
- API gateway deployment

API design concerns

The APIs are meant to be consumed and define how the API can be consumed. APIs specify the list of commands/operations as well as the format/schema of those commands that are required for interaction with the API.

When defining a REST API, the key abstraction of information is the resource. A resource is defined as a conceptual mapping to a set of entities. API design is centered around the resource that forms the nucleus of the design. **Uniform Resource Identifier (URI)**, operations (using HTTP methods), and resource representations (JSON schema) are built keeping the resource in mind. It becomes very important to have the right abstraction of the resource to enable consumption, re-usability, and maintainability of the API.

The resource can point to a single entity or a collection of entities. For example, a product is a singular resource, whereas products are a collection of resources. We will cover the design guidelines at two levels:

- How to identify the right level of resource granularity
- How to design the API around the identified resource

API resource identification

The design of the API is tied to the underlying business domain model of the problem domain. The APIs need to be consumer-centric and focus on the needs of the consumer. The domain-driven design principles are applied to identify the right granularity. The bounded context pattern is the central pattern that helps in dividing the problem area into different bounded contexts and being explicit about their relationship. For an enterprise, the resource identification is also driven by the canonical models defined by the central/group architecture teams.

Furthermore, depending upon where the API is defined and what features/functionality it is exposing, APIs can be classified into three, broad categories:

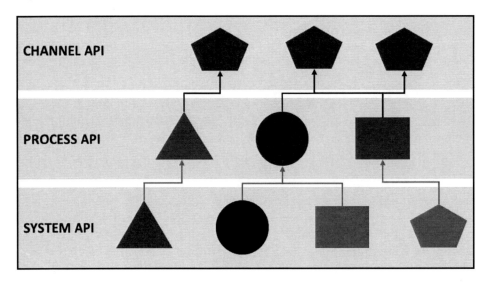

Let's discuss these categories in detail in the following sections.

System API

Key enterprise resources or systems of records need to be opened or exposed as a set of APIs for all downstream systems to build logic/experience around these services. For green field projects, system APIs typically represent the system of records or data stores that are being developed as part of the functionality. When it comes to enterprises, the system API represents all the enterprise systems, such as core **enterprise resource planning (ERP)** systems, operational data stores, mainframe applications, or many **commercial off-the-shelf (COTS)** products, such as **customer relationship management (CRM)**, and so on that run the core processes of the enterprise. Some of the distinguishing features of system APIs are as follows:

- The genesis of the domain-driven design stems from looking at the core system domains, and creating bounded contexts to define the system APIs.
- These systems of records typically map to the HTTP resource types—noun—and provide the entity services. For example, in the case of banking accounts, mortgages, securities, and cards are the core entities or nouns around which the system API is built.
- The model of bounded context defines that the services own their data stores. But in the case of existing systems, such as **enterprise resource planning (ERP)**, the services might share the same underlying system. This requires a careful study of the underlying business process, identifying the domain (aka nouns), and exposing them as system APIs. Accounts can be a system API but account transfer will be a process API that makes use of the underlying account system API to provide the service.
- System APIs are traditionally very stable and are agnostic of the change in the channel or the process API layers. These form part of the core, stable enterprise side.
- The composition and integration mechanism of this enterprise system defines how the system APIs integrate with the underlying systems. For example, a mainframe dictates the use of MQ as the integration mechanism, leaving the system API to implement MQ to expose the mainframe functionality as an API.
- The biggest issue with system APIs is their uptime and resiliency being tied to the stability of the underlying system. If the core application is going down frequently or has issues, these tend to get passed onto the system API layer.

Process API

The purists will say that the system API exposes the core functionality of the systems and the applications should mash up the functionality from system APIs to provide the requisite functionality to the end customers. This might work well for smaller applications or initial iterations of your application. As the application grows bigger, or you start to expose the functionality across multiple channels or devices, you start looking at scenarios where the functionality starts getting replicated, which means lack of reuse resulting in harder to maintain systems. Some of the distinguishing features of process APIs are as follows:

- Process APIs provide a richer functionality built on top of the system APIs. For example, instead of every channel writing an account transfer functionality, we can write the account transfer as a process API that gets reused across the channels to provide a consistent and reusable model.
- From a consumer's point of view, process APIs provide a simpler model for accessing functionality than trying to orchestrate multiple system APIs. This helps improve the ease of use from the client side and helps reduce traffic at the API gateway level.
- Process APIs can also be used to provide cross-channel/omni-channel capabilities to the application. Concerns such as channel context switchovers can be handled at this level.
- Applications tend to introduce process APIs to improve the performance of the overall systems. If the system API is tied to systems that are slow or can handle only limited throughput, a process API can be used to cache the data coming from the system API to avoid going to the underlying systems every time. In case of unavailability of a system of records and subsequently of the system API, the process API can be used to handle such requests by providing an alternate functional flow.
- Process APIs can also act as adapters to external third-party calls instead of applications making third-party calls directly. Using a process API allows us to handle scenarios where the failure of a third-party API does not impact the rest of the application. A process API can apply patterns, such as circuit breakers and throttling outgoing requests to handle multiple scenarios.

Channel API

The final API categorization is the channel API. As the name suggests, these APIs are channel-specific and mapped to the customer journeys that are being built as part of the application. These are also referred to as experience APIs or journey APIs. For example, if you are building your application using Angular or React, customer journeys that are part of the **Single-Page Applications (SPA)** need to be mapped to underlying services that can be provided by channel APIs. Some of the distinguishing features of channel APIs are as follows:

- Channel APIs are mapped to customer journeys, which are invariably tied to the channel. These are also called experience APIs at times. These APIs can be stateful since they serve customers during their journey and need to carry the session context. One can build stateless services, by externalizing the state to a session store such as Redis.

- Channel APIs will undergo change every time there is a change in the customer journey. The re-usability quotient among channel APIs is not very high. It usually ranges between 10-15%. For example, if a similar customer journey is mapped across Android and iOS applications, then there are chances of the same API getting reused.

- Channel APIs do not tend to have business logic or any service orchestration logic, as these concerns tend to be handled by the process API layer.

- Concerns such as security (CQRS, CORS), authentication, authorization, throttling, and so on are handled at the API gateway level and not passed onto the channel API layer.

- At times, during API development one might have done such a rigid differentiation and definition of APIs. But over the course of many application iterations, such differentiations start appearing in the API and one can start seeing the application moving toward these classifications.

- Next, we will cover API design guidelines that are applicable to the three classifications we saw.

API design guidelines

Once the right level of resource granularity has been identified, the rest of the API design guidelines help craft the right level of contract/interface to enable consumption, reusability, and maintainability.

The RESTful client should be able to discover all the available actions and resources required by accessing the URI path. The client should be able to handle the following:

- **Request**: Handle the inbound processing message that is sent to the server side
- **Response**: Encapsulated information provided by the server
- **Path**: Unique identifier of the resource being requested
- **Parameters**: Elements added to the request as key/value pairs to specify operations such as filter, subset, and so on to the request

As we begin designing the API, we are sharing some of the best practices that we have encountered over the years.

Naming and associations

The resource names are typically referring to the nouns extracted from the business domain. Once the nouns are identified, API contracts can be modeled as HTTP verbs against these nouns:

- The selection of the resource needs to account for the fine-grained versus coarse-grained model. Too fine-grained means too much chattiness, and coarse-grained means to narrow the focus resulting in support for variations. One can reason that by using the system versus the process API model to an extent. But the issue becomes, if the resources are too fine-grained, the number of system APIs rises leading to unmaintainable complexity.
- APIs are designed by looking at the needs of the consumer. Derive your API needs based on the customer journeys and how they will map to the underlying data store. This means, look at the API design using the top design approach. Using the bottom model of doing data modeling first, might not yield the right balance. In case you have existing enterprise assets, you will need to perform a meet-in-the-middle kind of approach, where you need to balance the needs of the customers by writing process APIs that help bridge the gap.

Base URLs for a resource

This depends on how you treat the resource—as a singleton or as a collection. So ideally, you will end up with two base URLs for one resource, one for the collection and a second for the entity. For example:

Resource	POST (Create)	GET (Read)	PUT (Update)	DELETE (Delete)
`/orders`	Create new order	Order list	Replace with a new order	Error (do not want to delete all orders)
`/orders/1234`	error	Show the order with ID: `1234`	If it exists update the order; if it does not, create a new order	Delete the order with ID: `1234`

Handling errors

Make use of the standard HTTP status code to indicate the problem/error:

- If using JSON, the error should be a top-level property
- With errors—be descriptive, correct, and informative

A sample error message is as shown in the following snippet:

```
{
    "type": "error",
    "status":400,
    "code": "bad_request",
    "context_info": {
        "errors": [
            {
                "reason": "missing_argument",
                "message": "order_id is required",
                "name": "order_id",
                "location": "query_param"
            }
        ]
    },
    "help_url": "http://developers.some.com/api/docs/#error_code",
    "message": "Bad Request"
    "request_id": "823323298092341249493"
}
```

Some examples of HTTP code usage are as follows:

- 400 Bad Request
- 401 Unauthorized
- 403 Forbidden
- 404 Not Found
- 409 Conflict
- 429 Too Many Requests
- 5xx API is faulty

Versioning

There are multiple models for service versioning:

- **URL**: You simply add the API version into the URL, for example: `https://getOrder/order/v2.0/sobjects/Account`. Used frequently, but not good practice.

- **Accept header**: You modify the accept header to specify the version, for example: `Accept: application/vnd.getOrders.v2+json`. Rarely used and cumbersome for the client.

- **Schema level**: Enforce the validation using schema, difficult to enforce with JSON, and works well with XML. Good practice/rare.

- **API facade layer**: Use the facade layer to hide the version complexity from the client.

Remember, a resource is a semantic model; a resource's representational form and state may change over time but the identifier must consistently address the same resource. Hence, new URIs should only be used when there is an underlying change in concept. The API facade layer can abstract the Northbound API from underlying service and schema versions. API management platforms support creating the API facade layer.

Pagination

Use the URL with the pagination information to handle results offset and limits. For example, `/orders?limit=25&offset=50`.

Attributes

The API should support provisioning of data attributes asked by the consumer using the query parameter model. For example, `/orders?fields=id,orderDate,total`.

Data formats

The API should provide support for multiple data formats based on what the consumer asks for. For example, `/orders/1234.json` returns data in JSON format.

Client support for limited HTTP methods

Depending upon the device and its limited capability to support HTTP verbs, you may want to provide support for HTTP methods using the following:

- **Create**: `/orders?method=post`
- **Read**: `/orders`
- **Update**: `/orders/1234?method=put&location=park`
- **Delete** `/orders/1234?method=delete`

Authentication and authorization

REST services use a role-based membership for each exposed method when appropriate and provide the ability to independently enable GET, POST, PUT, and DELETE based on any number of specific roles.

Typically, this concern should be handled at the API gateway level. You should not be handling this as part of the service.

Endpoint redirection

Service inventories may change over time for business or technical reasons. It may not be possible to replace all references to old endpoints simultaneously.

By adopting this design practice, consumers of a service endpoint adapt when service inventories are restructured. It automatically refers service consumers that access the stale endpoint identifier to the current identifier:

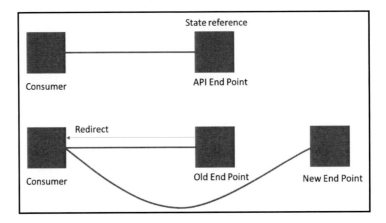

HTTP natively supports the endpoint redirection pattern using a combination of 3xx status codes and standard headers:

- 301 moved permanently
- 307 temporary redirect
- location/newURI

Content negotiation

Service consumers may change their requirements in a way that is not backward compatible. A service may have to support both old and new consumers without having to introduce a specific capability for each kind of consumer.

A service can specify specific content and data representation formats to be accepted or returned by a service capability negotiated at runtime as part of its invocation. The service contract refers to multiple standardized media types.

Secure

Always use SSL for your securing the URIs. SSL ensures guaranteed encrypted communications, which in turn simplifies authentication efforts—one need not sign each API request.

This covers some of the best practices that go with the API design. One can learn from how Google, Facebook, and Amazon are defining their public APIs and use those as the basis for your API design.

API modeling

There are two standards that are competing to describe the APIs—Open APIs and RESTful APIs. We will discuss them more in the following sections.

Open API

The Open API initiative is focused on creating and promoting a vendor-neutral API description format based on the Swagger specification. The Open API specification allows us to define a standard, language-agnostic interface for REST APIs, which allows both humans and computers to discover and understand the capabilities of the service without access to source code.

In the following figures, we have described a sample API definition based on Open API along with the various sections:

Code continues in the following image:

Definition of resources and methods with details wrt method calls like
- tag to identify the method
- description for the methods
- Operation name the method maps to
- Out put types
- Parameters definition along with description and type (array, string, integer etc)
- Expected response types
  - 200 along with expected output
  - 400 along with expected output
- Security policy applicable to these methods

```
paths:
  /playlist:
    get:
      tags:
        - playlist
      summary: get playlist by listening mood
      description: Multiple mood values can be provided with comma separated strings
      operationId: findPlaylistByMood
      produces:
        - application/xml
        - application/json
      parameters:
        - name: mood
          in: query
          description: Mood values that need to be considered for filter
          required: true
          type: array
          items:
            type: string
            enum:
              - heartbroken
              - sad
              - ecstatic
            default: available
          collectionFormat: multi
      responses:
        '200':
          description: successful operation
          schema:
            type: array
            items:
              $ref: '#/definitions/Playlist'
        '400':
          description: Invalid mood value
      security:
        - spotifystore_auth:
            - 'write:playlist'
            - 'read:playlist'
```

Code continues in the following image:

```
securityDefinitions:
  musicstore_auth:
    type: oauth2
    authorizationUrl: 'http://musicstore.swagger.io/oauth/dialog'
    flow: implicit
    scopes:
      'write:playlist': modify playlist in your account
      'read:playlist': read your playlist by mood
  api_key:
    type: apiKey
    name: api_key
    in: header
definitions:
  Playlist:
    type: object
    properties:
      id:
        type: integer
        format: int64
      playlistid:
        type: integer
        format: int64
      mood:
        type: array
        items:
          type: string
    xml:
      name: Playlist
externalDocs:
  description: Find out more about Swagger
  url: 'http://swagger.io'
```

Defines the security policy that
need is applicable to the API along
with the authorization model

Define the object structure that
are applicable for post and get
methods when using the API

RESTful API Modeling Language (RAML)

RESTful API Modeling Language (**RAML**) is a standard language to describe the RESTful
APIs. RAML is written in the same way as YAML, which is a human-readable data
serialization language. The goal of RAML is to provide all the necessary information
required to describe API. RAML provides a machine-readable API design that can be read
by various API management tools.

In the following figure, we have described a sample RAML along with the various sections:

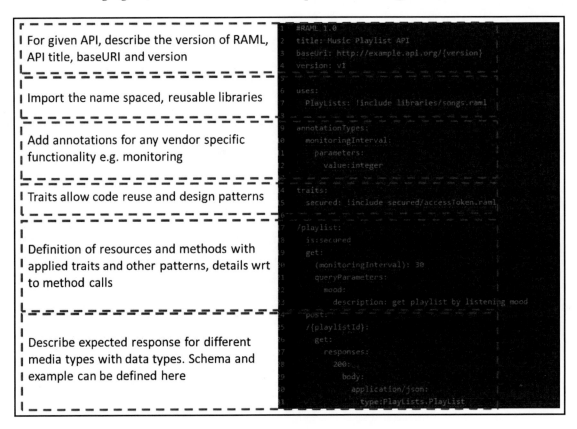

RAML maps to the full API design life, which can be categorized as follows:

Let's have a look at the flow:

1. **Design**: API vendors provide editors as part of the API development suite to help design/write the API/RAML definition, resulting in faster development and fewer errors. The generated RAML can be augmented with mock data and allows iterations with respect to design with the business owners/consumers for validation and correctness.

2. **Build**: The generated RAML provides the specifications for the build of the API. The development suites can generate stubs based on the RAML for plugging in the logic.

3. **Test**: RAML can be used to generate test scripts. Tools such as Postman and Abao allow RAML specifications to be imported and tests generated that are used to validate the API. In addition, tools such as API Fortress and SmartBear, can also test for response latency, payloads, and errors.

4. **Document**: The RAML specification can be converted into an HTML-based model. Tools such as RAML2HTML for PHP, API Console, and so on provide an easy way to expose the documentation specified as part of the RAML. This model allows any changes in the specification to be reflected in the documentation and keep them in sync.

5. **Integrate**: The last stage of the API lifecycle is the ability to integrate or consume the API. Usage of RAML allows vendors/tools to create multiple ways to integrate and consumer the API. Using RAML, API-specific SDKs can be built. Vendors also provide tools that can make use of RAML to integrate with client-side logic.

The choice between the two standards depends upon the API gateway product stack chosen by the organization. Most of the products have a preference of one standard over the other although every product claims to provide support for both standards.

API gateway deployment models

The API gateway provides a facade pattern that encapsulates the inner workings of the system providing a single point of entry for all incoming clients. An API gateway can provide an API tailored for each type of client, all the while addressing concerns such as security, authentication, authorization, throttling, load balancing, and so on.

Let's look at the factors that impact how the APIs are deployed on the API gateway.

- **Type of client or channel**: Depending upon the device or channel from where the request originates, the API might need to serve different subsets of data. For example, the desktop version of the service might be asking for more details as compared to the mobile client. There can be a difference in data even between phone and tablet. How do we make sure that the same microservice can service all device type requests and still handle these variations? In this case, we create multiple APIs for different device types that meet the specific needs of the client without the microservice being bothered.
- **Data transformation**: At times, the service on the backend is built to service JSON content. A requirement originates asking for an XML response or vice versa. In this case, the API gateway exposes an API that provides the XML as a response while doing the data transformation at the gateway level, allowing the service to work without any changes or knowledge of the client's needs.
- **Versioning**: For public APIs or APIs tied to a resource where versioning has not been added to the URI, an API gateway can route the incoming requests based on the client and the version used to the correct service. In this case, the API gateway can decipher the service version by using multiple techniques:
    - Client identifiers can be used to identify whether they have moved to a new version or are using an older version.
    - Clients can be segregated into multiple categories based on SLAs. When the new version is released, the lowermost category, or low usage clients, can be asked to move to a new version. As clients upgrade, the API gateway can redirect them to the right version of the service.
- **Orchestration**: At times, the API might require multiple backend services invoked and results be aggregated. In this case, the API gateway must invoke multiple services concurrently and aggregate the results. At times, there can be a dependency between the service calls. For example, incoming requests might need to be authenticated before actual service invocation, or additional client or session information might need to be pulled for invoking the call. One can write the entire orchestration logic in the API gateway layer as some of the products provide runtime support. Another option could be to write a process API that does the orchestration across the other services and provides a consolidated API for consumption. This helps reduce chattiness and improves the overall performance from a client's perspective.
  We covered the orchestration patterns in `Chapter 3`, *Designing Your Cloud-Native Application*.

- **Service discovery**: With the service instance going up and down, the service registry is the only true source of data in terms of the endpoints of the service that are available at any given point of time. An API gateway should be able to invoke the service registry to get the service endpoint at runtime and use that to invoke the service. A service registry can be used as a mechanism to load-balance the service calls across the registered service instances.

- **Handling timeouts**: For services that do not respond within a reasonable time, the API gateway allows you to timeout the request. This allows the gateway to handle timeout failures and even provide a failure mode for the clients. One option can be to provide cached data (if applicable and depending upon the type of service) or fail fast model, where the gateway can return an error or failure immediately without invoking the service.

- **Data caching**: The API gateway can also cache data for service calls that provide static data or data that does not change frequently. This model allows the traffic getting reduced on the service instance. This improves the overall response latency and the overall system resiliency. The cached data can also be used as a secondary failure flow, in case of failure of the primary flow.

- **Service invocation**: The service getting deployed can be using multiple interfaces or protocols. For example, you might have services that make use of an asynchronous messaging based mechanism (such as JMS, MQ, Kafka, and so on) or others can make use of synchronous models such as HTTP or Thrift. The API gateway should be able to support multiple service invocation models and provide orchestration models on top of these invocation methods.

- **Service metering/throttling**: For certain categories of clients, you may want to limit the number of service calls they can make. For example, if you are providing a freemium model of service with reduced functionality, along with limits of calls that can be made in a time frame. The ability to meter and throttle the incoming requests based on type of client (free or paid) helps provide a business model around your API and underlying services. This can also be helpful if you are making external API calls to another SaaS provider, routing those calls through the API gateway can help predict/manage the number of outgoing calls and give unnecessary shocks when the usage bill comes up.

- **API monitoring**: Another important concern is monitoring your API calls for any deviation, whether in terms of response latency across various percentiles, failures rates, API availability, and so on. These metrics need to be plotted on a dashboard with appropriate alerts and notification systems. Based on the type of failure, one can automate the recovery scripts to overcome them.

This concludes the various usage scenarios and patterns that can be applied to an API gateway to expose your services as API to the consumers.

Summary

In this chapter, we saw how an API can be categorized into different models based on its primary usage and underlying resource. We saw the best practice with respect to the overall API design and the standards available to model the API through Open API or RAML specification. Next, we saw how the API gateway can be leveraged to address concerns not handled at the service levels.

In the next chapter, we will cover the impact of cloud development on the existing landscape of an enterprise, and how it can achieve the transformation of moving toward a digital enterprise.

12
Digital Transformation

The advent of cloud computing is impacting every facet of the enterprise landscape. From the core infrastructure to the client-facing applications, the enterprise landscape is seeing the impact of the forces of change. Some enterprises are the leading harbingers of these transformations, while others are still trying to figure out where to start and what to do. Depending upon the maturity of the industry domain, the transformation journey can be very different. Some domains are the first to adopt technology trends (such as BFSI), while others wait for technology obsolescence to adopt new technology (manufacturing, utilities). In this chapter, we will cover the following:

- Mapping the application portfolio for digital transformation
- Breaking an existing monolithic application into a distributed cloud-native application
- Changes required at the process, people, and technology levels
- Building your own platform services (control versus delegation)

Application portfolio rationalization

The decision for digital transformation is typically mapped to a larger application portfolio. The external forces in terms of customer-centricity, better customer experiences, compliance/regulatory, the advent of cloud computing, open source, and so on lead to enterprises looking at their entire application landscape and identifying areas to improve, enhance, and rework.

The initial step is to identify the opportunities or the applications that need to be transformed for cloud deployment. In this step, we typically do an overall portfolio analysis across business and technical parameters. These parameters help provide a weighted score of the portfolio. Using the score, we can map the applications across four quadrants. These quadrants help us identify where to focus and where we will see the maximum value.

Portfolio analysis – business and technical parameters

The application is measured and scored across business and technical parameters.

The parameters for technical value are as follows:

- IT standards compliance
- Architecture standards compliance
- Quality of service
- Maintainability
- Operational considerations
- License/support cost
- Infrastructure cost
- Project/change cost
- Application maintenance cost
- Sourcing (insourcing/outsourcing)

The parameters for business value are as follows:

- Financial impact
- Application user impact
- Customer impact
- Criticality
- Business alignment
- Functional overlap/redundancy
- Regulatory / compliance risk
- Service failure risk
- Product/vendor stability

You can rate these parameters on a scale of 1-5 (one being the lowest and five being the highest).

Mapping these parameters helps us identify cost and complexity hotspots and segregate applications based on business capability areas. These application categories are further analyzed for inter-dependencies, touch points, integration points, and the underlying infrastructure. Using all these, we can analyze the benefits and provide recommendations for a transformation roadmap. The next step is based on the business value and technical value; we plot the applications in one of the following quadrants:

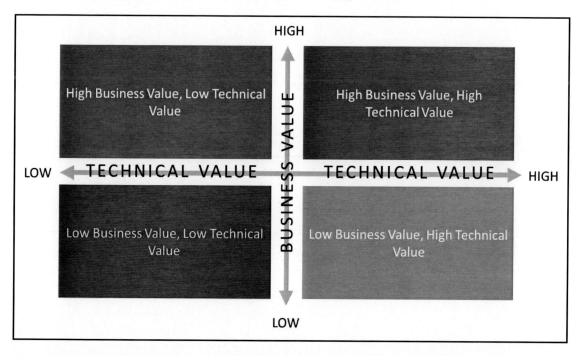

The scores help us provide the cost-benefit analysis at the application and portfolio level. It also helps to identify where there is a functional overlap (because of mergers and acquisition activities), understand the lack of business, IT alignment, and where the business priorities lie. These can help identify where the investment opportunities are and the potential non-core areas.

Using the preceding basis, the applications in each of the quadrants can be further mapped to one of the dispositions as shown in the following diagram:

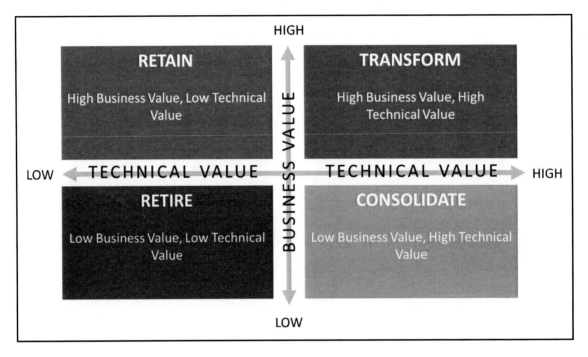

These dispositions provide us with rational opportunities for application across the areas which we will discuss in the following sections.

Retire

All the applications that fall into the low business value and low technical value can be marked for retirement. These are typically applications that have either lost relevance in a different business environment or had new functionality implemented.

These applications are marked by low usage and come with a very low business risk. One can also identify such applications by aggregating the tickets against these applications and usage volumes. Applications with low usage and lower numbers of tickets are typically candidates for decommissioning.

Retain

All applications that come with low technical value and high business value fall into this category. The technical maturity might be low, but they provide significant value to the business. These applications do not cost too much to run from an IT perspective. We can keep the lights switched on for these applications, as these still provide significant value to the business.

Consolidate

All applications that come with a high technical value and low business value fall into this category. The high technical value might be a result of the high cost of technical support, lack of people with technical skills, lack of documentation, and so on. The business can articulate the value of the applications, but the current spend on these applications might not be justifiable. These sets of applications need to be migrated and consolidated to upgrade the technical currency.

Transform

These are the applications that have high technical value and high business value. This means the applications have a large user base, multiple releases, a large number of tickets, and high infrastructure support costs, but still provide a significant advantage to the business. These applications are where the effort needs to be put in, because they provide significant differentiators for the organization.

Using the preceding methodology, we can identify the applications that are ripe for transformation. For our example, we can take an existing Java/JEE application that is currently running on-premises and needs to be transformed for a distributed application design model.

Monolithic application to distributed cloud-native application

The advent of the J2EE specification coupled with application servers providing the requisite services led to the design and development of monolithic applications:

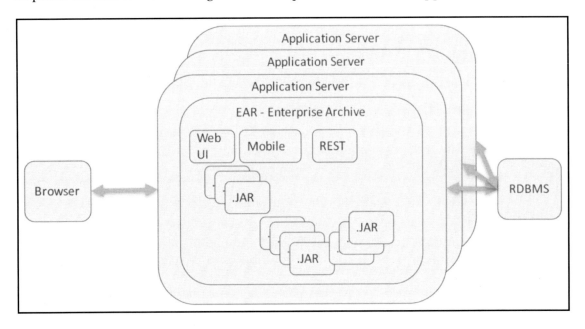

Some of the characteristics of the monolithic application and its ecosystem are:

- Everything is packaged into a single .ear file. The single .ear file requires a multi-month test cycle, which results in a reduced velocity of change in production. Typically, a *big* push to production once or twice a year.
- Application build complexity is very high with dependencies across various modules. At times, there is a clash between the versions of the JAR files used by the application.
- Reuse between application is primarily performed by sharing .JAR files.
- Huge bug and feature databases—from a backlog perspective, there are many feature sets/bugs across the various application modules. At times, some of the backlogs might be at loggerheads with each other.
- User acceptance criteria usually undefined. There are some smoke tests, but by and large, new features and integration is mostly visible in production only.

- Requiring multiple team involvement and significant oversight (business team, architecture team, development team, testing team, operations teams, and so on) for design, development, and operations management. During the release cycles, coordinating between the various teams is a Herculean effort.
- Technical debt accumulation over a period of time—as new features/functions are added to the application, the original design never undergoes any change/refactor to account for new requirements. This results in a lot of dead and duplicate code accumulating in the application.
- Outdated runtimes (licenses, complex updates)—the application might be running on an older version of JVM, older application servers and/or database. Upgrade costs are high and usually very complex. Planning an upgrade means foregoing any feature release during that development cycle. The involvement of multiple teams requires complex project management models. The absence of regression test scripts makes this even worse.
- The technical design-led approach followed by the team. The architecture and design is frozen upfront before development starts. As the application grows, new features/functions are getting added, there is no second look at the application architecture/design.
- Barely any business components or domains are used. The application design is usually sliced horizontally based on the tiers (presentation tier, business tier, integration tier, and database tier) and on the customer/application flows into specific modules/patterns. For example, applications making use of the MVC pattern will create packages along the lines of model, views, and controllers, with value and common thrown in.
- Usually, there is a single database schema for the entire application. There is no segregation of the functionality at the database level. The domains are linked to each other with foreign keys and databases following the third normalization form. The application design is usually bottom-up, with the DB schema determining the application database tier design.
- The average enterprise application will have more than 500k lines of code, with plenty of boilerplate code. As the application grows, there will be plenty of dead and duplicate code in the source code base.
- Applications typically supported by heavyweight infrastructure—the abilities of the application are managed by adding more and more hardware. Server clustering is used to scale the application.

- Thousands of test cases lead to increased time to run the regression test suite. At times, the release will skip the regression test suite to speed up the cycle.
- The team size is higher than 20 in most of these projects.

We can see that, in the case of monolithic applications, the business velocity and rate of change is very low. This model may have worked 10-15 years back. In today's competitive market, the ability to release features/functions at an incredible pace is paramount. You are not just competing with other large enterprises but with a lot of smaller nimbler start-ups that do not have the baggage of legacy applications, technologies, and processes.

The advent of open source growth of consumer companies, and growing mobile devices, among other factors, led to innovation in the application architecture space and more distributed applications driven by microservices and reactive models. The monolithic applications got decomposed into smaller sets of applications/services.

Next, we will explore the key architecture concerns that go with a distributed application. We will see how these key concerns map to the overall application technical capabilities and what capabilities should be hired and what should be built:

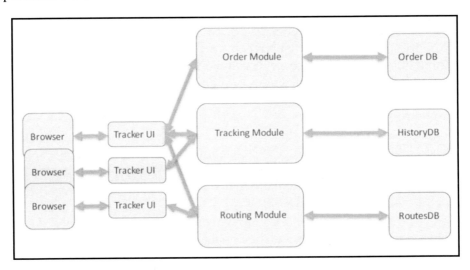

Some of the characteristics of the distributed application and its ecosystem are:

- **Lightweight runtime containers**: The advent of microservices correlates to the demise of the heavyweight JEE containers. As the applications morph into microservices with a singular purpose and loose coupling, there is a need to simplify the container managing the component lifecycle. The advent of Netty led to the development of the reactive framework that was just right for the purpose.

- **Transaction management**: Another causality of the application simplification was transaction management. Bounded context means the services are not talking to multiple resources and trying to do a two-phase commit transaction. Patterns such as CQRS, Event Store, **Multi Version Concurrency Control** (**MVCC**), eventual consistency, and so on, helped simplify and move the application to model a where locking resources are not needed.

- **Service scaling**: Breaking the application allows individual services to be scaled up and out independently. Using the Pareto principle, 80% of the incoming traffic is handled by 20% of the services. The ability to scale these 20% services becomes a significant driver toward the higher availability SLAs.

- **Load balancing**: Unlike the monolithic application, where the load balancing was between the application server cluster nodes, in the case of distributed applications, the load balancing is across the service instances (running in Docker-like containers). These service instances are stateless and typically can go up/down very frequently. The ability to discover the instances that are active and which are not active becomes a key feature of the load balancing.

- **Flexible deployment**: One of the key abilities of the distributed architecture is moving from a rigid cluster deployment model to a more flexible deployment model (cattle versus pets), where the deployment instances are deployed as immutable instances. Orchestration engines such as Kubernetes allow the optimum utilization of the underlying resources and take away the pain of managing/deploying hundreds of instances.

- **Configuration**: As the service instance becomes immutable, the service configuration is abstracted out of the services and held in a central repository (configuration management server). The service at boot time, or as part of the service initialization, picks up the configuration and starts in the available mode.

- **Service discovery**: The use of stateless immutable service instances running over commodity hardware means the services can go up and down at any time. The clients invoking these services should be able to discover the service instances at runtime. This feature, along with load balancing, helps maintain the service availability. Some new products (such as Envoy) have merged service discovery with load balancing.

- **Service versions:** As the services start getting consumers, there will be a need to upgrade the service contracts to accommodate new features/changes. In this case, running multiple versions of the service becomes paramount. You will need to worry about moving the existing consumers to a new service version.

- **Monitoring**: Unlike the traditional monolithic monitoring that focused on infrastructure and application server monitoring, the distributed architecture requires monitoring at the transaction level as it flows through the various service instances. **Application performance management** (**APM**) tools such as AppDynamics, New Relic, and so on are used to monitor the transactions.

- **Event handling / messaging / asynchronous communication**: Services do not talk to each other on a point-to-point basis. Services make use of asynchronous communication through events as a means to decouple them from each other. Some of the key messaging tools such as RabbitMQ, Kafka, and so on are used to bring asynchronous communication between the services.

- **Non-blocking I/O**: The services themselves make use of the non-blocking I/O models to get the maximum performance from the underlying resources. Reactive architecture is being pursued by microservices frameworks (with the likes of Play framework, Dropwizard, Vert.x, Reactor, and so on) used to build the underlying services.

- **Polyglot services**: The advent of the distributed application and using APIs as integration allows the service instance to be built with best-of-breed technologies. Since the integration model is JSON over HTTP, the services can be polyglot, allowing the use of the right technologies to build the services. The services can also make use of different data stores based on the type of service requirements.

- **High-performance persistence**: With the services owning their own data stores, the read/write services need to handle large volumes of concurrent requests. Patterns such as **Command Query Request Segregation** (**CQRS**) allow us to segregate the read/write requests and move to the data store to an eventual consistency model.

- **API management**: Another key ingredient of the distributed architecture is the ability to abstract out concerns such as service throttling, authentication/authorization, transformation, reverse proxy, and so on and move to an external layer called API management.

- **Health check and recovery**: Services implement health checks and recovery in order for the load balancer to discover the healthy service instances and remove the unhealthy ones. The services implement the heartbeat mechanism which is used by the service discovery mechanism to track healthy/unhealthy services across the application landscape.

- **Cross-service security:** Service-to-service invocation needs to be secured. Data in motion can be protected by a secured communication (HTTPS) or by encrypting the data over the wire. The services can also use public/private keys to match which client services can call the other services.

We saw some of the architecture concerns needed to build a distributed application. To cover the scope of the overall application, built as a bunch of microservices, we are looking at the following key architecture concerns across the various areas:

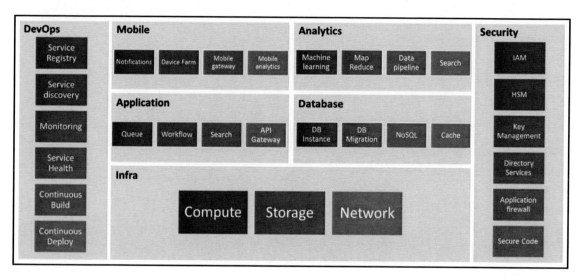

For the application to be cloud-native, it is important to build the application using SaaS/PaaS offered by the cloud vendor. This model allows you to focus on the pivoting on the business functionality, improve your innovation cadence, and improve the customer experience. Unless technology is not a key differentiator for the organization, the running of the core infrastructure and platform services should be left to the experts. In cases where there is a huge variability in demand, cloud elastic scale models provide an impetus. I do not want to do the marketing for cloud vendors, but unless the infrastructure is not an important aspect of your business, you should not be running the infrastructure.

The only downside of this is you are getting tied to the services offered by the cloud provider. Organizations are going with multi-cloud vendor strategies, where they spread their application and they take advantage of the key differentiators of the cloud vendors. For example, GCP provides a rich library of analytical and machine learning capabilities, with the ability to run your analytical workloads and decipher meaning insights, and **Machine Learning** (ML) models are one way to use the best-of-breed features. Similarly, for consumer-facing applications, AWS provides a rich set of PaaS services that can be used to launch and pivot on client-centric solutions.

Transformation of a monolithic application to a distributed application

In this section, we will take a monolithic application and see what steps are required for it to be architected into a distributed application.

We are assuming a typical Java application running on an application server, scaled through a clustering model and using a typical RDBMS. The application is already in production and needs to be refactored/migrated to a distributed architecture.

We will talk about multiple parallel tracks that need to work together to refactor/roll out the distributed application. We will cover individual tracks initially and then see them all come together. In your organization, you might choose to have separate teams for each track or one team managing more than one track. The idea is to provide you with a glimpse of the activities involved in actual transformation of a monolithic application.

Customer journey mapping to domain-driven design

The key driver to start the digital transformation is defining new customer journeys and building a new customer experience. This customer-centricity is what pushes the business to fund the digital transformation program. For our case, we can assume that the business has approved the digital transformation program and we proceed from there.

From a service decomposition perspective, we need to follow the steps mentioned here:

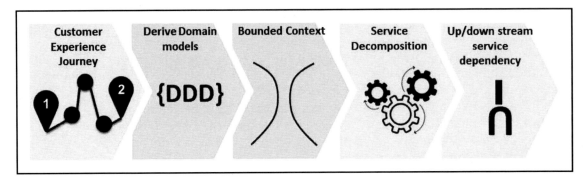

- **Customer experience journey mapping**: One of the key drivers for digital transformation is defining new customer journeys. A customer experience journey is a map of initial contact point of customer, through the process engagement model. This exercise is typically done by specialists and involves customer focus studies, touch points, actors/systems involved, business requirements, and competition analysis, among other things. The customer journey is typically created as an infographic.

  A customer journey helps identify the gaps as the customer interactions move across devices, channels, or processes. It helps plug those gaps and identify means and ways to enhance the overall customer experience.

- **Deriving the domain models**: The customer experience journey maps are mapped for the current and future requirements. These requirements then form the basis for the user stories. For new applications, the requirements can form the basis for functional decomposition of the system. In case of an existing application, the system might already be decomposed into identifiable domains/sub-domains.

  Once we have the requirements, we can start identifying the various sub-domains within the system. The domain model is documented using ubiquitous language. The whole idea is to use a language that is understood both by business and technology teams.

  The domains are modeled around entities and their functions. We also consider dependencies which interoperate among the functions. Usually, as a first pass, we end up with a big ball of mud, where all the known entities and functions have been identified. For smaller applications, the domain model might be the right size, but for larger applications, the big ball will need to be broken down further, and that's where the bounded context comes in.

- **Defining the bounded context**: The big ball of mud needs to be broken down into smaller chunks for easy adoptability. Each of these smaller chunks or bounded contexts has its own business context that is built around a specific responsibility. Context can also be modeled around how the teams are organized or how the existing application code base is structured.

  There are no rules to define how the context is defined, but it is very important that everybody understands the boundary conditions. You can create context maps to map out the domain landscape and make sure that the bounded context is clearly defined and mapped. There are various patterns (for example, Shared Kernel, Conformist, Producer/Supplier, and so on) that can be applied to map out the bounded context.

- **Service decomposition**: Using the bounded context, we can identify the teams that will work as part of one bounded context. They will focus on the services that need to be produced/consumed to provide functionality as part of the bounded context. The business capabilities are decomposed into individual microservices. The service can be decomposed based on the following principles:

  - **Single responsibility**: First and foremost is the scope of the service and the capability that will be exposed by the service
  - **Independent**: Changes in function/feature requirement should be limited to one service, allowing the one team to own and complete the same
  - **Loose coupling**: The services should be loosely coupled, allowing them to evolve independent of each other

- **Mapping the up/down stream service dependency**: As the services are identified in each of the domains, the services can be mapped as for dependency. Core entity services that encapsulate the system of records are the upstream services. Changes from the upstream services are published as events that are subscribed or consumed by the downstream services.

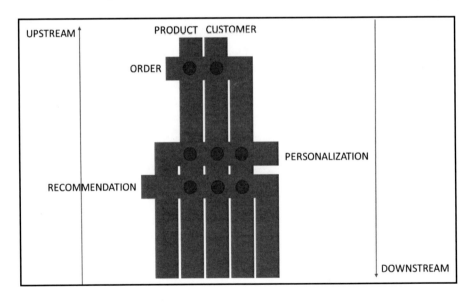

Defining the architecture runway

The business application needs to sit on the shoulders of a platform. The platform can be built or bought, depending on the business and application needs. The organization needs to define an intentional architecture model and define the rail guards to make sure the teams are building services within the given technical constraints. The platform team owns this overarching architecture, chooses the architecture and technical components, and helps build any common concerns required for successful running of the application services.

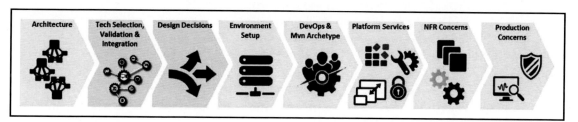

- **Platform architecture**: One of the key ingredients of a successful distributed architecture is the underlying platform. One can choose to build the platform by using off-the-shelf, open source / commercial software (Red Hat OpenStack, Cloud Foundry, and so on) or can choose a strategic cloud provider (such as AWS, Azure) to start building the platform. The elastic nature of the underlying infrastructure (compute, network, and storage) provides the fundamental building blocks for the platform.

- **Tech selection, validation, and integration**: To build the platform services, you might want to evaluate multiple sets of technologies to determine what works the best in your ecosystem. The tech stack evaluation is typically a multiple-step process where the requirements are mapped to the available technologies/products, and a detailed series of steps to validate is undertaken, resulting in a matrix with regards to the integration of the technologies.

- **Design decisions**: The result of the technology evaluations is mapped to the underlying requirements, resulting in a matrix. This matrix is used to determine the best fit and help take a design decision. This step works in close conjunction with the previous step.

- **Environment setup**: Once the key design decisions are in place, we need to start with the environment setup. Depending upon whether the choice is on-premises or the cloud, there will be variation in the setup and the related steps. You can start with the setup of the development, test, pre-production, and production environment. The environments are built in the order of complexity and go through multiple iterations (to move from manual to script/automated).

- **DevOps/Maven archetypes**: Next, we start working on the **continuous integration (CI) / continuous deployment (CD)** part of the application build and deployment. For applications being developed in the Agile model, the CI/CD model helps do multiple releases in a day, and bring higher velocity to the entire process. We can also develop accelerators to aid the CI/CD process. For example, Maven archetypes that come with requisite bindings for creating the deployable artifact.

- **Platform services build**: Next comes the set of platform services that need to be built/provided to the users of the platform.

  The services are in application development (for example, queuing, workflows, API Gateways, email services, and so on), database (for example, NoSQL, RDBMS, Cache, and so on), DevOps tooling (for example, CI/CD tools, service registry, code repos, and so on), security (such as directory services, key management services, certificate management services, **hardware security module (HSM)**, and so on), data analytics (such as Cognitive Services, Data Pipelines, Data lake, and so on).

  You can buy these services from multiple vendors (such as Tiles, offered as part of the **Pivotal Cloud Foundry (PCF)**, Iron.io platform) or subscribe to services provided by cloud vendors or create your own platform services on top on products.

- **Non-functional requirements (NFR) concerns**: Once the key platform services are in place, and the first set of applications start getting onboarded to the platform, we need to start worrying about how to handle the NFR concerns of the applications. How will the application scale based on the incoming load, how to detect failures, how to maintain minimum threshold of the application, and so on. Again, you may want to integrate existing products to your platform that provide/support these NFR concerns.

- **Production concerns**: Last of all, we need to start worrying about the production concerns such as service management, monitoring, security, and so on. We will need to build services and requisite portals from an operations point of view to monitor, detect, and take appropriate actions in case of deviations/defined rules. The services are usually built using the organization standards in mind. The services mature as more and more uses cases are identified. The idea is to automate all possible operations to make sure the platform is ticking all the time, without any human intervention.

Developer build

Another key aspect of the digital transformation is to focus on your existing team managing/maintaining the existing application. The team needs to be upgraded in terms of skills and technologies, to be able to refactor/build/deploy the existing application into a distributed application. We will cover the steps needed to reskill the teams to handle the distributed application story.

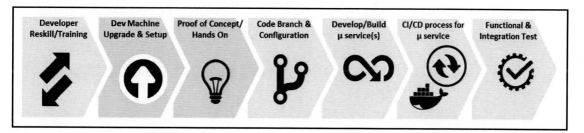

- **Developer reskill/training**: First and foremost is teaching developers new skills for the new application architecture techniques and design patterns. This means classroom training, online technology training, vendor product sessions/training, and so on. Another way to raise the skill of a team is to hire people with relevant skills and have them spearhead the overall development with support from existing developer teams.

  At times, you might want to have two teams—one that changes the business and a second that runs the business. In this case, the first business team brings the new skills to the team. The other business team manages and operates the existing application during the transformation period.

- **Dev machine upgrade and setup**: The new technology stack requires upgrades of the developer machines. If the machines are running on 4 GB RAM, we might want to upgrade them to minimum of 8 GB RAM, better still 16 GB RAM. The newer stack requires virtual machines, Docker engine, IDEs, and other software for development and unit testing. Slower machines increase the time to build/test the code. Without adequate horse power, the developer is simply not productive enough.

- **Hands on lab / proof of concept**: Once the machines are upgraded and developer training is done, the developer can start doing hands on lab and/or proof of concepts with the new technology stack to familiarize themselves with new development techniques. The developer can be given small projects or be involved as part of stack evaluation to enable them to become familiar with the technology stack.
  The work done by the developer team should be evaluated by an SME in the area to point out what they are doing wrong and the correct way of doing it. Having an external consultant (either SME or vendor consultant team) helps bridge this gap.
- **Code branching and configuration**: Once the developer team is ready to start working on the distributed application, the next step is to branch off the code from the monolithic application. You may want to branch off the configuration data also.
  Remember, even with branching, the existing application maintenance continues on the main code trunk. The branch version is used to refactor the code. We will see more details in the next section.
- **Develop/build microservices**: Once the code is branched and refactored, the developer should start packaging them as microservices. The team can also start creating new microservices that map to new requirements of the application. The code on the branch is regularly synced with the trunk to ensure changes made to the trunk are available in the branch code.
  Movement to specific PaaS services provided by the cloud vendor is also part of this phase. If you want to make use of services such as queuing or notification, or any of the other services, then this is the phase where you make the relevant changes.
- **CI/CD process of microservices**: Developers will start creating pipelines for continuous integration and deployment of the microservices. Service dependencies are mapped out and considered. Various code analysis checks are run as part of the CI process to ensure production readiness of the code. Additional service governance processes can be built into the various stages of the pipeline.
- **Functional/integration test**: Last but not least, developers will write functional and integration test suites to verify the correctness of the services. These test suites are integrated as part of the CI pipeline. As and when the new code is deployed, these tests are run as part of the regression to ensure the functional correctness.

Breaking the monolithic application

One of the key steps of digital transformation is the actual refactoring of the monolithic application. In this case, we are assuming a Java-based application that needs to be refactored/broken down into a distributed application:

- **Initial state**: Before we begin, we take the initial state of the monolithic application. In this state, the application is composed of a deployment unit (such as a WAR file), which is internally composed of multiple JAR files. The code is laid out in a logical manner, with some semblance of logical structuring across presentation, business, and data tiers. Each of the layers is further bifurcated by the modules or sub-packages modeled based on modules. If not, there is some distinction based on the class names to identify the modules. The configuration is stored as a set of external properties files. Code coverage is decent (more than 60%) and there is potential to write more test cases.

- **Code refactoring**: The next step is to carve pieces of the code from the monolithic application that potentially go together. For example, classes across the module can be packaged as a separate Java project. Common files or utility classes can be packaged as separate JAR(s). As you refactor the code from a single code project, you will create multiple, interdependent Java projects. Package the JARs as part of the larger WAR or EAR file only. Remember, we are working on the master trunk of the code base. Changes are integrated and synchronized back on the branch code.

  Besides the code, you will also need to refactor the application configuration. As you refactor the code, the configuration needs to be mapped to the respective Java projects. The configuration might be specific to the project/module, be shared across modules, or global, which is used across the application.

- **Build process update**: As you work on the code refactoring part, creating smaller independent Java projects, you will need to update your project build process. The Java projects need to be built in the order that they are dependent on each other. As you carve out the projects, the build process keeps going through iterations. The build process is updated in conjunction with the code refactoring steps.
  As the code gets refactored, the updated WAR/EAR needs to be deployed to production. This ensures that the code refactoring works, and other metrics—code coverage, unit test, regression test, and so on are factored in. This makes sure that the work you are doing gets incorporated on a daily basis to production.
- **Java version update**: Multiple times, we have seen that the JVM version being used on the project might not be current. Some of the newer reactive frameworks usually work with Java 1.7 upwards. This means the base JVM version needs to be upgraded. This might require application code to be refactored for features that got deprecated. Some pieces of the code might need to be upgraded for newer features. The refactored code needs to go into production along with the upgraded JVM version.
- **Introducing circuit breaker / reactive patterns**: The next step in the code refactoring is to upgrade the code for resiliency patterns. You can bring in patterns such as a circuit breaker by implementing a Java library such as Hystrix. You can also improve the code across the modules by implementing patterns such as decoupling the modules by implementing async messaging, bringing in reactive frameworks (such as Spring Boot, Vert.x, Dropwizard, and so on), and improving concurrency (such as Akka, RxJava, and so on). All the changes are to the production code and integrated with branch code.
- **Feature flag implementation**: At times, you might be integrating code coming from the branch. In this case, you may not want some piece of code going live. You can introduce feature flags in the code, controlled through configuration. So you can take code into production which might be dead till the feature is ready to go live.
- **Ongoing functional updates**: The application will be undergoing regular functional changes/updates. The changes are made to the code and synchronized back to the branched code on regular basis.

Bringing it all together

We saw how the four tracks are working at the application in their individual capacities. Now we bring all four tracks together in a collaborative manner. As the monolithic application undergoes transformation, the other tracks set up the base platform for carving out the bounded context and related microservices:

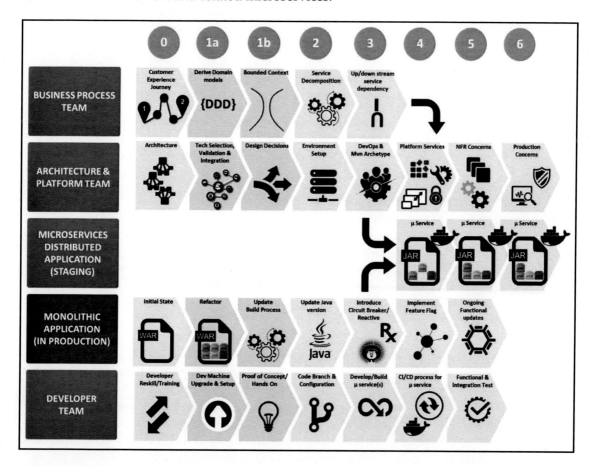

We can see how the two tracks change the business, run the business overlap, and provide the perfect balance to migrate from a monolithic model to a distributed application model.

This is akin to changing the tires of a moving car.

Building your own platform services (control versus delegation)

Another key decision for enterprises is how to choose your platform:

- Should I be building my own platform?
- Should I subscribe to an existing platform and develop my application on top of it?

This decision boils down to the factor how do you see technology, as an enabler (control) or a differentiator (delegation)?

At the core, all companies are technology companies. But the question is whether controlling technology provides you with the additional edge over your competition, or helps build a moat that can potentially discourage new players from coming. Let's take a couple of examples and see how it plays out:

- If you are to planning to compete with a company such as Amazon in the retail space, you need to have deep pockets. The low margin business of Amazon retails is bankrolled by profitable business from AWS. So, unless you have a sugar daddy or alternate revenue models, competing with Amazon is not going to be easy. But assuming you have deep pockets, can you start modeling your retail platform on top of AWS or any of the cloud providers? Yes! You can start with any of the public cloud platforms and once you have predictable demand, you can move into a private cloud model. This model saves you the upfront capex.
- Let's take an example of a manufacturing domain that sells physical products. They can potentially augment their product with **internet of things (IoT)** devices that provide a regular stream of data about the performance and usage of the product. The company collects this data and provides analytics services (such as predictive maintenance) as digital services around these products. Now, you can model and build the analytics model on any of the cloud providers. The choice of the platform can be determined by the choice of cognitive or data churning capabilities. You can choose the cognitive services from the platform or even create your own. The underlying platform capabilities are delegated to the cloud provider. You focus on building the right model to predict.

There is no right or wrong model. You may start with a delegate (going with a public cloud provider) initially, and then go to a control model (private cloud) where you have full control over the features/functionality of your application. It is easy to pivot on the cloud provider model without a lot of upfront investment and lock in. The idea is to identify where the differentiator lies for you!

Summary

This brings us to the end of digital transformation. We saw how we need to evaluate our application portfolio for transformation opportunities. We saw the reasons why monolithic applications are becoming a hindrance to achieving our business goals.

Once a transformation opportunity is identified, we can take an existing monolithic application and move to a distributed application model. We saw various steps that need to be taken across people, process, and technology levels.

This also brings an end to the overall journey for building cloud-native applications in Java. We saw the various tools/technologies to build new age microservice-based applications, how to build them, how to take these applications to production, how to monitor them, and how we adopt these applications for cloud providers such as AWS and Azure. We also saw some of the best practices in building API-based platforms, and how to take an existing monolithic application and transform it into a distributed microservice-based application.

Other Books You May Enjoy

If you enjoyed this book, you may be interested in these other books by Packt:

Mastering Microservices with Java 9 - Second Edition
Sourabh Sharma

ISBN: 978-1-78728-144-8

- Use domain-driven design to design and implement microservices
- Secure microservices using Spring Security
- Learn to develop REST service development
- Deploy and test microservices
- Troubleshoot and debug the issues faced during development
- Learning best practices and common principals about microservices

Building Serverless Architectures
Cagatay Gurturk

ISBN: 978-1-78712-919-1

- Learn to form microservices from bigger Softwares
- Orchestrate and scale microservices
- Design and set up the data flow between cloud services and custom business logic
- Get to grips with cloud provider's APIs, limitations, and known issues
- Migrate existing Java applications to a serverless architecture
- Acquire deployment strategies
- Build a highly available and scalable data persistence layer
- Unravel cost optimization techniques

Leave a review - let other readers know what you think

Please share your thoughts on this book with others by leaving a review on the site that you bought it from. If you purchased the book from Amazon, please leave us an honest review on this book's Amazon page. This is vital so that other potential readers can see and use your unbiased opinion to make purchasing decisions, we can understand what our customers think about our products, and our authors can see your feedback on the title that they have worked with Packt to create. It will only take a few minutes of your time, but is valuable to other potential customers, our authors, and Packt. Thank you!

Index

Printed by BoD™in Norderstedt, Germany